SOME WAYS OF
Writing:

Second Edition

A Supplemental Guide to Writing for Composition and Sophomore Literature

Jim Sanderson
Lamar University

Kendall Hunt
publishing company

Cover image © 2012 Shutterstock, Inc.

Kendall Hunt
publishing company

www.kendallhunt.com
Send all inquiries to:
4050 Westmark Drive
Dubuque, IA 52004-1840

Printed in the United States of America
10 9 8 7 6 5 4 3 2

Contents

Rationale for this Manual

This manual hopes to give students a concise overview of basic rhetorical concerns, essay organization, paragraph organization, and grammar and style. In other words, in terms of traditional components of rhetoric, this manual limits itself to arrangement (essay and paragraph organization) and style (writing for the proper audience and grammar)—although Christensen does combine invention and arrangement. Students and instructors will find hints at invention in all of the sections. I trust that instructors have their own methods of encouraging invention. Burke's Pentad appears in a lot of textbooks, and I refer students and instructors to him and to those textbooks.

Also, because students so rarely have essays to compare with theirs and because students always want to know "what the instructor wants," this manual includes a collection of student essays from Engl. 1301 and 1302 and sophomore literature courses in American and African-American literature. Students, many of them from Lamar University, wrote these essays for the courses listed.

This is a supplemental manual for students. It does not take the place of a required text. Instructors may or may not use it or refer to it. It is not as thorough or as informative as a handbook, reader, or rhetoric.

While this manual addresses instructors and gives advice to them, it is primarily **written for students—in any course.** Students may want to keep it throughout their study to remind themselves of certain processes or techniques. Students should not be intimidated by its length or heft. Over two-thirds is a collection of student essays, which are examples.

Students should read this manual closely. Certain passages refer to themselves, refer to sentences that students have just read, refer to previous or upcoming parts of the manual. In other words, the manual attempts to illustrate the points that it makes.

The exercises and techniques are based on over thirty years of teaching. The student essays are collected from over twenty-five years of teaching. The content is very old. The tone, method, and organization are sort of new.

Organization, Style, and Grammar

INTRODUCTION FOR INSTRUCTORS AND STUDENTS _____

Instructors: As you can see, I've organized this manual according to the basic writing skills that most instructors hope that composition students achieve: essay organization, paragraph organization, and sentence structure. This manual, an elaboration on a manual that I used for years to teach composition, designates skills and then makes *suggestions* about teaching those skills.

Students: No one likes to write, not professional writers, not students, not professors. Writing hurts; it is not fun. If writing seems to be fun and easy, then it probably isn't very good—no pain, no gain, so to speak. So a good writer should make writing hurt. The only satisfaction in writing *is having written well.*

An instructor should insist on the rigors for writing. On the other hand, the marks on the papers are not directed at the student. These marks critique a persona (a mask that the writer wears) not the student. No English instructor means to comment personally on a student. Unfortunately many students take writing personally. Language is what we use to define ourselves to ourselves. But students should make an attempt to see their language and thus their writing as a tool, something distinct from what they are. Therefore, they should try to be as objective as possible about this tool so as to make it a good one.

A HINT ABOUT PROCESS:

Any writer needs to try to keep the grammar/mechanics/spelling Nazi in him locked up at first. In a first draft, especially for beginning writers, composition students might focus on getting the content without worrying about form or the conventions of standard written English. This is the discovery stage. Writers shouldn't let the grammar Nazi interfere at this stage. In the next draft or two, students should try to shape their writing. They should be concerned with organizing the entire essay and then paragraphs and then sentences within the paragraph. This may take a couple or three drafts. This stage is the benevolent dictator stage. Not until the last draft or two should the student allow the Nazi to take over and demand exact precision and correction. An instructor and a writing center can help a student through these stages. For more advice about the writing process, see the commentary, "Final Thoughts about Rhetorical Modes and Process," after the Rhetorical Modes Section.

RHETORICAL CONCERNS FOR ESSAYS

MAXINE HAIRSTON

Students often think that writing is just content. Instructors hear students say that the instructor just didn't like what they wrote. But composition instructors are as interested in the form as in the content. On the other hand, some academics assume that students should learn to write in one manner, for one particular discipline. They assume that the writing should suit their particular discipline. But both students and instructors sometimes overlook the nature of rhetoric.

Maxine Hairston identified writing as composed of Audience, Purpose, Persona, and Content (33–45). *Persona* is a Greek word. It literally means the mask that the Greek actors wore in their plays. Older folks have seen these masks displayed in old TV programs and in theaters. Halloween masks and Mardi Gras masks are meant to represent something other than the wearer. Rhetoric adopted the term to mean the mask that the writer wears. Audience, of course, concerns whom the writer assumes will be reading the essay. (A mother will like whatever a son or daughter writes, so a writer should discount her and write for other people). Purpose implies a desire beyond the thesis: what the writer hopes to achieve with the essay: entertainment, information, political action, apology, etc.

As Hairston explains, each of these components influences the others. Therefore, she describes these components as forming a square, and any essay must address all four (33).

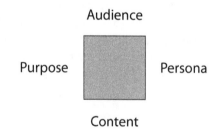

But I believe that, in different writing projects, the writer wants to emphasize different aspects of writing: audience, persona, content, or purpose. So the square stretches and contorts into a parallelogram or a trapezoid or some weird, four-sided geometric form—depending upon the writer's emphases. For example, this section of my manual looks like the following:

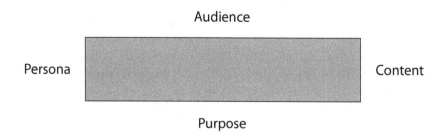

The writer still considers all of the components but emphasizes one over the other. In technical, business, bureaucratic, or scientific writing, bosses and researchers want objectivity. They falsely assume that a piece of writing can be purely objective, as though no one wrote it, and thus the use of **passive voice** shows up. The only objectivity, then, is an objective sounding persona. If you are going to urge some political action, you would write one essay or speech for those folks whom you know support you and another for those folks whom you know might be opposed to you or even neutral. A writer in a business or industry may write one report for the people who will actually perform the task or procedure, another for the administrator, another for experts, and yet another for accountants. In any scientific or technical field, the hardest audience to write for is the lay (or common, non-expert) audience.

For instance, in this manual, I am writing for both students and instructors. The audience is the hardest part for me. While I want to be serious, I don't want to be completely formal. So I want to project the idea of an observant but not an authoritative or intrusive persona. My purpose is to offer some ideas about writing that instructors can use as supplements to their own knowledge or to the textbooks and to simultaneously explain some of these ideas to students. Thus, audience and purpose blend together (see above). Content is pretty old hat to me. I've taught composition enough to see what I say here as nearly boring—to me, not to the reader, I hope.

Still reading, whether you are an instructor or a student? If you are, what do you think of me? You know nothing about me. But you may be devising some notions. Perhaps you are wishing that I would just shut up. Your vision of me has nothing to do with the real me. But I am working on creating a mask for myself. A reader should have a sense of a consistent type of person talking to him.

A Note on Using You

Look at my use of *you* in the above paragraph. I will have more advice about using *you* throughout this section of the manual. Once I start using *you,* whom am I talking to? I am talking directly to the readers, whom I believe are students. So language and persona shift once my audience shifts. However, you really should not shift your audience in mid-essay as I have just done. But excuse me for my example. When I go back to the original audience—both instructors and students—in the next paragraph, you will notice a jarring shift in persona.

Composition students will of course be preparing to write college essays. Therefore, their content will be academic, informative, or argumentative. They won't be writing many "how I spent my summer vacation" essays. So they would probably appreciate some practice in writing future college essays. However, college composition instructors may not have expertise in all college areas. So in the past, I've assigned students one assignment for the whole course, to be redone over and over (catch the redundancy?). That assignment is for students to turn their notes from some college course into an essay. Some course that is not too technical works best for instructor and student. This essay based on class notes will inevitably be contrast and comparison, classification, process, or cause and effect. But what the student must figure out is whom he is writing for, what sort of persona he wants to project, and what his purpose is. He should know the content—and perhaps this assignment will even force him to study and pay more attention to the class supplying the notes for his essay.

For most college essays, a student should use an objective persona so as to emphasize the content, which for him is most important in getting a grade. I've probably just mentioned the purpose. Besides a grade, the student wants to give the illusion, appearance, suggestion that he knows the content. But the student should assume that the audience is a lay audience, yet a very intelligent lay audience. The student should assume that his audience knows nearly as much as he does. Therefore, he need not do much plot summary, briefing, preparing, explaining background, etc. Therefore, typical college essays should look like the following:

Audience

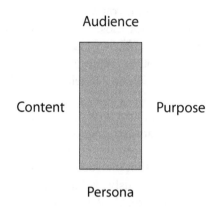

Content   Purpose

Persona

The essay that I describe above is the history, sociology, business, or psychology essay that a student will have to write in classes beyond freshman composition. Of course, English teachers like students who take chances. Students should look at the essays collected and see if they can determine the audience, persona, purpose, and content of these student writers.

Thus, I hope that students think beyond just content. And I hope that instructors will be gentle but firm and insightful in looking at audience, persona, content, and purpose in student essays. And I hope that students will apply this rhetoric to other college writing and to writing out there in the real world. Finally, most important, just as persona, audience, and purpose effect content, so do they effect organization and style. So the lessons about organization and style that follow depend upon the choices about audience, purpose, and persona.

A Note on Using I

I cautioned students about using *you*. But what about using *I*? Look back over this section. Look at upcoming "essays" that I wrote in this manual. How hard would reading this essay be if I removed the *I*? Look back at the sentences that I just wrote. How hard would these sentences be to read if I didn't use *I*? I could replace *I* with "this author" or "the writer." Wouldn't this rewrite sound both stupid and pretentious? Wouldn't this rewrite destroy the informal persona that I tried to create? Or even worse, what if I went back and removed *I* by writing passive voice sentences? You can look ahead at the problems caused by passive voice.

Purpose and persona should determine the use of *I*. On the one hand, if you are writing about something outside of yourself, if you are not writing an anecdotal essay about your own experience; then you really don't need to mention your experience; you thus don't need to mention *I*. If you are writing a critical essay, your name will be on the essay, so you do not need to write, "I think" or "in my opinion." This statement would be redundant. So you rarely need to use "I" in a critical, college essay. I have used *I* in scholarly articles—usually as a joke. Sometimes I got away with using *I*. Other times, editors made fun of me and rejected my articles.

On the other hand, if you are working on creating a certain persona, if you are writing about your personal experience, if you are writing a report, memo, or process report on the results of your work; then you can hardly avoid saying *I*. Avoiding *I* would invite clumsiness, misunderstanding, passive voice, and other grammatical problems.

A Note on Works Cited

Students should notice my Works Cited citation here and throughout the different sections of the manual. Normally, a works cited entry should be on a separate page, but I am trying to save space. Handbooks should have the correct documentation for citations. Similarly, Works Cited should be double spaced in essays turned in for class. But once again, I am trying to save space, paper, and thus trees.

Students may not be studying documentation until their second course in composition, but they might want to study ahead, or they might want to retain this manual for the second composition course. Online documentation has changed since some of the student examples were written. See a current handbook for proper form.

WORKS CITED

Hairston, Maxine. *A Contemporary Rhetoric.* Boston: Houghton Mifflin Company, 1974.

WAYNE C. BOOTH

A Note about Booth and Other Sources

Instructors could best use this section for teaching fiction. Students might want to skip it. I first read Wayne C. Booth's *Rhetoric of Fiction* way back in the dark ages when I was in graduate school. After three years, I sort of understood this incisive but difficult book. For more than twenty years, I've taught Wayne C. Booth. So in a way, I think that I may be plagiarizing. The problem is that, over years of using Booth (as with Maxine Hairston and Bill Pixton), I'm not sure what's me and what's him (or Hairston and Pixton) and what's common knowledge. (**Notice** that I use the wrong pronoun case above: *me* instead of *I, him* instead of *he.* But notice how my persona would shift if I used the correct pronoun. I'd sound uppity.) Common knowledge is that knowledge that any person in the field would be aware of, knowledge that is easily found in any work about that subject or person (birthdays, publication dates, etc.). Further, a writer isn't really stealing when he takes what several critics say, puts their thoughts together, and comes up with his own ideas. My point here is that the writer gets confused as to his influences. So writers do the best they can to document what they can.

Look at the squares and shapes preceeding. Suppose that I took one of those shapes and banged it into a straight line so that I had something like the diagram below:

Audience ——————— Purpose ——————— Persona ——————— Content ——————— .

This is the shape that Booth uses to describe fiction. But he uses some different names since he is writing about fiction. Instead of content, he says **"story."** By story, he means what most people assume fiction is: just "the what happens," just the basic plot. But as Booth well knows, that plot is delivered to us through words; thus fiction is a rhetorical medium. A drama is a performance medium. The story is delivered through literal actions, dialogs, scenes. So to understand a story presented through a drama, a viewer needs to know about set design, acting, and staging. The same is true for a story presented through a movie. To fully understand the movie, the movie viewer must understand film technique. So to understand a story presented through writing, one must understand the rhetoric.

Controlling the story, manipulating it, in fact delivering the very words that form the story, is what Booth calls the **narrative persona,** or as most textbooks will say, the narrator. This narrator is some distance away from the story. Some time may have passed since the story took place. Perhaps the narrator is telling about a time when she was a girl. The narrator may be in a different locale from the story and may be missing that locale. The narrator may be talking about someone other than himself. The narrator may not even take part in the story or may not even mention himself (as what happens in third person limited omniscient point of view). The narrator may seem to know everything (as with omniscient point of view). So as you can see, in writing about a narrator or narrative persona, Booth is talking about what textbooks discuss in their chapters on point of view.

The point that Booth makes is that the narrator is at some personal, moral, emotional, psychological, spatial, or temporal distance from the story that he is telling. This distance equals irony. For instance, a narrator may lie, a narrator may be pompous, a narrator may not be of sound mind, a narrator may be bigoted. As some of you may have guessed, now I am talking about the reliability of the narrator. But it is not just the reliability of the narrator that concerns Booth but the whole nature of the narrator. We should be concerned with how he tells the story, with what is on his mind, with what he chooses to discuss (yes, this is true even of omniscient narrators).

However, the author ultimately controls the narrator. And the author has a point, **a purpose,** a theme. When we talk about the theme of a fiction, we say the author's name and use a present tense verb. We attribute what the fiction means to the author. This theme is not the flesh and blood author. So Booth says that we ascribe a controlling force to the fiction. He says that this is the **implied author**—or purpose, theme, point. In my first paragraph for this section, I use the names of authors and professors as the names of themes, purposes, or ideas.

The implied author is at some moral, emotional, psychological, temporal, chronological distance from the narrator. The implied author may be younger or older than the narrator. The narrator may be unreliable, may be a bigot, may be a liar, may smell bad, so we should trust the implied author more than the narrator. If a reader thinks that narrator Huck Finn is implied author Mark Twain and that Mark Twain agrees with him, then *The Adventures of Huckleberry Finn* is not a very funny book. But if one sees the distance between Mark Twain and Huck Finn, if one sees how the implied author manipulates and controls Huck so as to satirize society, then the book becomes very funny.

Controlling everything is the Reader—or the audience. The Reader can shut the book, can quit reading, so the reader has the most power.

Now what Booth is doing here, see, is he's saying we don't get the whole story if we just think the happenings is all that a story is. A story ain't just plot but gots a lot more to it than the happenings. That lots more gots to do with the thing what tells the story, which is a narrator thing. And then there's this force, this guy, behind that narrator making him jump through hoops and saying things so as to make some theme. The narrator, see, is like this ragged ol' puppet boy, and the implied author is the fella pulling the strings.

What on earth did I do in the paragraph above? Why do you want me to stop? Why did I ruin my essay? I switched narrators. The narrator above uses a more colloquial language than the narrator or persona that you are reading now. Perhaps, because of your associations with that type of language, you assume that the narrator above wasn't as smart, as sophisticated, or as literate as the previous narrator. You were probably annoyed. The distance between the implied author and the narrator became greater. So you were wondering more about how I talked than about what I was saying. Now that my guise, my persona, my narrator is closer to the content and to the implied author and is in a language you would associate more with a textbook, you can trust me and look more closely at what I am saying, rather than how I'm saying it.

So once you establish a method of telling your story or your essay, once you establish a persona, don't change it. If I had started out talking like I do in the bold paragraph above, you might have been confused, but you would have eventually gotten used to it.

What Booth says is that the rhetoric of fiction depends upon these distances. Here are some maps of some stories.

In the following, the narrator would be close to the story, but she might be unreliable because she is so far away from the point of the story.

I.A.   N.P.   Story

In the following, the narrator is looking back at his story, weighing it, judging it. Perhaps he is commenting and making fun of what happened. But we can trust him because he is close to the I.A.

I.A.   N.P.   Story

A Note on Satire and Sarcasm

In the first example, the distance between the N.P. and the I.A., shows what happens in **satire.** The speaker, the narrator, doesn't realize that he is showing himself to be foolish. In the second example, the narrator is aware that he is making fun, so that narrator may be **sarcastic.** The difference is in the speaker's awareness. (Students, sarcasm is neither a crime nor a moral fault).

In the following example, the plot, the content, or "the what happens" is most important. We can generally trust what happened.

I.A.   N.P.   Story

In the following, perhaps a narrator tells about someone else, but we can't trust all that the narrator says, or we don't really know what to make of his own story.

I.A.   N.P.   Story

The point is that there are as many different relations between the I.A. and the N.P. and the N.P. and the Story as there are stories. You may have noticed that I left off the term reader. Generally, very generally, if there is a great distance between the reader and the I.A., the theme, the point, the purpose of the fiction, the reader quits reading. Now of course, many contemporary literary critics will say that this is precisely what happens, but that point is best addressed by another writer in another course.

Of course Booth is talking about fiction, BUT his ideas, which are more difficult to understand than Harriston's, can be applied to nonfiction. As writers, students will want their narrators to change with different assignments, just as their writing purposes may change. So they will want to look at the distances. For an essay in freshman composition that is about a personal experience a student may have the following arrangement.

I.A.   N.P.   Essay

A student may look back at himself and make fun of himself.

I.A.   N.P.   Essay

As student may be sarcastic and make fun of a fellow student or, God forbid, an instructor.

I.A.   N.P.   Essay

A student may write an editorial in which she attacks some local legislation.

I.A.   N.P.   Essay

Or the student may wish to appear to be perfectly objective, and emphasize the material.

I.A.   N.P.   Essay

A Note on Objectivity and Passive Voice

I would like to add that I believe that there is no objectivity, not in a lab report (passive voice does not make a lab report objective), not in a textbook. Someone, some intent, has to make the narrator/persona/narrative persona choose what to write and how to write it. The only thing that is objective is an objective narrator. Objectivity is really no excuse for writing passive voice.

The point is that understanding Booth's concepts gives a writer more ammunition. Booth is simply looking at the age-old components of rhetoric and coming up with another way of presenting them. With Booth's idea about distance and narrators in mind, students might start reading newspapers, magazines, and editorials a bit differently. With Booth as a guide, students might see satire, might see that the point that the narrator makes might not be the point of the essay at all. Students might also see the wondrous possibilities in writing. They might also see the wondrous ways that they might adapt their writing to the situation.

A Note on Traditional Point of View

Eager students anticipating composition II and instructors may have noted that Booth gives more in-depth discussion of point of view. As presented by most composition II or introduction to literature courses, point of view consist of four different ways to narrate a story.

1. First Person: An "I" narrates the story and, to varying degrees, takes part in the story.
2. Third Person Limited: The story is sifted through the consciousness of a "he" or a "she." Some textbooks explain that the main character, or the character delivering the story, or the character who does the thinking, is referred to as "he" or "she."
3. Third Person Omniscient: The narrator is god like, jumping from one "he" or "she" to another, commenting about the whole of creation, or going from commentary to the thoughts of a particular "he" or "she."
4. Third Person Objective: The narrator looks only at sight, smell, sound, or touch common to anyone observing. The narrator does not go into any character's head. The narrator, as such, is like a camera.

According to Booth's logic, in first person the "I" narrator is close to the story, but we might have to wonder how distant the "I" is from the implied author. We should wonder how much we can trust that narrator. A little more distant from the story than most "I" narrators, the third person limited, "he," narrator may be distant from the implied author—because the details and events are sifted through his mind, even though the narration is not in his words. An omniscient narrator can get close to the story or a character and then back up, but overall he still creates a way of telling the story that is his own. An objective point of view will not go into any character's mind, so this point of view will be more distant from the characters than first or third person.

But Booth will allow that this point of view is like a spectrum, with as many "voices" or point of views as there are stories. As Moffet and McElheny say, "every story is first person, whether the speaker is identified or not" (588). That is, each narrator is distinct. Each story has a narrator that has a distinct way of telling the story. That narrator may say "I" or not, may take part in the story or not, may offer a lot of commentary or not.

Works Cited

Booth, Wayne C. *The Rhetoric of Fiction.* Chicago: The University of Chicago Press, 1961.

Moffett, James, and Kenneth R. McElheny. eds. *Points of View: An Anthology of Short Stories.* revised ed. New York: Penguin, 1995.

BASIC ESSAY ORGANIZATION

(I got the information below from a hand out in pre-computer, dinosaur age from my composition instructor and director, Dr. William Pixton. I hope that he intended for me to plagiarize; in fact, I believe that he intended that I commit it to memory. I'm not sure where he got it).

Title: The title should give a hint of the thesis. The title indicates the limits of the topic, the specific elements of the topic to be dealt with, and the thesis—the assertion about the elements.

Introduction: The introduction, written as if there were no title, provides background information, states limits, states specifics, and states the thesis, including subject segments.

Main Body: The main body consists of several paragraphs, usually one for each subject segment (or one paragraph block for each segment). The typical Main-Body Paragraph contains:

1. *a topic sentence,* placed at the beginning, or at the end, or at both places (with appropriate word variation) when the paragraph is long and detailed. The topic sentence is rarely appropriate in the middle of the paragraph (it is buried).

2. *several supporting sentences,* demonstrating coherence (order, logic, and unity); these establish the truth of the assertion made in the topic sentence.

3. *adequate detail and development*—an essential aspect of the supporting sentences.

[This discussion of the paragraph is only half-true, as Christensen says. Not all paragraphs are diamond shaped as suggested here. See the section on "The Generative Rhetoric of the Paragraph"].

Conclusion: The conclusion restates the main points of the essay (the subject segments), usually in grammatically subordinate structures, and reasserts the thesis, usually in the main clause of the same sentence. The conclusion thus answers the question implied (or asked) by the title; it ends with a sentence indicating finality.

TITLES

A title is not just something witty, nor is it the title of the work that the student is writing about; that title has been taken. A student should not write an essay called simply, "The Great Gatsby." F. Scott Fitzgerald has already written a novel called *The Great Gatsby,* and thus Fitzgerald has already used that title. The title of an academic paper should indicate what is coming. A title in an academic essay should indicate the topic or work under the discussion. Students should think of the title as a classification device for a library. It should explain to the librarian and the potential reader where to place the book. If a student goes to the library, researches for an essay on Chillingsworth in the *Scarlet Letter,* finds a title such as "Wings of Scarlett Letters," finds the article, and realizes that it is a review of a Romance Novel, then he will have wasted a lot of effort.

SPECIFICS IN THE ESSAY

Eighty percent of the essay should be the specifics in the main body. These specifics are the nitty gritty. These specifics make writing hard. Getting specific will take most of the writer's time. This specificity should hurt. I will discuss the main body paragraph in the section on Christensen's Generative Rhetoric of the Paragraph.

Following, though, are some observations about introductions, conclusions, theses, and subject segments.

LISTING SUBJECT SEGMENTS AND THE THESIS AND MAIN BODY

Not all instructors recommend listing subject segments (main points, plan of development, over view) after the thesis. But if a writer does list them, he commits himself to following them. This commitment helps the writer as much as the reader. And as I explain later in this manual, perhaps the writer may write these last. I can make several observations about this list of subject segments. In business and technical writing, in lab reports, in social work and criminal justice reports; writers often spell out and highlight the different elements: purpose (thesis) and plan of development (subject segments). These types of writing are usually very explicit. "This report will show . . ." or "In this investigation, we will . . . ," they might say for the thesis. So I recommend that students list subject segments. Doing so might not be graceful, might not be the best way to write the personal essay or creative nonfiction, but listing them helps prepare students for writing in other fields.

1. The subject segments listed should appear in grammatically equal units (if one is a word, then all should be a word, a clause, then all should be a clause) attached to the thesis. Parallelism (equal information should be in equal structures) plays an important role here. The first sentence of the conclusion should be a mirror image of this thesis. In other words, students should present their subject segments first and then their thesis. See the section on the **conclusion** for more information.

2. Another option for the writer is to list these subject segments in grammatically equal elements in a sentence unto themselves after the thesis. A writer **should not** put each subject segment in its own sentence. A sentence for each subject segment will confuse the reader as to what is the subject segment and what is the thesis.

3. A writer **should not** discuss his subject segments in the background of the introduction. Their appearance after the thesis is the first instance that the reader will see the subject segments even mentioned. They are a list, not a discussion. The writer discusses them fully in the main body.

4. The subject segments are important only in so far as they reveal the thesis. Therefore, the thesis should be as narrow as possible. Oftentimes, if the thesis is not narrowed, the writer will address the subject segments in the main body but not prove the thesis. In other words, the writer will end up writing about the subject segments as though they were independent of the thesis.

5. So again, a narrowed thesis is vital. I tell students that a good thesis is one in which the writer thinks that she has nothing she can possibly say. Such a situation forces the writer to really dig deeply and thus get more specific. To narrow a thesis, a writer might write a thesis with subject segments, then choose one of the subject segments as the thesis and thus divide this new subject segment promoted to a thesis into some more subject segments.

6. Essays usually have two or three subject segments. Our Western minds work better with dualities or trinities. An essay expands, not by adding more subject segments or main points to the main body, but by going into more depth about each subject segment. As an essay grows, each subject segment may become its own essay (see the Christensen section for advice about how to expand).

7. In the hands of more experienced writers, the thesis and subject segments blend together. But still, after reading thesis and/or subject segments, the reader should know what is coming in the main body. Look at this thesis from an academic article:
Through a close analysis of the epistolary exchange in Terrence Malick's *The Thin Red Line* (1998) combined with socio-historical contexts, this article examines this characterization and the narrative function of these intimate and yet distant correspondents (306).

Students may not know what this thesis means, but can they can sense what will be in the main body.

WORKS CITED

Walsh, Susie. "Friendly Fire: Epistolary Voice-Over in Terrence Malick's *The Thin Red Line." Literature/Film Quarterly.* 33 (2005): 306–312.

INTRODUCTIONS & CONCLUSIONS

1. The background section of the introduction may expand quite a bit, perhaps even requiring two or more paragraphs for an essay. In some literary essays, particularly in the past, and in some other fields, a background section might appear after the introduction as a review of literature (see my essay on Christensen). The other alternative, of course, is to simply get through the background information before leading into the thesis.
2. Often, students use *you,* especially in an introduction, to avoid naming the audience. By getting more specific, students can alert the reader as whom the essay is addressed. *One* is not any more specific than *you,* nor is *people. The reader* at least tells us something. But the more specific the reference to the audience, especially in the introduction, the better the sentence or paragraph or introduction will announce the audience. Giving hints as to the intended audience of an essay early on, such as in the background of the introduction, is a good idea.
3. Since the reader has just read through the subject segments in the main body, then the writer should list them first in the conclusion. Now, in the conclusion, the writer can go into some detail about them. He can then reassert the thesis. The first sentence of the conclusions, as said, might be a mirror image of the thesis. What I mean is that the thesis should present the thesis and then the subject segments while the first sentence of the conclusion should present the subject segments and then the thesis restated.
4. Often a thesis in a scholarly paper will pose a question. Though the thesis will not be a question, it will make the reader ask how the thesis statement is true. The writer of the scholarly essay will develop the answer to the question posed by the thesis throughout the main body of the essay. This is a much harder plan than simply stating the thesis and listing the subject segments. Research and experience show that unconfident writers do better with a more rigid structure.
5. Often, an essay will have a mini-conclusion. A writer will come to logical conclusions or answers in a paragraph before the actual restatement of subject segments and conclusions. However, this plan works best for essays that have more than five paragraphs.
6. Journalism has a different form. The journalist opens with a "lead" that tries to get the who, what, where, when, and why, but also gives the most important information first, then works down to the lesser information. The journalist knows and fears that the reader will stop reading partially through the report.

7. In creative nonfiction and the feature article, the writer searches for his points in the very writing itself. So the thesis may not be as apparent. Most of the essays in the students' reader or essay collection usually are like the creative nonfiction or the feature article. Probably, most of the essays that a student reads outside of class—a *Time* magazine essay or Sunday supplement article, for example—are editorial or feature articles. The classic personal essays in most collections are like these. So:

   a. Examples in essay collections sometimes confuse students.
   b. Basic essay organization and the rigid five paragraph essay can get boring for both students and teachers.
   c. But, the basic essay paragraph, at the very least,
       i.   keeps an unconfident writer on track,
       ii. keeps him from veering off,
       iii. and is very useful for the in-class essay.

So I think that students, once they gain some experience and confidence, ought to expand the basic essay format and the five paragraph essay: by adding paragraphs to the main body (See Christensen coming up) and by playing with smoother ways to present the thesis and the list of subject segments. And once students gain some experience and confidence, they should try to pose questions for a thesis—as in the academic article—or should imply it or even lead to it as in creative nonfiction, some personal essays, and feature articles. And then there usually is an advanced nonfiction writing course somewhere on campus.

COHERENCE, UNITY, AND CHOPPINESS IN INTRODUCTIONS

The paragraphs below are all introductions. Look at how hard it is to follow the point of the **first paragraph** because of the lack of unity. Notice, too, how the writer gives a preview of the subject segments and thus destroys unity.

Notice how the **second paragraph** seems to hit you in the face as you read it because of its choppiness. The obvious solution for choppiness is to combine sentences; however, you should try to maintain coherence. Maintaining coherence will mean that you will have to rewrite words that remind the reader of previous sentences. Look at the **third paragraph,** a rewrite of the second paragraph.

Notice how only the **fourth paragraph** is coherent and unified. Each of its sentences echoes some point or word from the previous sentence. For now, the easiest way to maintain unity and coherence is to repeat key words, to use pronouns, and to use transitions. But, again, if you overuse any of these methods, your essay will become needlessly repetitive.

The weather in West Texas may change from hot to cold, from wet to dry, or from calm to windy in just a short period of time. The scenery is composed of tumbleweeds, mesquites, sand, and caliche. Many objects cannot be kept clean in West Texas because of the sandy, dirty, environment—especially a car. The unpleasant weather, the type of scenery, and the fact that automobiles cannot be kept clean are the major reasons that I dislike West Texas.

I moved to Odessa because I liked its location. Odessa is located in Central West Texas. Because of its location, Odessa is noted for its dry climate. The lack of moisture here causes Odessa's scenery to look like a desert. Odessa scenery includes tumbleweeds, wildflowers, and rocks.

I moved to Odessa, which is located in central West Texas, because I liked its climate. However, the lack of moisture in West Texas causes the scenery to look like barren desert. Most people do not enjoy this barrenness, but I find some beauty in it, especially in the tumbleweeds, wild-flowers, and rocks.

I arrived in this desolate, dusty area in June. The dryness of the climate came as a shock to my system. As the sun evaporated the natural juices that my body possessed, I was forced to resort to artificial tears and an assortment of creams. However, as the sun began to descend, some of the good points about West Texas became apparent. Among this desert's vast qualities, starry nights, clean air, as well as cool summer nights were vital in my adjustment to this climate.

FRANCIS CHRISTENSEN'S GENERATIVE RHETORIC OF THE PARAGRAPH

(Ignore "Paragraph level" markings until later in this section)

Paragraph level 1   Way back in the 1960s, Francis Christensen devised rhetorics for writing sentences and paragraphs. He set himself the task of making both his rhetoric of the sentence and his rhetoric of the paragraph descriptive of the way that sentences and paragraphs work. He also wanted his rhetorics to be generative (creating something to write about). He was mainly concerned with style. The result was first "A Generative Rhetoric of the Sentence" followed by "A Generative Rhetoric of the Paragraph." His descriptive and generative rhetorics are based on a system of subordination and coordination, and both use what I have taken to calling modification, texture, and depth as assessments of the sentence and paragraph. Here, I will concentrate on the paragraph.

Paragraph level 2   1) Most students hear that paragraphs should be unified and coherent, should have a topic sentence, and should also be free of choppiness. 2) Several textbooks say that students can make their paragraphs coherent through the repetition of key words, the use of transitions, and the use of pronouns. 3) Sentences basically move forward—to the right, but unless they refer backwards—to the left—just a little, then they lose coherence. 4) So pronouns, transitions, and key words move the reader backwards just a little. 2) Students might also have been told that the topic sentence should be the first sentence and that it should designate the contents of the paragraph. 3) Sometimes a writer may have sort of an introductory sentence or a sentence of transition from a previous paragraph, or a writer may put the topic sentence last. 3) But these are rare cases, especially the latter. 2) And students have probably had exercises in sentence combining in order to avoid choppiness. 3) Besides just losing variety, short, choppy sentences aren't coherent; they don't *adhere* to each other.

Paragraph level 2   Christensen gives instructors and students a way to think about paragraphing that incorporates all of the qualities stated in the above paragraph. Christensen's method at once makes the paragraph more complex yet easier for students.

Paragraph level 3   Christensen started with no predispositions about paragraphs but asked himself how they worked and noted some of the errors that we use in thinking about them that were contrary to their actual composition. Christensen says that a typical paragraph is not a "dash" from general to specific, as many texts and teachers describe them, but more of a "pirouette" done by a dancer, with the topic sentence being the outermost circle and the other sentences a series of circles within that larger one (234). To further the analogy, the paragraph does not have the straight, steep, slanted edge that we describe the paragraph as having. A paragraph is not a diamond shape (although the introduction should be, see later in this essay). The edge of a paragraph should be jagged, going in, then coming out, then going back in, like a very poorly made and irregular saw blade.

Paragraph level 4   Christensen's points imply that the rhetorical modes are not the best way of teaching paragraph writing. The Greeks intended these modes for analyzing speech, not for writing. They are best used for analyzing what *has been written,* not for *what is being written.* Therefore, the rhetorical modes aren't generative. Further, any one paragraph may contain a number of rhetorical modes; in fact most good ones do.

Paragraph level 4   Paragraphs work, to Christensen, first simply by **addition,** one sentence is added to the next and so on, simple enough. But as sentences are added, the "writer and reader must see the **direction of modification** [bold mine] or *direction of movement."* This direction in turn creates *"levels of generality"* [bold mine], which in turn create a *"denser texture"* [bold mine] (Christensen 235–236). To me, I like to say that adding sentences based on their coordination or subordination makes for depth and usually some texture.

Paragraph level 3   To achieve the three aims described immediately prior and to address the actual construction of paragraphs, Christensen devised his rhetoric of the paragraph. Christensen suggests labeling sentences (or better yet writing them) in a paragraph according to their generality, which is a matter of their coordinate or subordinate structure (Christensen 237). A student can do so by labeling or writing sentences according to its **subordination** or **coordination** to other sentences. A subordinate sentence is more specific than some other sentence in the paragraph; a coordinate sentence is equal in specificity to some other sentence in the paragraph—and ultimately subordinate to another.

Paragraph level 4   **What Christensen does not say is how sentences become subordinate or coordinate to one another. This is simple. If a sentence semantically—and sometimes but not necessarily grammatically—adds information to the predicate (anything from the verb to the right) of a sentence previous to it, then the sentence is subordinate to the previous sentence. If it adds information about the subject of the sentence, then it is coordinate to that sentence.**

Paragraph level 4   Ninety-nine percent of the time, the topic sentence is the first sentence. It must also be the most general sentence in the paragraph. **(*I will also add that the topic sentence should not just tell what is in the paragraph but should also fix the paragraph within the context of the whole essay. See the discussion about Christensen's Rhetoric of the Paragraph applied to the Essay*).** So a writer should label his first sentence a 1. The next sentence must be subordinate. So a writer should label this second sentence a 2. The next sentence can either refer back to the predicate of the first sentence and become another 2, or it can refer back to and elaborate on the second sentence and thus become a 3. Christensen's system is very logical.

Paragraph level 5   For example, if the third sentence of a paragraph is subordinate to the 2 above it, then it is a 3. The next sentence could be another 3, a 2, or a 4. The only thing that it could not be would be another 1—that would be a new paragraph. In other words, the more sentences that the writer writes, the more possibilities she creates for another sentence. The more depth that the sentences in a paragraph get, the more they suggest other sentences.

Paragraph level 4   **Thus this simple method is generative. If a student can write one sentence, then he can elaborate on its predicate and thus write another sentence, and so on.**

Paragraph level 2   Christensen, then, with his "Generative Rhetoric of The Paragraph," gives instructors and students a valuable tool. He gives us a method for creating sentences within a paragraph and for evaluating paragraphs. An instructor might tell a student to put a 4 in a particular paragraph or add more 3s. So I would urge students and instructors to give a good honest try in understanding and using Christensen's "Generative Rhetoric of the Paragraph."

Works Cited

Christensen, Francis. "A Generative Rhetoric of the Paragraph." *Contemporary Rhetoric: A Conceptual Background with Readings.* ed. W. Ross Winterowd. New York: Harcourt, Brace, Jovanovich, 1975. 233–252.

EXAMPLES OF PARAGRAPHS LABELED ACCORDING TO CHRISTENSEN

Because I was a little worried about getting the rights to use paragraphs, rather than using Christensen's examples, I applied his method to paragraphs that I wrote. I gave myself the rights to do this. And though it is silly, I cite myself with a work cited "page."

1) Despite my early fondness for Roy Rogers' TV series, in which Pat Brady drove his jeep around and in which Roy and Trigger could gallop up to a speeding car; I just knew that World War II era soldiers did not mix with nineteenth century cowboys.
    2) I could prove it too.
        3) I had kid and sometimes grown up history books from the Mobile Library, a trailer that would bring mostly kids' books from the downtown library to local neighborhoods.
    2) If I was going to be stuck being a kid, and if I was going to play, then I was going to play right, just like adults did.
        3) So I primarily read histories to research my playing.
            4) Reading, then, for me became preparation for playing, and then reading became like play. (Sanderson, "Justifying My Existence," 202–203).

1) Further, through rejections and advice, I've been told what not to write about.
    2) For me, writing is intertwined with professoring, which is what I know.
        3) But a professor story means immediate rejection.
            4) So I can't write about what I know.
            4) Instead, I've faked writing about more interesting people than professors: alcoholics, pimps, criminals, psychotics, loose women, looser men, ignoramuses, and the morally challenged.
                5) As a boring professor, I hope that I know nothing about these people.
    2) People who know tell me not to write about the weather.
        3) Since I've lived in Texas nearly my whole life, the weather, especially the varyir kinds of heat across the state, is really important to me.
            4) I can't send a Texas character outside without mentioning the degrees of mis and sweat.
        3) (I've really put one over on *Langdon Review* because my submitted story con￼ ￼s a professor and a dean—characters whom I may know about—and opens with the we ￼r, but in this case something I know next to nothing about—snow) (Sanderson, "Jus￼ ng My Existence," 202).

1) Our most appealing and artistically satisfying Western heroes are not young.
    2) As Wills points out, the essential Wayne, as well as the essential Westerner (Harry Carey, William S. Hart, Randolph Scott), I would add, is middle-aged.
        3) These middle-aged American heroes have been expelled from or have chosen to escape from the feminine, civilized world, and now aging, they want the comfort that femininity and the civilization that we associate with femininity offer.
            4) The nostalgia in the Western is not for the wide-open wilderness, but for the hero's remembered or imagined feminine life.
            4) In the narratives that we see on the screen, he tries to come back into society or reconcile himself with the feminine, but his wild life and his time in the company of men in the wilderness have made him unfit for the feminine world and values.
                5) As with Oedipus, his past creates his tragic flaw and thus dooms his present desires.

4) Thus, the Western hero, from William S. Hart to Clint Eastwood, with Wayne standing between them, and in all sorts of manifestations in other genres, is Huck Finn grown up.

5) He has lit out for "the territory ahead of the rest" to escape Aunt Sally who hopes to "sivilize" him.

5) But when he gains psychological, sexual, and moral awareness, my guess is that he will miss what he has given up—those feminine values back in society (Sanderson, *"Red River* and the Loss of Femininity in the John Wayne Persona," 40).

1) No discussion of business and the oil boom and West Texas would be complete without at least a cursory glance at Odessa's neighbor fifteen miles to the east: Midland.

2) Another example of West Texas development and of American corporatism, Midland is the home of the white-collar accountants and managers in the oil industry, unlike working class Odessa.

3) Midland bills itself as the "Tall City" because it has a business district with four or five high-rises.

4) To the north of these buildings is the rest of Midland, to the east and south is mostly empty land.

5) Rather than expanding out into vacant lots, Midland expanded up, like Dallas or New York, and thereby created parking garages and traffic jams, just like those in Dallas or New York.

3) The West Texas God looks down and smiles upon corporatism, which Midlanders confuse with free enterprise, and corporatism can be comforting.

4) Claiming to be a Texan, but an obvious Yankee who did his time in Midland, ex-president George Bush is a good example of a Midlander.

4) Of course with his Daddy's money behind him and his past yearning for good times, W. Bush is also a good example of a Midlander.

2) Midlanders say that you raise kids in Midland and raise hell in Odessa (Sanderson, "The Twentieth Century Frontier in Odessa, Texas," 7–8).

1) So unlike some of my colleagues and fellow students who had richer parents, I and my fellow colleagues and students with poorer parents saw neither laziness and lack of ambition nor nobility and character in workers and their work.

2) We noticed crumpled bodies, sun burned faces, and physical and intellectual misery.

2) So we figured to be true to our parents' often unarticulated urging to escape work.

3) Work, as any oil field hand, plumber, laborer, or even mid-level manager knows s sweat.

4) We saw college as a way to find a job that wouldn't force us to sweat.

4) And in college, some of us found that we could actually get paid for sta   ig in college.

5) Now we teach in college, and as my friend and colleague Truett H liard, a New Mexican from the broad plains around Portales whose father worked at a variety of odd jobs, says, college teachers have "a bird nest on the ground."

5) Barry Phillips—an artist and a native Odessan whose father sold tires—confesses that, as infuriated as he gets at his job, he would beg for his or any college teaching job (Sanderson, "'They Can't Take an Education Away from You: Sweat and Professors," 83–84).

1) In the same class with Debi, was another "older" woman in her mid-thirties who had dropped out of school in the ninth grade to get married, have kids, and subjugate her life to her husband.

2) In order to remain inferior to her husband, an out-of-work oil-field hand, Anita had to be "dumb," and admitted her dumbness every day of class to anyone who would listen.

2) But in studying language, she realized that she already instinctively knew a lot about it and about the world.

3) Anita was crude but not dumb.

3) So as language became a more useful and easy tool for her, the world started shifting into new and more intriguing shapes.

4) For her last essay, she did read Alan Bloom's book along with E. D. Hirsch's *Cultural Literary* (finding out from Hirsch's questions that she was a lot more literate than she had thought) and several articles about college education from the *Chronicle of Higher Education* and wrote a remarkable essay about the possible problems with the education awaiting her daughter.

4) But along with her insight came more arguments with her husband about school and growing absences from church.

5) Anita didn't sign up for any classes the following semester.

2) Now, she consciously chose to remain "dumb."

2) She had learned the consequences of education (Sanderson, "Students: Chasing Grades and Looking Askance"; "They Can't Take an Education Away from You: Sweat and Professors," 96–97).

1) Though he rarely spoke, he wrote well, with a terse, no-nonsense sort of style.

2) His first couple of essays began to intrigue me.

3) From them, I learned that he had literally been pulled across the Rio Grande as a three-year-old child.

3) He and his migrant parents then lived in a deserted boxcar in Pecos, Texas.

3) Gradually, they moved to a better home, got Juan into the public schools, where he learned to speak English, and then he got himself a scholarship and a loan to go to Odessa College.

3) Later I saw that Juan did very well with grammar.

4) I talked to him about his ability with grammar and his language.

5) He told me that he had essentially taught himself English by memorizing the words, the orders, and the structures.

6) As an elementary school student, he would read, then try to grammatically analyze the sentences, and then write some like them.

4) When one of my Anglo students indignantly asked what use grammar had to anybody in the real world, I asked Juan to answer him.

5) In the first words that he ever spoke in class, Juan said, "It's how I eat."

6) Juan then told the class how he had learned to speak English.

2) After that point in this class and in another class that Juan took with me, I always called on him in order to get him to talk and to hear what he had to say.

3) I suspected that Juan knew and felt something that I never would.

4) I could only glimpse his world now and then, maybe by looking askance.

4) His world was far more profound than the academic and social world of my students, of the Odessa College Counselors, and of Odessa College.

4) And Juan's world gave him the strength to tolerate the O.C. world (Sanderson, "Students: Chasing Grades and Looking Askance"; "They Can't Take an Education Away from You: Sweat and Professors," 101).

Works Cited

Sanderson, Jim. "Justifying My Existence." *Langdon Review of the Arts in Texas.* 2 (2005–2006): 201–204.

_____. "*Red River* and the Loss of Femininity in the Development of the John Wayne Persona." *Literature Film Quarterly.* 32: 39–45.

_____. "Students: Chasing Grades and Looking Askance." *A West Texas Soapbox.* College Station: Texas A&M University P, 1998. 92–106.

_____. "They Can't Take an Education Away from You: Sweat and Professors." *A West Texas Soapbox.* College Station: Texas A&M University P, 1998. 81–91.

_____. "The Twentieth Century Frontier in Odessa, Texas." *A West Texas Soapbox.* College Station: Texas A&M University P, 1998. 3–15.

RHETORICAL QUESTIONS FOR SAMPLE PARAGRAPHS

What is the tone of each of the following paragraphs? Whom are they written for? Which are the scholarly essays? What is the persona (the mask that the writer wears) for each? Which persona is funny, satiric, teasing? Which persona is serious? What are the purposes of the paragraphs? In other words, how would you apply audience, purpose, content, and persona from the earlier section to the paragraphs that you just read?

EXERCISES

1. Look at the second paragraph of my essay on Christensen. See how it follows Christensen's rhetoric? Notice that the paragraphs grow shorter. For the more difficult sections, I try to present less complex paragraphs, basically a 1 and a couple of 2s, maybe a 3 in there.
2. Look at some of the examples. Make up sentences that would be on a 2 level. Make up sentences that would be on a 4 level. Place them in the correct places.

Try the following exercises on a computer. A computer naturally follows Christensen's reasoning. So compose with a word processing program. Try it!

3. Write (or type or process) a sentence—or use the following: "I fondly remember my grandmother's stained lace tablecloth and dilapidated refrigerator." Label it as a 1. Now write a 2. Now arbitrarily put a 3, 4 and then another 2, 3, 3. Fill them in. How did you fill them in? Try once going in order 2, then 3, then 4 then so on. Now try filling in the 2s. Then go back in fill in the 3s, then the 4s. Which way works best for you: a) going in order, b) filling in level by level, c) some combination?

Look at the sentence above again. Does your first 2 concern the tablecloth and the second concern the refrigerator? Or does each 2 concern the image of the tablecloth and refrigerator together? Either is okay as long as the 2s fit.

Here's another try. Fill in the following paragraph.

1) The biggest irritant in my English Class is Harold Baker, that jerk who sits behind me.
   2)
       3)
       3)
   2)
       3)
           4)

4.   Now simply write a paragraph and ignore Christensen. Once you have written the paragraph, go back and see if you can label the sentences. If you cannot, then the paragraph is probably not unified and coherent. Try to rewrite your sentences so as to make them clearly 2s or 3s or 4s. Try to revise them so that the reader can clearly see them as 2s, 3s, etc.

OBSERVATIONS AND CONCLUSIONS ON CHRISTENSEN

1.   The sentences in an introduction should generally be slanted, should go from general to specific: 1, 2, 3, 3, 4, 5, for example, where the 5 would be the thesis. Or maybe the thesis would be the 4 and the 5 would be a list of the subject segments to appear in the essay. The sentences in a conclusion should not go into much depth but simply restate the subject segments and thus reassert the thesis. A conclusion is also generally short. It should look like 1, 2, 2.

2.   For a freshman composition essay, a main body paragraph that has the following organization—1, 2, 2, 2, 2, 2, is generally not a very good paragraph. It is simply listing. It does not have depth or texture. But wait; don't throw it away. Put in some 3s. Then try some 4s. See what is happening? Maybe each 2, in turn, could become a paragraph itself. Wait! Think! It would then become a topic sentence (or a 1) of its own paragraph.

Look at some of the paragraphs in my Christensen essay. See how they could be a part of the paragraph above them? Put them back into the paragraph above them and see if they fit. Look at my purpose and audience. See why I have a 1, 2, 2 or 1, 2, 3 approach later in the essay.

3.   Following this method, you may write choppy paragraphs, ones composed of very simple sentences. For example,

1) My brother, Tim, likes mysteries.
   2) His favorite mystery is *The Last Good Kiss* by James Crumley.
       3) James Crumley is now his favorite author.

Combine the sentences:

1) Since my brother Tim, a mystery fan, read *The Last Good Kiss,* his favorite author is James Crumley.

Now you are ready to add 2s and 3s. Suppose you add them, and they too are choppy? Wait! Think! That's right, combine them.

4. Say you have a 3. It must have a 2, and it can only fit under that particular 2. You cannot simply move it up under another 2. However, you could conceivably exchange 2s, dragging the 3s and 4s and such forth with them—if they stay under the same 1.
5. If you have a paragraph that you can label, then can you add some 3s or 4s? Some 5s? Can you add some more 2s?
6. Some options:

A) Use the Generative Rhetoric of the Paragraph to write paragraphs. Try to get at least to a 3 level. This level will guarantee depth. Can you come back out, say to a 2? This broadening will add texture.

B) As you write your paragraph, try to label each sentence as you write it. Thus force yourself to a 3 or 4 level.

C) Ignore this method, but use it to check coherency and unity. If you do use it, then you need not worry so much about repeating key words, pronouns, or transitions. They will be there. A hint: Where might you use transitions? That's right, when you "come back out," when you go say from a 4 back out to a 2, you may want to give the reader a little help with a transition to fix him in the right place.

D) Your instructor can quickly tell you how you might fix your paragraphs. She might say that she cannot discern your 3 or 4 level sentences. She might say that you need to add 4s.

Notes—Grammatical Questions and Comments on You, Imperative Mood, Passive Voice, Singular/Genderless Pronouns, Who/Whom, Restriction, and Use of Indefinite Pronouns

1. You should not use **you in a formal essay.** *You* literally means the reader. Is that your intent?
    a. **A special note about you:** When students use *you* in formal essays, they are either writing like they talk, or they are not thinking about the audience.
        i.   You know how we talk, right? We always say "you know" or something with *you*. *You* literally means the reader, but it rarely means the reader in a formal essay.
        ii. Students also use **you** to avoid specifying the audience: freshman students, scholars, high school students, parents, etc. Students should attempt to specify the audience by naming it rather than using *you*. **A good place to name the audience is right up front, in the background section of an essay.**
    b. Why, then, do I use *you* throughout this essay? You are right if you guessed that the purpose and audience shifted. During the essay, I was hoping to get an instructor's attention. In the exercises, I shifted my attention to students. These exercises are like instructions (see **imperative mood).** The *you* literally is *you*, the reader. And I hope that readers are students and that the *you* applies to students.
    c. Throughout this manual, I have asked, suggested, ordered, or commanded. When I do so, the first word of the sentence is a verb. But this verb is not the subject. What is the subject? The subject is the person reading, or *you*. This is the **imperative mood** (see the grammar chart and the description of verbs in grammar). It is a mood that gives a command, a suggestion, or an order. You rarely need to use it, unless you are writing questions like these or a manual like this one. **Again, your persona and purpose will determine your rare use of *you*.**

    d. Now look at the use of *you* in some of the excerpts. Here, *you* in the informal paragraphs, written as entertainment, is a **rhetorical *you.*** The use of *you* in these paragraphs approximates the way we talk, you know. You understand? Thus, you should go back to the original advice, you should not use *you* in formal essays. See **point of view errors** in grammar mistakes. See my earlier discussion of the use of *you.*

2. Notice the times that I use *I.* **I use *I* when it is convenient to do so.** It is better to use *I* than the passive voice: "The essay is written . . . ," for instance. Or here is another passive voice that I've written to avoid the use of *I:* "The exercises were presented . . ." However, a writer should avoid **"in my opinion," or "I think"** because obviously what I have written is what I think. See my earlier discussion of the use of *I.*

3. Look at the pronouns throughout the essay in the advice about applying Christensen's method to the essay. How do I deal with the **singular pronouns for either gender?** English does not have a singular pronoun for either gender. Therefore, either shift unobtrusively between *he* or *she,* or better perhaps, try to use plural terms, *students* for instance, and use *they.* What is the subject of these last sentences? Whom are they addressed to? *You,* imperative mood, right? See why?

4. Why do I use *whom* instead of *who?* Notice my **use of *who* and *whom*** throughout this manual. *Who* should always be in the subject slot. *Whom* should always be in the object slot. Try the following. In declarative sentences, if the nasty *W* word has a verb after it, it should probably be *who.* If it has a noun after it, it should be a *whom.* This simple rule, like most rules, works most of the time. See pronoun case errors in grammar mistakes section.

5. Look up at sentence 1 under exercise 3. Huh? That sentence is "My brother, Tim, likes mystery novels." How many brothers does the writer of that sentence have? He has just one brother. How do I know? *Tim,* with commas around it, is a non-restrictive **appositive.** It simply renames *brother.* "My brother Tim likes mystery novels." Now how many brothers does the writer have? He has more than one. Tim is a restrictive appositive. It specifies which brother. Do you see the importance and efficiency of commas? See restriction and non-restriction in punctuation.

6. Make sure that indefinite pronouns have a clear antecedent.

    a. In the examples of paragraphs and in the essay, look for my use of ***this*** and ***it.*** How many sentences begin with ***it* or *there?*** *It* is a pronoun and is perfectly acceptable to use. However if *it* is simply an expletive, if *it* simply fills the subject slot, then you should avoid it. The same is true of *there.*

    b. ***This,*** unlike *it, he,* or *she,* usually refers to an idea expressed in a phrase or clause or whole sentence. Therefore, *this* is indefinite; *this* can get confusing. So put a summarizing noun after it. *This principle, this progress,* this practice is better than simply using *this.* Do any of my *this*'s confuse you? If a writer uses a linking verb—*is, are, was*—then *this* alone as the subject may be okay. With the linking verb the *this* is equated to the adjective or the noun on the other side of the verb.

    c. Often, students and other writers also throw ***which*** around. It too is indefinite and can cause confusion about what it refers to.

    d. Look at these bad sentences:
    It is apparent that we can't know this. There is, though, no reason that we should understand this. It is best then just to forget this, which is my point. That which is apparent is best forgotten.
    What in the world am I talking about? Those sentences say nothing but were easy to write. Have you heard or read sentences like them before? Politicians, bureaucrats, and people who have nothing to say but like easy writing write like this. Be very careful about using these indeterminate pronouns. Make sure that they have a referent. See pronoun reference in grammar mistakes.

Generative Rhetoric of the Essay

Christensen did not apply his method for describing sentences within a paragraph to the essay. But a student or instructor can very easily apply Christensen's method to paragraphs within an essay.

First, students and instructors should look at my essay on Christensen. They should look at the paragraph levels that I marked. How many paragraphs in the introduction? Where is the thesis? How many subject segments? What level are they at?

After looking at my example, a student should try writing his own essay using this method. A word processing program is an immense help.

An essay, unlike a paragraph, can indeed have two 1s. Those two 1 paragraphs would be the introduction (if the essay has a one paragraph introduction) and the conclusion (if the essay has a one paragraph conclusion). The rest of the essay should have paragraphs that are 2s that develop the thesis. If the student has subject segments listed after the thesis, then he should have as many 2s as he has subject segments listed. If she has three subject segments, then she should have three 2s.

Each 2, should in turn become a topic sentence that is labeled a 1.

So the basic five paragraph essay should look like the following: 1, 2, 2, 2, 1. Thus, if a student can write a thesis with subject segments attached, he can in turn write three topic sentences. Then he can restate those topic sentences and reassert the thesis for the first sentence of the conclusion. Thus, the student can have a ready-made outline in his head if he just has the thesis. Thinking as such, he can easily write an in-class essay.

A computer is especially helpful for writing in this manner. A student should sit down at a computer and write his thesis with subject segments listed afterward. Now, that student should write a topic sentence on the first subject segment and label it 1. Now, the student should skip a few spaces (hit enter) and write subject segment two as a topic sentence and label it a 1. Now, the diligent student who is following this essay should do the same for subject segment three. Then the persevering student should put the listed subjected segments in front of the thesis and put this sentence down as the first sentence of the conclusion. Now, with these five sentences; the tired, sweaty, confused student should go back to each topic sentence and write sentences using Christensen's method of paragraphing.

With his main body now complete, maybe the newly resuscitated and enlightened student can look at his main body. Perhaps he can add paragraphs that are at 3 levels. Perhaps she has a very long paragraph, something like 1, 2, 3, 4, 5, 5, 5, 2, 3, 4, 4, 4. She could hit enter and tab on her computer at the second 2 sentence. Now, she would have two paragraphs. Since the first is a 2, the second would be a 3. She would now change the 2 sentence in that newly created paragraph to a 1 and have a 1, 2, 3, 3, 3 paragraph. Maybe there's another more complex or complicated 3 sentence that could become the topic sentence of yet another paragraph that would become a 4. Now, she has some depth and texture within her essay and is moving beyond the basic five paragraph essay.

If a writer breaks a paragraph into two paragraphs, the second paragraph will be subordinate as long as it addresses something in the previous paragraph. The topic sentence will thus indicate the level from the previous paragraph that the new paragraph will elaborate. Thus, as I have said, the topic sentence should fix the paragraph within the context of the whole essay.

Maybe the drooling, tired, but encouraged student now sees that he has a main body that looks like the following 2, 3, 2, 2, 3. Any fours around? Now, that future A student writes his introduction and the conclusion.

Thus, the student is writing "from the inside." The main body creates itself. And thus, just maybe, the introduction will be easier to write. Following this process will, of course, be very difficult at first. But a student should give it a good try in order to see what works best for her. As I said in the first discussion, if a student can write one sentence, with Christensen, she can write a whole essay.

Now, I'd like to return to some bold and italicized comments from my essay: (**I will also add that the topic sentence should not just tell what is in the paragraph but should also fix the para-**

graph within the context of the whole essay. See the discussion about Christensen's Rhetoric of the Paragraph applied to the Essay).

Instructors should note (and students should pay very close attention) that, given the above quote, an instructor could relatively easily grade an essay just by finding the thesis and then looking at each topic sentence. Since each topic sentence fixes that paragraph in the context of the whole essay—in other words declares the paragraph as a 3 attached to the 2 right above it or that it is the second 2—then the grader should know where she is in the essay just by reading the topic sentences. So an instructor could grade an essay just by looking at topic sentences, thesis, and first sentence of the conclusion.

If the sentences in the paragraph are now clearly following subordinate and coordinate patterns, then the student has an organized essay. With any attention now not just to content but to grammar, mechanics, punctuation, and style, the student is not just writing a passable essay but an eloquent one.

Assignment on Christensen

As I said earlier, I believe that composing on a computer matches Christensen's method. I also think that composing on a computer, since it is so much faster than writing long hand or even typing, and since it allows you to quickly change or move text, makes writing easier.

Try using Christensen on your next out-of-class writing assignment. Compose on a computer. Label the levels of your sentence, either on your computer or afterwards with a pencil. Find a fellow student and go over each other's essay. Turn this essay with your marked levels of generality in to your professor. See if she can offer any advice.

GRAMMAR

A Note to Instructors

I use the term *grammar* here rather loosely, as any method of understanding how the language works. My view of grammar is a writer's perspective. I try to find what elements of the language work and what elements don't. But I try to use traditional terms and definitions to describe my notions. I think that anyone could come up with his own way of understanding language, his own grammar, even a freshman composition student. I'd consider a computer program a grammar. Students and instructors both have been forced to use computer programs.

However, most folks will assume that grammar means the very formal grammar of linguists or grammarians. These confusions in meaning account for our thinking about the teaching of grammar. Just as students assume that they can't learn grammar, so many teachers assume that we can't teach grammar or that teaching grammar does little good for students. This pedagogical assumption depends again upon how we interpret "grammar." The famous Braddock, Lloyd-Jones, and Schoer dictum does not say that teaching grammar produces no results or harmful results, but rather, this influential study says that the teaching of *formal* grammar produces questionable results. And most studies look at the result of teaching grammar after only one semester. A full understanding of language takes years, and in college composition we are given a year, or maybe a semester. So the jury is still out concerning **the benefit of teaching a formal grammar to most students** (my qualifications are deliberate). As Rei Noguchi and Constance Weaver explain, students don't so much need a complete grammar as a method of understanding basic sentence structure and sentence elements. They each come up with a grammar. From a writer's perspective, I think that beginning writers need a logical way of understanding subjects, verbs, objectives, and modifiers and then different types of words, phrases, or clauses that function as the above. Application to students' own writing and a systematic "grammar" (or way of understanding sentences) seems to work best. What most students have as a grammar is a list of "do nots," which are often wrong, incomplete, or partial. So, most important in teaching grammar is not necessarily to insist on memorization but on teaching some logic, or why a mistake is a mistake.

In defense of grammar, from my own experience, knowledge of grammar is absolutely vital in publishing one's own works. Editing, copyediting, and the insights and compromises that they bring require a firm understanding of grammar, punctuation, and mechanics. Yet no one, least of all me, can master all of the problems in his own writing.

A Note to Students
Many students assume that either humans have a grammar gene or they don't. They then assume that if they don't have the gene, then they can never learn grammar.

A Note on Qualifiers
(Notice that I said "many." I did so to make a qualified statement so as to not insult all students. Words like *very, quite,* and *rather* are mostly needless qualifiers while words like *most, many,* and *some* are wisely chosen qualifiers).

But those scientists studying our genetic makeup have yet to find a gene for grammar. So students can learn grammar. But learning grammar takes a lot of work, just as learning math or a language does. A teacher can't simply teach a student grammar. The student must struggle with the material. And yes, a student can teach himself grammar. And the acquisition of a grammar can change a student's writing life; can give him the keys to heaven.

With knowledge of how the language works, a student can start to *consciously manipulate the language.* This conscious manipulation of the language is style. This conscious manipulation of the language enables the student to get an A or a B in composition. It gives the student's writing some eloquence.

Furthermore, when the populace at large, other professors, and potential employers complain about students' thinking and writing ability, they most often complain of style. So if a student is to do well in college and later on in life, he should learn grammar very early on. He should overcome that assumed genetic deficiency and use composition class as his entrée into grammar enlightenment.

In teaching myself and then others grammar, I found that I and others needed to learn the structure of the language before we could see why a mistake was a mistake. Let me repeat that: **We need to learn structure to learn WHY a mistake is a mistake.** Mistakes are mistakes not because the god of grammar or a bunch of blue-haired English teachers simply declared them mistakes. They are mistakes because they impede understanding. They cost the company money. So in order to understand the terminology that textbooks use to describe the mistakes, students need to understand that terminology and its application.

So before I start to talk about grammar mistakes, I first look very closely at the structure of the language. A funny thing happens when a student starts to study the structure of the language. She becomes a better writer. She sees how she should make sentences, put the words together. She sees the options that she has. She makes better grades and lives happily ever after. So students should buckle up, gird their loins, stick their chins out, and start studying the structure.

I first describe parts of speech. I do so by giving the name of the part of speech and then giving the **function** of the word. I define then by function. Then I give a grammar chart that students and I designed. This grammar chart will cover 90% of sentence making. A student should keep the chart with him. In looking at his own sentences, he should try to see what each grammatical element is and describe its function by looking at the chart.

After the chart, I give some axioms about writing. With a knowledge of function, a student can start to manipulate the language. Once students understand the chart, they can also more easily understand punctuation. So I discuss punctuation in this section also. Then I discuss grammar mistakes, which should now be obvious to students.

In my classes, I encourage students to simultaneously listen to me talk about the sections following, to study the chart, and to study the handbook. In doing so, students will get three presentations and perhaps understand one best. If they have difficulty, I encourage them to go to the writing center and seek help. Best of all, I hope that students might come up with their own way of understanding structure and thus mistakes.

I hope that what I suggest here is an outline with some commentary. Instructors should be able to elaborate on these ideas. Handbooks should more fully discuss these ideas.

A Note to Students and Instructors on Parts of Speech and Chart

You may want to skip past this section on Parts of Speech and phrases and clauses to the chart and the comments about it—and then come back to this section (Why did I put that dash there? Read on, and then see if you can figure out if I need it). You may find that the chart and its comments answer more questions than this section. Wouldn't it be neat if this manual were hypertext and you could click on the link that you want? We will work on the hyperlinks.

A Note on the Subjunctive Mood

Look at the verb above, *were* instead of *was*. This is not hypertext so this is a condition contrary to fact. That condition requires a special type of verb: the subjunctive mood.

PARTS OF SPEECH

Let's start with this premise. All sentences have a subject and a verb. Most have a subject, a verb, and some sort of object(s). Besides subjects, verbs, and objects, words, phrases, and clauses can function as modifiers. Modifiers are adjectives or adverbs. So the chart and my description below define parts of speech by their function—as a subject, verb, object, adjective modifier, or adverb modifier. Students should perhaps study this section and the grammar chart simultaneously. Those hyperlinks are coming.

name   function

Nouns are used to make subjects and objects.
Pronouns are used to make subjects and objects (be aware of case: nominative, objective, possessive, and reflexive. Pronouns used as subjects must be in nominative case; pronouns used in objective case must be objects; pronouns used in possessive case must be adjectives.).
    Relative Pronouns join subordinate adjective clauses to the independent clause and also make noun clauses.
Verbs, as words, function as the verb in a sentence (see comments on the chart). Verb indicates tense, mood (indicative, imperative, question), and voice (active or passive). Verbs can be transitive, intransitive, or linking.

Verbals are manipulated verbs used as nouns, adjectives, or adverbs.
Participles are the verb form + *ing* or past tense form used as an adjective.
Gerunds are the verb form + *ing* used as a noun.
Infinitives consist of to + base form of the verb used as an adjective, noun, or adverb.
Adjectives are used to modify nouns—so it will modify those words functioning as subjects, and objects or those words in a subject or object slot, which, of course, would be nouns. Sometimes an adjective functions as an object complement.
Adverbs modify verbs, other adverbs, or adjectives.

(**A Note:** for adverbs and adjectives, be aware of degrees: positive, comparative, and superlative).

Prepositions make preposition phrases that can be used as adjectives or adverbs. (See comment under noun phrases).
Conjunctions join words, phrases, and clauses.
Coordinating conjunctions join grammatically equal elements.
  Correlative conjunctions are like scorpions; they run in pairs: <u>and</u> and <u>or</u>, <u>not only</u> and <u>but also</u>; <u>either</u> and <u>or</u>. They increase emphasis or equal grammatical elements.
  Conjunctive adverbs join independent clauses and show relationship between two clauses also used as transitions within essays, paragraphs, or sentences.
  Subordinating conjunctions join <u>adverbial clauses</u> to the main clause of the sentence.
  Interjections are simply words added to a sentence to add emotion. Avoid them in formal writing. Avoid them in formal writing because they can be cheap or redundant.

A Note on the Exclamation Mark and on Interjections
Nothing is less exciting than an exclamation mark. The words and the context should indicate excitement, importance, or surprise, not an exclamation mark or an interjection!

SENTENCES, CLAUSES, PHRASES

A sentence may be:

  Simple—one main clause
  Compound—two independent clauses joined by a comma and coord. conj. or a semicolon
  Complex—a main clause and one or more dep. clauses
  Compound-complex—two indep. clauses and at least one dep. clause

A **subordinate or dependent clause** is not grammatically complete and cannot stand alone like a main or independent clause. A subordinate clause will be an adjective, adverb, or noun clause.
Relative pronouns and **subordinating conjunctions** make clauses.

  Adverb clauses have a subject and a predicate but have a **subordinating conjunction** in front of them. And adverb clauses thus modify the main verb of the main clause.
  Adjective clauses modify a noun in the main clause and are joined to the main clause by a **relative pronoun** (will be either restrictive or non-restrictive).
  Noun clauses function the same as a single noun.

A **phrase,** unlike a clause, has no subject and verb. A phrase basically has a noun or an object with a "phrase-maker" (a **preposition, infinitive, participle,** or **gerund)** in front of it.

Adverb phrases may be **prepositional phrases, gerund phrases,** or **infinitive phrases. Adjective phrases** may be **prepositional phrases, participle phrases,** or **infinitive phrases. Noun phrases** may be **gerund phrases** or **infinitive phrases. *Most grammarians** say that **prepositional phrases** cannot be noun phrases. Yet some professional and amateur grammarians say that prepositional phrases can function as the direction object, indirect object, or even the subject complement of a sentence. So these phrases would, by my logic, be nouns. My point is that prepositional phrases in noun "slots," thus the slots that I just mentioned, can be clumsy or misleading.

SPECIAL PHRASES AND CLAUSES

1. An **absolute phrase** does not directly modify anything in the sentence. It comments upon the relation between the subject and the verb. It usually consists of a noun and an -ing verb.

Feet pumping the ground, head down, shoulders dropped, Barry Sanders got the first down.
   Absolute phrases are usually short, and they cannot dangle. Try putting the absolutes in the above sentence anywhere in the sentence. Thus, absolute phrases are very helpful constructions for combining sentences and for streamlining sentences.

2. An **elliptical clause** is an adverbial clause. However, its subject is also the subject of the sentence. Therefore, the subject of the clause has been "elliptisized." The subject of the sentence must then be right next to the clause, or the clause will dangle. An elliptical clause has a subordinating conjunction followed by an -*ing* verb.

After running for four miles a day, John drank four glasses of water.
Before finding a skirt that fit, Joan went to the mall every night for six days.

Note: some textbooks and teachers call this construction an adverb phrase with a gerund or gerund phrase as their objects. See why? I think that my definition is closer to the process that we go through to get such constructions. And, if thinking of these as elliptical clauses, a writer is less likely to write dangling modifiers.

Similarities:

1. A **participle or gerund phrase** has an -*ing* verb followed by a noun or a noun phrase or a clause.
2. An **absolute** usually has a noun and then an -*ing* verb. Or, it has what looks to be a noun and a participle.
3. An **elliptical clause** has a subordinating conjunction (which you can mistake for a preposition if you don't look at function) and an -*ing* word.

GRAMMAR CHART OBSERVATIONS

Concerning Function 1: The problem, to me, is that we use the same word for both "function" and for the word that fulfills that function for **verb, adjective, and adverb.** We use different words for function and words that fulfill that function for subject—noun, pronoun, etc. So I think that when we say "verb," we confuse students because we don't imply whether we are talking about a function or a word. Also, I avoid the term *verb phrase.* A sentence may have more than one word in the verb slot or verb function, but I see all those words having the same function. They are "the verb." In other words, they help the verb.

Verb: I don't believe that students really have that much trouble with verbs. They have grown up speaking and thus learning about helping verbs. What they learned or rather heard may have problems (agreement errors). But students generally can use transitive, intransitive, helping verbs, voice, and to a lesser degree mood. If students have problems just with mood and voice, then they are rather grammatically healthy with verbs. The main problem is with tense. Students often shift tenses in a section of writing and (I believe) local colloquialisms and speech patterns contribute to agreement errors (see grammar mistakes). Also, at this level, students should be aware of linking verbs and active verbs.

Concerning Function 2: Students should be very careful to look at the labels for the function: ACTORS, ACTIONS, RECEIVERS OF ACTIONS, and MODIFIERS. Watch someone do something. Throw an eraser, for instance. Now describe what that person did. You will say, "He threw the eraser." What you did, then, was to divide the action into an actor, an action, and a recipient of that action. Now you can add modifiers. We see the world in this manner, so this is the way our language works.

1. If students start thinking about function, they can also start thinking about position. Where in the sentence should the subject be? Instructors might try to make sentences with non-sensible or made up words and then see if students can spot the subjects, verbs, and objects. With this idea in mind, while sniffing sentences students may become able to generally find or sniff out subjects, objects, and verbs. The purpose of the chart is to give a simple theoretical idea about languages. In reading it, students should see that some word, phrase, or clause could *logically function* as some part of a sentence. However, in practice we may hardly or never use such a construction. But this is another lesson.

2. Because students and instructors say that students are genetically predisposed to misunderstand or to be incapable of understanding grammar, I note that students designed this chart.

3. People who work with language will disagree with my chart and my advice about punctuation and grammar mistakes. These disagreements may be frustrating, but they can teach. For example googling "preposition phrases as indirect objects" shows disagreements. Also, polling several friends, most could not think of a gerund serving as an indirect object. The best thing for any writer to do is to be able to adapt his style, mechanics, and punctuation to the task and the taskmaster. **So I'd encourage students to learn the following, to get advice from other texts and from teachers, and get as far along as possible. Learn as much "structure" as possible so that you can adapt your writing to the task.**

GRAMMAR CHART

Perception	Actor	Action	Receiver of Action					Modifier	
			Objects (four types)						
Function	Subject	Verb	Direct Object	Indirect Object	Subject Complement (Noun OR / Adjective)	Object Complement (Noun OR / Adjective)	Object of the Phrase	Adjective	Adverb
Words	Noun Pronoun (subjective case) Gerund Infinitive	Verbs: transitive or intransitive Linking Indicates tense, voice, mood	Noun Pronoun (objective case) Gerund infinitive	Noun Pronoun (objective case) Gerund infinitive	Noun Pronoun (subjective case) Gerund Infinitive OR Adjective Participle Infinitive	Noun Pronoun (objective case) Gerund Infinitive OR Adjective Participle Infinitive	Noun Pronoun (objective case) Gerund Infinitive	Adjectives (positive, comparative, and superlative degrees) Participle Infinitive Possessive case pronoun	Adverbs (positive, comparative, and superlative degrees) Infinitive
Phrases	Gerund Infinitive		Gerund Infinitive (Sometimes, but clumsily, a prepositional phrase)	Gerund (maybe never) Infinitive (Sometimes, but clumsily, a prepositional phrase)	Noun phrase: Gerund Infinitive Adj. phrase: Preposition Participle Infinitive	Noun phrase: Gerund Infinitive Adj. phrase: Preposition Participle Infinitive	Gerund Infinitive	Preposition Infinitive participle	Preposition Infinitive
Clauses	Noun (Relative Pronoun)		Noun clause (Relative Pronoun)	Noun clause (Relative Pronoun)	Noun clause (Relative Pronoun) Adjective (relative pronoun)	Noun clause (Relative Pronoun) Adjective (relative pronoun)	Noun clause (Relative Pronoun)	Adjective clause (relative pronoun)	Adverb clause (subordinating conjunction)

Absolutes: outside of chart.

Sentence Patterns and Grammar Chart
Instructors and students might notice that this grammar chart covers the traditional possible sentence constructions:

1. Subject-intransitive verb:
    Joe shook.
2. Subject-transitive verb-direct object:
    Joe shook his hand.
3. Subject-linking verb-subject complement: noun or adjective:
    Joe was our leader.
    Joe was nervous.
4. Subject-transitive verb-indirect object-direct object:
    Joe sent the department a letter.
5. Subject-transitive verb-direct object-object complement:
    Joe declared Sally his leader.

Of course, I left out the question. I'll leave questions about the question to students.

Students should take a look at these five patterns and then look at the chart. Students can write perfectly acceptable sentences just by following these patterns and/or the chart. Students should note too, if they can, what constructions these patterns do not cover. That's right, passive voice. Again, passive voice is a problem.

Students should further note that so far, with the sentence patterns mentioned, we are talking about the first row (or two rows given my meager computer abilities) of the chart. Now, students should note that we have left out modifiers—or adjectives and adverbs. So below are the same sentences with modifying words, phrases, and clauses added. These modifiers, of course, will be adjectives or adverbs.

1. Subject-intransitive verb:

Joe vigorously shook. A single word modifier, an adverb, was added.
   Cold Joe vigorously shook. Another single word modifier, an adjective, was now added. (What is peculiar about the two sentences of explanation? That's right. They are both passive voice construction. Can you see why? Can you see what passive voice is? Can you see why it distorts normal sentences? See why it is used? See all the questions that I ask and their form?)

2. Subject-transitive verb-direct object:

Spreading his fingers, Joe shook his hand. A phrase was added. This modifier is a participle. See the chart. As a participle phrase, it is an adjective.
   To warm his fingers, Joe shook his hand. A phrase was added. This modifier is an infinitive phrase. It is an adjective. Or I could also be convinced that it is an adverb. See why I can see it as either? Infinitives can make adjective or adverb phrases.
   Joe shook his hand over the plate. A phrase was added. This one is a prepositional phrase. What things, words, stuff, make a prepositional phrase? The placement of the phrase suggests to me that it is an adjective or an adverb because it is close to the object **and** to the verb. Such is the case with prepositional phrases. They can be adjectives or adverbs (or nouns. See the Chart). Here, now resorting to meaning, not placement or function, I'd guess that this particular prepositional phrase is an adverb. I think, maybe. See why it is confusing?

3.   Subject-linking verb-subject complement: noun or adjective:

After he subdued the aliens, Joe was our leader. A clause was added. This clause begins with a clause-making word called a *subordinating conjunction*. Subordinating conjunctions make adverb clauses. So this is an adverb clause.

   Joe was nervous because the aliens were ugly. Once again, as in the sentence above, an adverb clause was added. What kind of word, then, is *because? More rambling:* Who is doing all this adding to sentences? I am adding these clauses, phrases, and words. But I don't want to call attention to myself. I don't want to take credit—or blame. I might make a mistake. I want to hide. So I'm writing all those **passive voice** sentences.

A Note on Passive Voice

Writing passive voice sentences is a way to avoid responsibility. Now look at my sentence before this one. What is the subject of the sentence? What would you call the subject of this sentence? Can you use one of these gerund phrases as a subject in a sentence? (Whoops, I gave the answer away). You can use gerunds or gerund phrases and thus the actions that they express as subjects and thus cut the need for many passive voice constructions.

4.   Subject-transitive verb-indirect object-direct object:

Joe sent the department a letter, which he spent hours composing the night before. Now I added a clause (I'll take credit now and try to avoid passive voice). This clause begins with a relative pronoun. Relative pronouns make adjective or noun clauses. This is an adjective clause. I put a comma before it because it is a non-restrictive or non-essential adjective clause. Also, I keep in mind that *which* usually starts non-restrictive adjective clauses.

   Joe sent the department a letter that detailed his complaints. This clause also has an adjective modifier. This adjective modifier begins with a relative pronoun. This adjective modifier, I think, is restrictive or essential. It specifies which letter. I also know that *that* generally starts restrictive or essential adjective clauses.

5.   Subject-transitive verb-direct object-object complement:

Joe declared Betty his leader. I'm tired. I'm quitting. Look below.

An Exercise and Assignment on Sentences, Phrases, and Clauses

Here is a good, standard sentence. It has an active verb. It has a concrete subject and object.
   Joe shook his hands.
   Now I'm going to play with it.
   After he had been outside in the cold for two hours, shivering, holding his fingers stiff and spreading them; pale, cold, frosty Joe urgently shook his hands over the hot oven.
   Can you spot the phrases, clauses, and words doing the modifying? Can you identify them as adjectives or adverbs? Why did I put that semicolon after *them?* Take it away. Erase it. Imagine it gone. Now replace it with a comma. What happens to your reading of the sentence? What is the subject? Can you tell? So to repeat, why did I put a semicolon after *them?*
   Now try again.
   Shivering, shouting, cussing in a low deep growl; pale, cold, frosty Joe shook his opened hands, which were chafed to a pink rawness.

Get your teacher to write some more sentences. Or better yet, you write some.

Write a simple Subject-verb-object sentence. Now add as many words, phrases, and clauses as you can. Keep writing phrases and clauses until the sentence stops making sense. Go on; see how long you can do this. When it stops making sense or if you are exhausted, look at your sentence.

Are all your phrases, clauses, or words adjectives and adverbs?

If the sentence stopped making sense, try to find a spot where it stopped making sense.

Now, is it not making sense because of placement? Will it make sense if you move some phrases or clauses around? Did it stop making sense because you added too many of the same type of phrases, particularly prepositional phrases?

Look at your beastly sentence again, could you help it make more sense just through punctuation? Could you possibly replace some commas with semicolons? With dashes?

Assignment: Now look at your own writing. Can you combine sentences? Can you make longer sentences? Can you cut sentences shorter? Can you use active verbs?

A Note on Phrases and Clauses as Subjects and Objects (nouns)

Both phrases and clauses can be nouns and can thus function in the subject and object slots (even the object of a preposition). That is, you can use phrases and clauses as subjects and objects. Get your instructor to write some. Or go look for examples. And then, write some. The hard part is a subject that is a clause. These noun subjects would start with a relative pronoun: *how, which, who, that, which,* or something like them. They would not start with a subordinating conjunction. See why? Below are some noun clauses and subjects and objects.

The professor knew that the class had not read the assignment. (See why the *that* is really important in this sentence and in the one below?)

That the class had not read the assignment was obvious.

How he graded the essays caused the students the most confusion.

The students hated how he graded the essays.

Where he is going is unclear.

He knows not where he is going.

I read that these sentences are no good.

Which one of these sentences could be written more simply and efficiently?

ANOTHER NOTE ON PASSIVE VOICE—USING GERUNDS

Writing passive voice sentences is a way to avoid responsibility. Now look at my sentence before this one. What is the subject of the sentence? What would you call the subject of this sentence? Can you use one of these gerund phrases as a subject in a sentence? Why isn't this a participle phrase? See when you could use gerunds or gerund phrases in your writing?

PUNCTUATION

Comma Usage for Words, Phrases, and Clauses:

1. Put commas after any clause **before the main clause.** If you have two or more phrases put a comma between these introductory elements and the subject. Conjunctive adverbs

should probably have a comma. Coordinating Conjunctions should not. Other single words may or may not. Basically, the reader is expecting to see the subject first. If any element impedes the reader from logically and quickly getting to the subject, then the writer should put a comma after it to separate it from the main clause (the sentence).

2. If you have an **adverbial clause** (thus a subordinating conjunction) before the main clause, then you should put a comma between it and the main clause. If you put the adverbial clause in the middle of a sentence, then you should put commas around it. If you put it after the sentence, then percentage-wise, you should not put commas between the main clause and the adverb clause. In this case, meaning plays a part. If the adverb clause offers a contradiction or an exception, most editors will put a comma.

3. For **adjective clauses and phrases** you should ask yourself if these are restrictive or non-restrictive phrases or clauses. If you have a restrictive element, then you should not punctuate it. If you have a non-restrictive element, then you should surround it with commas. For adjective clauses (and thus the use of relative pronouns), you should use *which* for non-restrictive clauses and *that* for restrictive clauses.

4. For **adverbs in the middle of the sentence**—phrases or words—you should ask yourself if these elements "impede" the flow of the sentence. If these elements do slow the reader, then put commas around these elements. This practice is mostly a matter of taste or style.

5. For **compound sentences** (now we are talking about the use of coordinating conjunctions) you should use a semicolon if you join the independent clauses without a coordinating conjunction. You should use a comma if you use a coordinating conjunction. A conjunctive adverb requires a semicolon before it and a comma after it when it joins two independent clauses. Two sentences joined with a comma make a punctuation error called a **comma splice.** A mere comma attempts to splice the two sentences together. Two sentences jammed together without any punctuation creates an error called a **fused sentence or a run-on sentence.** As a Catholic colleague of mine used to say, "A fused sentence is two sentences living in sin without benefit of a semicolon."

6. When you have a **participle phrase** at the end of the sentence, put a comma between it and the sentence, if the participle phrase refers back to the subject. If the participle phrase refers to the word next to it, usually a noun, then put no comma after it. If you have a participle phrase at the end of the sentence and it does not refer to the subject or to the last noun but to some other noun in the sentence, then the reader will become confused. Avoid this construction if possible.

7. Always put commas around **absolutes.**

8. Of course, when you have **items in a series,** you should put commas around that series. For example if I write that you should retrieve a "yellow, blue and green ball," would you know if that ball has three colors (yellow, blue, and green) or just two (yellow and a blue/green combination)? So put one less comma than items. Write "yellow, blue, and green" ball. Also be sure that your items within the series (the things between the commas) are coordinate, parallel, and equal in structure and meaning. See later in this manual.

9. Some editors prefer that you should use a comma to show negation, contradiction, or a reversal. For example, **punctuate my way, not any other way.** Remember that clauses usually require punctuation more so than phrases. Remember that commas are like scorpions for the punctuation of adjectives or adverbs. They run in pairs. Use two or no commas for the punctuation of adjectives or adverbs in the middle of the sentence. For adjectives, restriction and non-restriction govern the punctuation. For adverbs, your preference and the readers' ease govern the punctuation.

Use of Semicolons
1. Use a semicolon to join two independent clauses (or two sentences) (see above).
2. When a writer has internal commas within structures, then he might replace a comma with a semicolon.

When Joe, fully knowing the complications, took the job as our leader, thereby calling attention to himself, we all thought that he was foolish.

When Joe, fully knowing the complications, took the job as our leader, thereby calling attention to himself; we all thought that he was foolish.

Use of Colons
The colon has one use. A sentence precedes it and a list, an enumeration, or a statement about that sentence should follow it. A semicolon usually has a sentence on either side of it (except when you use it to make clumped up commas clearer). A colon most often has a sentence on the left side of it and a phrase, clause, or even some very emphatic word or words to its right.

Joe fully knew the consequences of his actions: that punishment awaited him.

Sally knew what Joe's entry into the political primary meant: a challenge to her political health.

Use of Dashes and Parentheses:
Both dashes and parentheses are stronger than commas, so a writer should use them for emphasis or in place of comma (or pairs of commas) to avoid confusion. Look at my use of dashes and parentheses throughout this manual.

The committee consisted of Joe, our leader, Sally, his opponent, Sam, our favorite candidate, and the dean. (How many people are on the committee? Four? Seven? Six? Five?

The committee consisted of Joe (our leader), Sally (his opponent), Sam (our favorite candidate), and the dean. (Now, four people are on the committee).

STYLE, AXIOMS, AND RHETORIC IN WRITING SENTENCES

The result of all language, as John Gardner says, is to transcend itself. The only way for language to accomplish this task is to create an image. Since imagery is vital to the quality that we call description and vital to the rhetorical mode that we call description, description is a part of all language. The axioms below provide for efficient description. Instructors can help explain why all these axioms are true.

1. Try to preserve S V O (subject-verb-object) order of sentences.
2. Use active verbs. Avoid state of being verb: *is, are, was, am.* Avoid making automatic verbs by adding *ize* to a noun: *finalize, maximize, theorize, categorize.*
3. Use concrete nouns. Or, try to use as many concrete nouns as you can. If you find yourself writing about abstractions, use examples that use concrete nouns, metaphors, or vital imagery. You may find, then, when writing about abstractions, that you begin to use concrete adjective and adverb clauses to illustrate your main clause; thus, your sentence structure will automatically grow more complex.

4. Avoid stacking like modifiers, especially prepositional phrases and infinitive phrases, because they can be either adjectives, nouns, or adverbs. See why? Also, try to maintain parallelism.

5. Avoid passive voice. Passive voice automatically perverts the S V O order of sentences. Here is a passive voice sentence. Passive voice should be avoided by writers.

6. Avoid expletives or indefinite pronouns (<u>it</u> and <u>there</u>), especially as subjects. This practice keeps you from having concrete subjects. *It* is a pronoun and is perfectly acceptable to use. However if *it* is simply an expletive, if *it* simply fills the subject slot, then you should avoid it. The same is true of *there*. *This*, unlike *it, he,* or *she*, usually refers to an idea expressed in a phrase or clause or whole sentence. Therefore, *this* is indefinite, it can get confusing. So put a summarizing noun after it. *This principle, This progress, This practice* is better than simply using *this*.

7. Whether you consider them noun phrases or not, as do most grammarians, generally avoid putting prepositional phrases in the subject slot. These constructions sound trite and cute. For example: **Over the moon jumped the cow.** Disregard this advice if a prepositional phrase works well.

8. Be as precise as possible. Remember that a good sentence starts with a concrete subject and an active verb. Then try modification. Again, be precise and simple. Prefer the word to the phrase or the clause. Generally, prefer the phrase to the clause. Again, with more complex subject matter, in essays about beliefs or ideas, you may find yourself losing concrete nouns and active verbs. So now modification becomes important. Now you may want to use metaphors (similes perhaps) as analogies to explain the concept. For example, try explaining a scientific principle, (say the theory of relativity) without a metaphor or an analogy.

9. Modifications give a sentence direction and texture. You should use them. But, as cited in #2, don't stack like modifiers. Try to vary the types of modifying you do. Participle phrases, absolutes, and coordinate constructions are useful for modification and texture.

10. When you have a subject, a linking verb, and an adjective, could you put the adjective in front of the subject? If so, then do so. Instead of **the cake is chocolate,** write, the **chocolate cake.** What will happen is that you will no longer have a full sentence but just an adjective and a noun. Good! Now work on writing an active verb and a concrete noun for the object. Also, when you use a prepositional phrase beginning with *of,* see if you can simply turn the noun that the phrase modifies into a possessive. Instead of **the lawnmower of John** write **John's lawnmower.**

11. See Section on Word Usage in section on argumentation.

For more advice, skip to the section on the use of **Figurative Language.**

SENTENCE RHETORIC

simple sentence: S-V-O (subject-verb-object)
compound sentences: S-V-O; S-V-O or S-V-O, **and** S-V-O
complex sentence: S-V-O + a dependent clause
complex compound sentence: a compound sentence with one or more complex clauses in it

Sentences consist of a subject, verb, object, and then some modification. Sentences that have clauses before the main clause (the S-V-O) are **periodic sentences.** A reader has to wait until the period to get the full meaning of the sentence. A periodic sentence creates suspense or mystery. Sentences that have the clauses after the main clause are **loose sentences.** The reader gets the main clause, the most important information, right away and then gets some elaboration. A balanced sentence hardly exists anymore. A balanced sentence is usually a compound sentence with exactly the same structure in each clause.

Most business and technical writers prefer loose sentences. Even fiction writers more often use loose sentences or simple sentences. The periodic sentence then contains more suspense—if it is used sparingly.

After studying Christensen's paragraphing techniques, you might suspect that sentences have coordinate and subordinate structures. If a student has two sentences and wants to combine them, he has several options given complex and compound sentences.

Coordination: If a student has information that is of equal importance, then he should put that information in equal structures, whether sentences, dependent clauses, phrases, or even words.

Parallelism: In creating a series of equal structures, a student should make sure that all of his grammatical structures are equal.

Subordination: If a student has information that is of unequal importance, where one unit of information is more important than another, then he should reduce the lesser important element to a subordinate structure, whether a clause, phrase, or even a word. Loose or periodic sentences both have subordinate information. The loose and periodic information governs **the placement** of that information within the sentence, not the importance of the information.

PRACTICE STRUCTURE TEST

1. She knows that the cat is a male.

    What is <u>that the cat . . .</u>, a phrase or a clause?

    _____

    How does it function, that is, what type of phrase or clause is it?

    _____

2. Driving to Dallas usually takes me over six hours.

    What is <u>Driving to Dallas</u>?

    _____

3. Driving to Dallas, I ran over a cat.

    What is <u>Driving to Dallas</u>?

    _____

4. No one knows what she might do.

    What is the direct object?

    _____

    Is this object a word, a phrase, or a clause?

    _____

    What is <u>what</u>?

    _____

5. Of the three dogs, Joe's is the smartest.

    What is <u>of . . .</u>? How does it function? What type of word is <u>smartest</u>? What type of degree is it in?

    _____

6. While he could not spell, Joe was an excellent grammarian.

   What would you call While . . .? What is its function?

   _____

7. During his trip to Europe, Joe got married.

   What is During his . . . , a phrase or a clause? How does it function?

   _____

   What is to Europe? How does it function?

   _____

8. Since his trip, Joe hates marriage.

9. Since he went to Europe, Joe likes cathedrals.

   Look at sentence 8 & 9.

   What is Since in 8?

   _____

   What is it in 9?

   _____

   What is Since his trip, a phrase or a clause?

   _____

   What is Since he went to Europe in 9, a phrase or a clause?

   What is the function of each grammatical unit in each sentence?

   _____

10. Since going to Europe, Joe likes cathedrals.

    What is Since . . .? A hint, it is a special kind of clause.

    _____

    What is the subject, then, of this clause?

    _____

38

11. Although he missed class, Joe made an A.

     What type of word is <u>Although</u>?

     _____

     What then is the grammatical unit that it forms, and what is the function of this unit?

     _____

12. Though missing class, Joe made an A.

     What type of clause is in the sentence? It is the same as in 11.

     _____

     What type of similarities do you see?

     _____

13. Ears back, nostrils flared, eyes rolling, the bull charged.

     What type of grammatical units are <u>Ears back</u>, <u>nostrils flared</u>, <u>eyes rolling</u>?

     _____

14. Arm stretching over his head, wrist turning in, feet planted, Troy Aikman threw the ball.

     What similar types of units are in this sentence as in 13? What are they?

     _____

15. Fingers down, the chemist shook his hands.

     Again, what are the similar grammatical units?

     _____

     What are they?

     _____

16. Jumping over the log, Mary strained her ankle.

     What is <u>Jumping . . .</u>?

     _____

17. Jumping over that log is easy.

What is Jumping . . .?

_____

18. The red ball is usually lop-sided.

What is usually?

_____

19. Setting out all night, the bottle of milk smelled bad.

What is Setting . . .?

_____

APPLICATION OF SENTENCE STRUCTURE TO ESSAY WRITING

Pictures of My Brother

When I look through old family photograph albums, I marvel at what time has done to my relatives. This inevitable change shows especially in the pictures of us children. The physical change also shows a gradual change in personality. A series of photos of my brother Bill shows a personality developing.

1. My favorite photo is one of Billy in the first grade. 2. He sits and wears a purple western shirt, head slightly tilted, his hair slicked back in the flattop that my father always insisted that he wear, his freckled face bright and clean, his mouth shaped into an uncertain half grin. 2. His eyes though are the compelling force in the picture. [Why does the writer not combine these two sentences? 3. In them, I can see a mix of emotions caused by that first year in school: fear at the newness of the surroundings and the people, uncertainty as to what was expected of him, and the pain of being separated from his mother and sisters. [see how this writer uses a list of nouns and modifies each with an adj. prepositional phrase] 4. However, in among these emotions, I can also see a spark of anticipated excitement at times yet to come and mischievous wonder at finishing his first year.

Looking at pictures of successive grades, I see the changes in those emotions displayed in his eyes. 2. As time passes, the fear transforms to distrust and resentment, and the excited spark flickers then dies. 3. This change is most obvious to me in his eighth-grade picture. 4. Billy now slouches in his chair, his denim jacket defiantly left on and buttoned up (unlike my sisters and I who proudly display a new or favorite outfit). 5. He sits with his shoulders thrown back, head thrust slightly forward. 5. He no longer has a little boy's half smile. 5. Rather, his jaw is clinched tightly, his mouth hard and unsmiling. 5. His eyes too are hard, as if to reject any invasion of his privacy.

A third picture of Billy is a snapshot taken of him on his graduation night. 2. He stands, dressed in his cap and gown, hands clamped tightly in front of him. 2. His eyes are small and cold, his mouth shaped into an expression of boredom, intolerance, and impatience. 2. Behind him on the shelf, almost out of the camera's focus is a baby picture of him, a chubby baby, eyes laughing, fist flailing at some invisible object. 2. Also in the background, I can see my younger sister, Cheryl. 3. She looks at Billy's cap and gown. 4. Her lips are pressed tightly together as she tries desperately to hold back her tears, knowing that tomorrow her big brother will be leaving home.

As I looked at these pictures, I wonder what had changed that laughing baby and slightly shy little boy into the belligerent boy in the denim jacket and finally into the stern young man in the cap and gown. And I wonder what picture and what memory I like best. And I wonder what way he best liked himself.

Notice the statement of the subject segments in the introduction and their restatement in the conclusion. Are these clear?

Notice the sentence combining in this essay. This writer could have had many more sentences in the paragraph but, by combining them, she achieved greater paragraph coherence, more textured sentences, and thus starts to develop a style. Try to determine or distinguish the types of phrases and clauses that she used to combine sentences. Note the underlined parts. She quite effectively uses infinitive and participle phrases and absolute phrases to combine sentences.

Notice the levels of specificity in the paragraphs.

GRAMMAR MISTAKES

Students may want to start here and skip the earlier test, then go back to the test. Students should keep their grammar charts close by when reading this section. They should read very slowly. A class might require several weeks to get through all of these mistakes. As instructors and students should see, I use the terms from structure and from the chart to define the grammar mistakes. I think it best to first understand the definition, to see why it is conceivably an error, and then to look at mistakes. Anyone gets confused when she is bombarded by mistakes, but if she has some logic, some plan, some way to twist her mind so that she can see why something would be an error, then those errors become much more apparent. Students should respond to mistakes not because they "sound" wrong, but because they violate some grammatical logic. My purpose here, as it is throughout, in case my readers can't tell, is to provide students with the ability to write well by guarding against making mistakes in the first place. I hope that, with an understanding of structure and thus with an idea of what constitutes mistakes, students can smell errors before they happen.

I give several symbols for the mistakes. Different handbooks and different proofreaders use different symbols. Some for instance include omission of *that*, faulty subject, and faulty complement under "mixed construction." So an instructor or a text should guide the markings. Or an instructor can easily abbreviate the following. **Students should not be bashful about bringing marked essays to the instructor to explain the symbols and the mistakes.**

Because I am lazy and bored, I've disregarded **mechanics** and barely touch on **diction** and usage. So this manual, once again, is a supplement.

Instructors may find it easier to concentrate on the more common mistakes. These divisions are, admittedly, just a bit better than arbitrary. And again, the best way for a student to understand these mistakes and to guard against them in her own writing is to learn the structure of the language—back to the chart. Student always seem to be creating new mistakes.

GRAMMAR MISTAKES: WORDS

The mistakes below concern usage or placement. Again look back at the chart, particularly at verbs and pronouns. What is difficult about verbs and pronouns? Verbs have to "agree" in number with the subject. Pronouns have to agree in number with their antecedents. Now think about these principles before you read the advice below. After you have read about the mistakes below, look back at this information and at the chart to see if you can see the logic.

Usage (ww, diction, usage,): This mistake usually involves standard written English usage in America. It involves the misuse of words or the use of the wrong words.

1. *Sit/set, lie/lay, farther/further* often get confusing. Look up the words above in a good dictionary.
2. Student should be aware of the positive, comparative, and superlative degrees in adjectives and adverbs.
3. Sometimes students simply use the wrong word.
4. Sometimes a grammar check will catch troublesome words.

Improper use of Adjectives or Adverbs (ad)—using adjectives for adverbs or vice versa, or misusing the comparative or superlative forms of adjectives or adverbs.

a. **Joe smells bad.**
b. **Joe smells badly.**

In which sentence does Joe's nose not work, and in which one does Joe stink? Smell functions as a linking verb and thus links *smell* to *Joe. Joe* equals *bad.* So with *smell* in between *Joe* and *bad,* Joe stinks.

In b, the **ly** adverb modifies the verb smell. Thus Joe's smeller doesn't work, so Joe has a bad nose.

Reaching into his empty pockets, Joe felt poorly.

Huh, empty pockets made Joe feel sick? So Joe should feel *poor* when he reaches into his pockets.

Joe smells good.
Joe smells well.

I'll let you figure these two sentences out.

Pronouns and verbs cause students many problems. So I'll start with those mistakes. Some textbooks treat these two together. **Note:** I'll have a note at the end of my discussion of mistakes about how to look for them on a computer. You might want to skip to the note.

VERBS

Subject Verb agreement (agr or s-v-agr)—disagreement in number between subject and verb.

Most of the trouble here occurs due to tricky words.

Either **the vice president or the dean** *are* **to speak to the student committee this afternoon.**

Either is singular, so the verb should be *is*. Better yet, rewrite the sentence to clear up the confusion.

Either the Vice President is to speak or the Dean is to speak to the student committee . . .

Lack or misuse of subjunctive mood (subj, verbs)—The subjunctive mood of the verb indicates a condition contrary to fact, a wish, suggestion, demand, or requirement. It requires that the writer use <u>were</u> for <u>was</u>, <u>be</u> for <u>am</u>, <u>are</u>, and <u>is</u>; or a form of the third person singular of the present tense that is s-less.

Instead of saying, as Tevye does, "If I *was* a rich man," because he obviously is not, Tevye should say, "If I *were* a rich man."

If Joe talked to an instructor, administrator, judge, or lawyer, she might *demand* that he *withdraw* his complaint. The police might demand that Joe release his hostage.

Passive voice: Try to maintain actor-action-receiver of action order. See the chart. Below are some passive voice constructions and their corrections. As you might notice farther on, officials often use passive voice to avoid blame. Thus, such an action is not just a grammatical fault but a moral one. Thus bad language, as George Orwell points out, makes for bad politics.

Mary was hit. John hit Mary.
The lecture was given. Professor Jones gave the lecture.
The eighty-yard run was made by Kiki Barber. Kiki Barber made the eighty-yard run.
Iraq was invaded. The United States invaded Iraq.
The attack was launched. The United States Air Force launched the attack.
Credit will be given. The Savings and Loans Association will give you credit.
Mistakes were made. I made a mistake. The Secretary of Defense made a mistake.

PRONOUNS

Pronoun without an Antecedent (ref, p-ant)—<u>This</u>, <u>that</u>, <u>it</u>, and <u>which</u> are pronouns most often used without a clear antecedent because they are used to take the place of an idea implied by the preceding word-group instead of a single word.

Read the following.

> **This requires simple tinkering. It is apparent that this is something that it doesn't take brains to figure out. It has a simple process to fix that.**

Look at the above sentences. Look at the *it, this,* and *that* s. What on earth am I saying? I have no idea. I can't even fix it. But the sentences were easy to write.

It is a pronoun and is perfectly acceptable to use. However if *it* is simply an expletive, if *it* simply fills the subject slot, then you should avoid it. The same is true of *there. This,* unlike *it, he,* or *she,* usually refers to an idea expressed in a phrase or clause or whole sentence. Therefore, *this* is indefinite; *this* can get confusing. So put a summarizing noun after *this. This principle, This progress,* or *This practice* is better than simply using *this.* This is the third time you've seen the sentences above. I think, at least I count three. Instructors are obsessed by *it.* Here is a mistake that a student can indeed easily find and avoid simply by searching for *it* on a computer.

Mistakes with *which* usually involve trying to use this relative pronoun as a subordinating conjunction. Remember relative pronouns create adjective or noun clauses while subordinating conjunctions create adverb clause. You can't mix them. As with *it, that,* and *this,* advertisers and politicians tend to over use the words and create vagueness. You can avoid a whole lot of mistakes if you see *which* as always making non-restrictive adjective clauses. Thus, the *which* clause **should always modify the noun next to it and should always have commas around it.**

> **Sally won, which angered her brother Tommy.**

Here *which* is trying to create an adverb clause to modify won. It can't. Replace *which* with *that.*

> **Sally won that angered her brother Tommy.** Huh?

Here too is a problem.

> **Sally won the writing contest, which angered her brother Tom.**

Did the writing contest anger Tommy? Did Sally? Or did Sally's winning? Usually you can change the *which* clause to an adverb clause or to a participle modifying the subject to fix the error.

> **Sally won, angering her brother Tommy.**

Here is another.

> **Joe knows that he didn't study for any of his classes in college, which should qualify him to be a state senator.**
> **Joe knows that he didn't study for any of his classes in college, qualifying him to be a state senator.**

Here is yet another mistake that students have created in the last twenty-five years.

> **In *Faulkner's* novels, *he* deals with both the upper and lower classes in Mississippi.**

As with any possessive case, *Faulkner's* is an adjective. The pronoun *he* must take the place of a noun. Since *Faulkner's* is an adjective, *he* has no noun for an antecedent. So here is a correct rewrite.

In his novels, Faulkner deals with both the upper and lower classes in Mississippi.

Pronoun-antecedent disagreement (agr, p-agr)—a pronoun must agree in number with its antecedent. Advertisers, some publishers, and some government officials endorse this mistake. They see the following sentence as correct.

Everyone should get their just due.

However, *everyone* is singular and should demand a singular verb. English does not have a singular pronoun for either gender. Therefore, either shift unobtrusively between *he* or *she,* or try to use plural terms, *students* for instance, and use *their.*

Everyone should get her just due.

All of the following sentences that use corporate nouns are grammatically right. But they make no sense.

The corporation applauded all of its employees.

An *it* can applaud?

The committee actually was stunned when Joe was introduced. It made no sound at all.

How much sound can an inanimate *it* make?

The football team ran out onto the field. It practiced for an hour before the game.

This thing, this team, has twenty-two legs and arms and uses them all at once?
Change the antecedent to plurals and the sentences make more since.

The corporate members applauded all of their employees.
The committee members were actually stunned when Joe was introduced. They made no sound at all.
The football players ran out onto the field. They practiced for an hour before the game.

Pronoun in the Wrong Case (case, ca, p-case)—a pronoun must be in the proper case; nominative or subjective if it is a subject, objective if it is an object, and possessive if it is possessive.

Just between you and I, I hate grammar.

I is trying to be the subject of the preposition between. Therefore, that pronoun needs to be in the objective case.

Just between you and me, I hate grammar.

Tommy always speeds, so Joe hated him driving to Dallas.

Him should be the possessive *his.*

Tommy always speeds, so Joe hated his driving to Dallas.

Who should always be in the subject slot. *Whom* should always be in the object slot. Try the following. In declarative sentences, if the nasty *W* word has a verb after it, it should probably be *who.* If it has a noun after it, it should be a *whom.* This simple rule, like most rules, works most of the time. All of the sentences below are correct.

I don't know who robbed the store.
Do not ask for whom the bell tolls.
Joe claims that he saw the man who robbed the store.
The judge had previously prosecuted the man whom Joe saw.

Point of View (pov, shift,): use of *you* when not needed. *You* literally means whoever is reading the writing. You almost never need to use *you* in a formal essay. The Army is not very particular. Their posters say that "Uncle Sam wants you." However the Marines are particular. Their posters say that they "are looking for a few good men," or the Marines urge you to become one of the "few, the proud, the Marines." Students often use you as they use this, there, it, and which—as a way to keep from getting specific. Students should try to name to whom the essay is addressed.

GRAMMAR MISTAKES: PHRASES AND CLAUSES

If you have studied the chart, you can use it to study this section as well as the other sections. Take your time in reading and think about what I say. If you can understand the reasoning, then you are well on your way to avoiding mistakes in the first place as opposed to constantly looking for them.

1. You know that subordinating conjunctions make adverb clauses.
2. You know that relative pronouns make adjective and noun clauses.
3. You know that infinitives and prepositions can make adverb, adjective, or noun phrases.
4. You know that participles can make adjective phrases.
5. You know that gerunds can make noun phrases.

So look at the places where these types of constructions can go. Look at how they can function. If they are in the wrong place or if they are attempting the wrong function, then they are a mistake. See the logic?

1. For instance, consider **adverb clauses.** They will start with a subordinating conjunction like *while, before, during, after, if, because,* or etc. Where can placement or function of adverb clauses cause problems? Look at dangling modifiers (where the adverb clause is "elipticized"), faulty subjects (where the adverb clause tries to be a subject), and faulty complements (where the adverb clause tries to be the complement of the sentence). Now think about how you would punctuate adverb clauses in a sentence. Look back at punctuation. Can you now see a design to dealing with adverb clauses in a sentence?

2. **Adjective clauses,** like noun clauses, are made with a relative pronoun. Be careful that they are not misplaced. Be careful about who and whom. Be careful about restriction. Remember that restriction governs the punctuation of adjectives.

3. **Noun clauses** have problems with omission of *that* from the noun clause when they are used as an object. Any reason to put a comma between the verb and the object? The answer is "no."

4. **Adverb phrases** can be misplaced. How would you punctuate them? Whether you put commas around them or not is mostly up to how much disruption you think that they cause the sentence.

5. Now consider **adjective phrases.** Look above and see what phrasemakers start them. They should be place close to what they modify. So they can cause problems with dangling modifiers and misplaced modifiers. How do you punctuate adjective phrases? Remember restriction and non-restriction?

6. Now consider **noun phrases.** They can cause problems with faulty complements and can sometimes make clumsy subjects. How would you punctuate noun phrases? Would you want commas around the subject or the object? Of course you wouldn't.

   Look at the mistakes described below, and then return to this advice. How can **you** best understand **why** these are mistakes?

Dangling Modifier (dm, dangl., mm/dm)—usually a verbal phrase (participle, gerund, or infinitive) or prepositional phrase that does not properly modify the subject of the sentence or an elliptical clause that does not properly refer to the subject of the sentence.

One of the biggest culprits in causing dangling modifiers is passive voice construction.

An elliptical clause, as defined previously, is a special adverb clause whose subject is also the subject of the sentence. So if a writer tampers with the subject, the elliptical clause has the wrong subject. Look very closely at the tampering with the following sentence:

After she worked hard writing her essay for three days, Sally went on a shopping spree.
Look at the adverb clause beginning with the subordinating conjunction *after*.

After working hard writing her essay for three days, Sally went on a shopping spree.
Now look at what happened to the clause. It is now an elliptical clause. The clause is the subject.

After working hard writing her essay for three days, a shopping spree was taken.

After working hard writing her essay for three days, a shopping spree was Sally's reward.

Now notice that I moved the subject of the sentence—and thus also the subject of the ellipticized clause. The first time I moved it because of the passive voice. The second time that I moved it I just emphasized the shopping spree. In both cases, the elliptical clause dangles.

Here is a dangling participle.

Running behind the car, mud sprayed my dog.

Why was mud running behind the car?

Running through the park, my dog was sprayed with mud.

And another dangling participle

Having taught composition for thirty years, Joe's brain was numb.

I suppose that Joe kept his brain in a glass jar so that it could teach.

Having taught composition for thirty years, Joe felt as though his brain were numb.

(Notice the subjunctive mood in the sentence above?)
Here is a dangling infinitive:

To do well in school, discipline and responsibility are needed.

This mistake is a classic dangling modifier. The passive voice switches the normal S-V-O, actor-action-receiver of action around. Then it drops the former subject or the actor. So we have no real person to do well in school. You probably don't have too many disciplines and responsibilities in class with you.

To do well in school, a student needs discipline and responsibility.

Here is a dangling prepositional phrase. Again passive voice causes the dangling modifier. Can you fix it?

By calling many potential buyers, the magazine sales were increased by the energetic staff.

Misplaced Modifier (mm, mm/dm)—an improperly placed modifier that thus causes the sentence to be unclear, ambiguous, or distorted. This mistake usually involves an adjective modifier that is in the wrong place. Make sure that any adjective phrase or clause is placed next to or as close as possible to the work that it modifies. Single words can also be misplaced.

Joe watched the pine trees running in the park.

Look out for those pine trees running through the park. *Running in the park* is a participle phrase that should modify *Joe*. Put it closer to *Joe*.

Running in the park, Joe watched the pine trees.

A NOTE ON DANGLING AND MISPLACED MODIFIERS

Dangling modifiers have nothing to modify, thus the term *dangling*. You cannot simply cut and paste a dangling modifier to correct the sentence. You must rewrite the sentence. A misplaced modifier can simply be cut and pasted into the proper place in a sentence. An instructor may circle the misplaced modifier and draw a circle to where it should be.

It only hurts when I laugh.

So whatever this injury is, it only hurts as opposed to killing you. Hurting is no problem. It is thus misplaced. The sentence should be written as below.

It hurts only when I laugh.

Now this injury appropriately hurts just when the speaker laughs.

Stacked Modifiers (stacked): Do not stack modifiers, especially like modifiers. See writing advice and Faulty Subordination. Try to make sense of the following sentence.

Any student will fail if he does not stack his books in the chair in the corner between the northwest and north wall of the classroom within the next twenty minutes.

How could that student help but fail? Look at all the stacked prepositional phrases.

Faulty Complement (mixed/inc, F-Compl)—the equation of a subject with an improper complement: a normally adverbial clause, a preposition phrase, or a construction that, although a noun, cannot logically be equated with the subject. The most common mistake here is putting an adverb clause (one beginning with a subordinating conjunction) after a linking verb. A linking verb should have grammatically and semantically equal entities on either side of it. **Note: Look back at the start of this section on mistakes and at the chart and then at the advice about writing. Linking verbs always give you problems. Be on guard against them.**

An F is when a student fails.
Sometimes the reason that a student fails is because he doesn't study.
A student's passing is if he studies.

Note: **Do a search and find on a computer to look for** *"is if,"* *"is because,"* *"is when."* The best way to correct this error is to change the verb to an active verb.

An F occurs when a student fails.
A student fails because he doesn't study.
A student passes if he studies.

You can also sometimes change the subordinating conjunction to the relative pronoun *that* to make an adjective or noun clause.

The reason that a student fails is that he does not study.

Look at the following sentences.

An *A* is a lot of studying.
Lamar University is learning.

An *A* simply is not a lot of studying. It may *require* a lot of studying. Likewise, going to Lamar *means* that a student must study a lot, but Lamar is not a lot of studying. It is a university composed of bricks and lumber. Notice that gerunds are the problems here.

Success in school is through going to math class.

What huh? A preposition after a linking verb is just a bad idea.

Faulty Subject (mixed/inc, F-Subject)—occurs when a phrase or cause that is usually a modifier in the sentence appears as the subject itself.

> **When he studies all night does not necessarily mean success.**
> **Because he tries hard makes John a good student.**
> **If he gives his instructor an apple will help him pass.**

All of these sentences begin with a subordinate conjunction. What do they do? They make adverb clauses. Thus all of these sentences are trying to pass off an adverb clause as a subject. And of course, checking the chart, an adverb can't be a subject; only a noun can.

A NOTE ON DANGLING MODIFIERS

Look at my sentence above. What is checking the chart? That's right, an adverb. Do adverbs check charts? So "checking the chart" is a dangling modifier. What caused this dangling modifier? Who should be checking the chart? A student! But where is the word *student* in the sentence. So I should have written, "Checking the chart, a student will see that an adverb can't be a subject."

Here are corrections to the previous sentences. Notice how I made the corrections.

> **Even though he studied all night long, John did not pass.**
> **John is a good student because he tries hard.**
> **If he gives his instructor an apple, John will pass.**

Notice that I started by putting a noun in the subject slot then moved or rewrote the adverb clause.

Here's another faulty subject. Can you correct it on your own?

> **After a person works out is no time for a beer.**

Omission of that from the noun clause (That, omt, mixed/inc)—The word <u>that</u> is often used to join a noun clause to the rest of the sentence, particularly when the noun clause is the direct object of main verbs such as <u>say</u>, <u>think</u>, <u>believe</u>, <u>know</u>, <u>realize</u>, <u>suggest</u>, <u>imply</u>, etc.

(While many times, writers can excuse the omission of *that* from an adjective clause, the omission of *that* from the noun clause after the verb shows up more and more. It is particularly disconcerting.)

Read the following sentence very slowly and trace your thoughts about analyzing its structure as you read it. That is, trace your understanding of the sentence word by word. Here is the sentence.

> **I know Suzy will do the right thing and she will give Brad his money.**

What's the subject? Quickly, as you read! *I,* right?

Now what's the verb? Quickly, as you read. *Know,* right?

Now you expect an object right. Quickly, as you read. *Suzy,* right? Now wait, what will you do with all those other words? What do they do in the sentence?

Now stick a *that* in between *know* and *Suzy. Suzy will do . . .* is thus a noun clause. And that whole noun clause is the object of the verb. Wouldn't it be easier and save wear and tear on your brain if you got some kind of signal that the object is not just one word but a whole clause, say maybe a relative pronoun, say maybe a *that?* See the logic? Now what does the *I* know? *I* knows two things. *I* knows that Suzy will do the right thing and

that she will give Brad his money.

GRAMMAR MISTAKES: SENTENCES

Think about what sentences are. Think about the different parts of a sentence: subject, verb, object, modifiers. Think about what type of punctuation joins two sentences. Now, shift and think about meaning and logic. These mistakes are mistakes of either structure and/or logic.

Sentence fragment (frag)—a word group that is not grammatically complete and thus cannot stand alone as a complete assertion. Remember **fused sentence** (fs, run on) and **comma splice** (cs)? Refer back to the punctuation section. Misuse of a semicolon between an indep. clause and a dep. clause is a semicolon fragment. Below is a common mistake. Check the chart. *Although* is a subordinating conjunction. Comma after it or not, *although* makes whatever follows it into an adverb clause. So the following is a fragment.

Although, Matthew still remained optimistic.

Faulty Comparison (mixed/inc, F-comp)—a comparison that is ambiguous, that omits the terms of comparison, that is grammatically incorrect, or that is illogical.

Joe likes hunting as much as his wife.

See how not being aware of this mistake could get you in trouble? The sentence above has two possibilities.

a. Joe likes hunting as much as he likes his wife.
b. Joe likes hunting as much as his wife likes hunting.

Let's hope that the answer is b) and that Joe is not headed for divorce court.

Here's another common mistake. It is an incomplete comparison.

She liked the play so much.

She liked it so much that she did what? **She liked the play so much that she praised it for three days to her husband Joe.**

Joe's discount shopping offers more.

Here's a popular advertising slogan. What is the *more* that Joe's discount shopping offers: bills, prices, defective goods?

Joe's discount shopping offers more bargains.

And yet another Faulty comparison.

> **Since he considers himself a traditional conservative, Joe likes the *views* of George Will better than *Maureen Dowd.***

Can you spot what is not equal? This sentence compares views with a person. Since he considers himself a traditional conservative, Joe likes the views of George Will better than those of Maureen Dowd.

Faulty Parallelism (//, parall): When listing equal information, a writer needs to put the information in equal structures. Faulty parallelism occurs when the writer, in presenting a second or third unit of information, violates the structure of the first. Students often violate parallelism in listing subject segments after the thesis.
Look at the violations of structures in the sentences below.

> **A few college freshmen seem to be either hard working or natural geniuses.**

> **Correct: A few college freshmen seem to be either hard workers or natural geniuses.**
> **In this essay, I shall explain the battle of Gettysburg and how both armies responded to the battle.**
> **Correct: In this essay, I shall explain the battle of Gettysburg and the responses of both armies.**
> **Because the essay was both admirable in content and its organization was good, the instructor disliked giving it a low grade for consistently poor expression.**
> **Correct: Because the essay was both admirable in content and organization, the instructor disliked giving it a low grade for consistently poor expression.**

Faulty Coordination (coord/sub, F-Coord) occurs when the writer treats secondary information as as if it were primary and places the secondary information in a main clause or in a coordinate structure.

> **Sam carefully played his online video games with opponents from across the nation, and then he took his final in English 4341, Advanced Writing.**

So according to this sentence video gaming is as important to Sam as his final. At least put taking a final in the main clause of the sentence.

> **The professor brought graded quizzes to class, handed them to the students, and announced that he had not received tenure.**

Tenure is a very big deal for professors. This fact should be in the main clause. **A note:** For those of you who can follow, this sentence creates irony by equating these instances. This stylistic feat is creative and belongs to creative writing class.

> ***The Bridges of Madison County* was the most popular novel, and Clint Eastwood made it into a critically successful movie in 1995.**

The popularity of the novel and the critical acceptance of the movie are not equal. The sentences prior to this one should give the writer a clue as to which is more important. Reduce one fact to a dependent phrase, clause, or word.

Faulty subordination (coord/sub, F-Sub) occurs when the writer treats primary information as if it was secondary and places the primary information in a subordinate structure.

> **A large truck hurdled over an embankment on I-10, killing three people.**

The truck's crash is more important than the death of three people.

> **Three people were killed when a large truck hurdled over an embankment on I-10.**

> **Cormac McCarthy won a MacArthur Prize in the early eighties, and his first successful novel was *All the Pretty Horses* in 1992.**

What is more important, the fact that the blind McCarthy won a McArthur or the fact that his first successful novel was published in 1992? What does the sentence say is more important?

> **A grade is a designated mark that attempts to assess the progress and knowledge that a student has exhibited in the progress and process of a college course.**
> **Students were confused where to go when the instructor told them to line up at the door next to the two windows on the north side of the last classroom in Maes Hall.**

These sentences simply stack up modifiers. Stacking up modifiers, especially like ones (as in the last sentence), makes a sentence confusing. Try to streamline these sentences, if possible.

Faulty transition (trans, choppy, paragraph sign, unity, coh) occurs when the writer either fails to indicate the relation between units of information or indicates the wrong relation.

> **Although Joey began sweating and coughing as soon as he saw the test, he made a very bad score on the test.**

Replace *Although* with *because*.

> **When the semester started, the students worked hard and asked questions; none of them made higher than a C.**

The sentence grows abrupt after the semicolon. Put a *however* or some other contraction after it. Put a comma after the conjunctive adverb *however*.

> **The glassed-in garden room had steel reinforced glass; the glass shattered in a mild thunderstorm.**

Try to put a subordinating conjunction showing contradiction before *The glassed-in garden room* to make that sentence a dependent adverb clause. If this direction confuses you, review parts of speech section and the grammar chart.

Choppy sentences (choppy, paragraph sign, unity, coh). Choppy sentences slap the reader in the face. Because they are so choppy, these sentences also lose unity and coherence. So a writer should combine these sentences. Refer back to Christensen discussion for advice here.

> The swamps smelled. The factories belch gas. The logging plants expel a gagging gas in the fall. Harold liked the soft East Texas air.
> Even though the swamps smell, the factories belched gas, and the logging plants expelled a gagging gas; Harold liked the soft East Texas air.

MANY EXAMPLES AND DEFINITIONS FROM

Pixton, William. *Some Conventions of Standard Written English*, 2nd ed. Dubuque, Iowa: Kendall Hunt publishing Company, 1978.

A hint for proofreading on a computer

Since students have probably heeded my advice and composed on a computer, they might use the computer to check for mistakes. Since linking verbs cause mistakes, go to the search or find function and type in *space is space*. Find all the *is* s. See if you can change them to active verbs. See if you have any faulty complements. Now try *space was space*. Can you change any of these? Now try the faulty complements *is if, is when, is because*. Now type in *space you space*. Can you eliminate any of these? Now try *space this space*. Can you put summarizing nouns after this? Now try *which*. Make sure that the *which clause* is next to the noun that if modifies and then make sure that it is not trying to function as adjective and thus forming a reference mistake.

PRACTICE GRAMMAR AND PUNCTUATION TEST _____

Note: Like any other grammar or punctuation test, this test might help students become better proofreaders. But it will not necessarily make them better writers unless they can apply these concepts to their own writing. Therefore, students should proof each other's papers, find these mistakes in their own writing, write obvious mistakes on their own and then revise them. Students should look very closely at their graded papers and try to fix the grammar mistakes. Again, grammar is like math. As such, understanding grammar, I think, starts with concepts and then application of concepts to specific incidents. Neither teaching nor understanding grammar should be a series of memorized rules, observations, half-truths, and old-wives tales. A good writer usually develops his own grammatical understanding.

Below are a series of grammar and punctuation mistakes. Go through this practice test and don't just try to fix the mistake, but try to figure out which mistake it is, and then try to figure out why it is a mistake. Try to describe the mistake in your own words.

1. When a team loses a game, it usually depresses the players and the fans who support them.

   _____

   _____

2. To write a good essay, attention must be paid to content, organization, and expression by the writer.

   _____

   _____

3. Sometimes, I fail the student who I like the most.

   _____

   _____

4. The award should be given to whomever makes the greatest contribution to the sales program.

   _____

   _____

5. The only reason that you should miss class is if you break a limb on the way to school.

   _____

   _____

6. The bewildering variety of items in the typical grocery store make shopping for food very difficult.

7. After running one mile, Jim's shirt was soaked with perspiration.

8. Bob believed that he performed as good on the test as any of the other students.

9. I wish that I was going to Dallas with my parents this summer.

10. Lamar University is learning.

11. Driving slowly down Sixth Street, almost every traffic light will be green when the car reaches it.

12. Because the race is so long is the reason that Joe dropped out.

13. Johnny knows that playing good is its own reward.

14. Because Johnny failed the T.A.S.P., it requires that he take English 301.

_____

_____

15. Joe knows that he didn't study for any of his classes in college, which should qualify him to be a state senator.

_____

_____

16. Johnny rarely went to his mathematics class. That, no doubt, caused him to fail.

_____

_____

17. She liked the class so much.

_____

_____

18. After completing the test in record time, the scores were surprisingly high.

_____

_____

19. Joe often stands around campus looking dejected at the library.

_____

_____

20. In my class, I demanded that Charlie Johnson completes his work.

_____

_____

21. If the president of Lamar would appoint more students to administrative posts, it would increase his popularity.

_____

_____

22. I asked the clerk who I was supposed to see, but he gave me no answer.

_____

_____

23. Growing up, my teeth were crooked, so I wore braces.

_____

_____

24. Bill says that the time for a beer is when a person wants one.

_____

_____

25. Sometimes, I think that I should just shoot someone who tells me that they can't do grammar.

_____

_____

26. This university expects composition students to know how to write a coherent and unified essay and writing grammatical sentences.

_____

_____

Correct the Punctuation in the following sentences.

27. Joe knew that he and Jim would eventually get caught but he still kept stealing from the company's treasury.

28. Professor Flunkemoften whom Natalie saw go into the exotic dancers' bar is that distinguished looking gentleman going in office twenty-two.

29. First and foremost a student should study at least two hours a day.

30. The courses we hate are: History, English, and Philosophy.

31. However, we all need those core courses; History, English, and Philosophy.

32. Joe ripped up the paper, after he found out he had made a D.

33. Joe ripped up Sally's paper, because she had made a D.

34. Because he ripped up her paper, Sally swore that despite her friendship for Joe she would never trust him again.

35. Joe went home to pout but after crying for two hours Sally determined that she would never speak to Joe.

36. Prof. Flunkemoften looked upon this whole episode or at least what he knew of it with amusement.

37. **Sample or Diagnostic Grammar Test**

ENGLISH 1301, GRAMMAR AND PUNCTUATION TEST _____

Do not write on this test. Fill out your answers on a scan-tron sheet. Respond to the question or complete the statement with the best answer. Make sure that you know what the question asks. Some questions may give you hints. You may disregard the hints if you like and discuss them with your instructor at a later date. Consider this also as a test on test taking skills, logic, and reading comprehension. This test will be scary, but if you relax, try hard, and then **study your textbook and its webpage,** talk to your instructor, and make use of the writing center, your grammar skills and thus your writing should improve. The bold material in the parentheses indicates where you find explanation of this mistake in your textbook, *The Little Brown Handbook.*

Grammar, diction, parts of speech

1. Fused sentences (two sentences jammed together without any punctuation, also called "run-on sentences"), comma splices (two sentences joined with a mere comma), and fragments (sentences that lack a subject and/or a verb) usually result from overlooking punctuation, using the wrong punctuation, putting the wrong word in front of a sentence (usually a subordinating conjunction), or combining sentences in the wrong way. **Which one of the following is correct? (frag, cs, fs)**
    a. Bill Drool just couldn't pass Professor Flunkemoften's test. Although, he studied at least an hour a day.
    b. Bill Drool just couldn't pass Professor Flunkemoften's test, although, he studied at least an hour a day.
    c. Although he studied at least an hour a day, Bill Drool just couldn't pass Professor Flunkemoften's test.
    d. Bill Drool just couldn't pass Professor Flunkemoften's test, he studied at least an hour a day.

2. *Find the complete, correctly punctuated sentence.*
    a. After he began yoga, Bill Drool finally saw sense in grammar.
    b. After beginning yoga, finally seeing sense in grammar.
    c. Because, he began yoga.
    d. Bill Drool started Yoga he saw a connection between grammar and body.

3. Subjects and verbs should agree. You must simply practice to overcome this mistake. Oftentimes some indefinite singular nouns and coordinating conjunctions around the subject confuse students. Notice that subject/verb agreement can get really picky. So the best advice for such confusions, incidents, or discrepancies is to rewrite or revise the sentence to avoid the mistake. *Pick out the correct sentence.* **(agr-verb)**
    a. The subordinate clause, like so many adverb constructions, disrupt sentences when students put them in the middle of the sentence.
    b. To start a sentence with phrases prevent the reader from getting to the subject.
    c. Punctuation of sentences and clauses are the chief cause of student errors.
    d. Sentences and clauses with proper punctuation are not distracting.

4. Dangling Modifiers are usually constructions that appear before the subject. They either don't properly modify or refer to the subject. They usually sound silly. Since they have nothing to sensibly modify, they "dangle." You can correct them only by revising the sentence. **Which of the following is correct?** (dm)
   a. After slamming the book down, Professor Flunkemoften's podium shook.
   b. After Professor Flunkemoften slammed his book down, his podium shook.
   c. Shaking his fist at the students, the podium began to wobble.
   d. After shaking his fist at the students, the podium began to wobble.

5. Look at the silly things that three of the previous sentences' subjects are doing. **Try to find another correct sentence.** (dm)
   a. At the age of ten, a Ph.D. in physics was described by Professor Flunkemoften as his goal.
   b. To begin his college career, physics was studied by Professor Flunkemoften.
   c. After studying cosmology, it became evident that aptitude was Professor Flunkemoften's problem.
   d. After studying cosmology, Professor Flunkemoften decided to change his major to English.

6. Notice that passive voice constructions cause a lot of the mistakes. How many of the previous sentences are caused by passive voice constructions? If you can avoid it, passive voice is just not worth using. Passive voice takes what would normally be the object and puts it in the subject slot. **Which of the following is <u>not</u> a passive voice construction?** (vb)
   a. Literature was studied by Professor Flunkemoften.
   b. Professor Flunkemoften took up English by default.
   c. A college teaching job was sought.
   d. A college teaching job was eventually found.

7. Are you starting to be able to smell dangling modifiers? Can you smell them in your own writing? Here's a hint—if you have the time. The following sentences have *full* adverb clauses. *After Bill went to the movie, he drove home in his soaked convertible. While Bill watched the movie, rain drenched his new convertible.* A full adverb clause cannot dangle. A full adverb clause will have a subject and a verb and then a word before it that could also be a preposition. This word is a *subordinating conjunction* (the *when, before, during, after* type words that could also be prepositions). However, look at what I can do to full adverb clauses. I can pull the subject of the clause out of the clause and make it the subject of the sentence and the clause. *After going to the movie, Bill drove home in his soaked convertible.* However, look at the dangling modifier that occurs when I move the subject in the second sentence. *While watching the movie, rain drenched Bill's car.* See what happened? So if you can pick out the *full, complete* adverb clauses, then you can spot the correct answer. You now know another trick in avoiding dangling modifiers. **So which one of the following sentences does not have a dangling modifier?** (dm)
   a. When Professor Flunkemoften first went to graduate school, his grades were very poor.
   b. When first going to graduate school, Professor Flunkemoften's grades were very poor.
   c. After applying himself and studying harder, his writing improved.
   d. Consequently, while improving his writing, his grades got better and better.

8. A misplaced modifier is simply misplaced in the sentence so that it causes confusion or silliness. A writer can correct it, especially with a computer, simply by moving it to another place in the sentence. **Which sentence does not have a misplaced modifier? (mm)**
    a. Ms. Tolerance always walked her dog in a short skirt.
    b. The dog once chased Billy Drool with a choker chain.
    c. The dog almost choked himself twenty times.
    d. The dog choked himself almost twenty times.

9. Here is another general rule. Use concrete nouns and active verbs. Active verbs are verbs like *run, hit, stab, mutilate*. A linking verb is *is* or *was*. Look at how much more the active verbs repulse or shock you. The structures on either side of a linking verb must be equal in meaning and structure. The structures on the right side of the linking verb must be nouns or adjectives. We call those things to the right of the linking verb *complements*. Look at the sentences in this question, and find the linking verbs. Are the elements on either side equal? **Now, find the sentence with an active verb. (vb)**
    a. Professor Screwy is just not a scholar.
    b. Because he now faced a year of dealing with factions, Billy slapped himself in the forehead.
    c. The best way to write is to apply the cloth against your butt to the seat of a chair, stay in the chair, and write.
    d. Billy Drool was elected class president.

10. Subordinating conjunctions make adverb clauses—they usually modify a verb. They suggest time or movement, the type of things that a verb suggests. Thus these clauses **cannot** be used as subjects or complements. Remember that a complement is the object that comes after a linking verb. It should be to the right of the linking verb. Remember that linking verbs are like an equal sign. The subject must be a noun (word, phrase, or clause) and the complement (the thing on the right side of the linking verb) must be equal to the subject. A complement must be a noun or an adjective. Prepositional phrases usually make weak complements and sometimes unclear subjects. **Which one of the following sentences is correct? Or to ask the question another way, which one of the following sentences does not have the wrong sort of construction as a subject or a complement? So which one is used correctly? (mixed/inc)**
    a. While bathing or painting toes is not the time to study.
    b. If a student drools in class is a sign that he is confused.
    c. Because his mind is full of words, Professor Tolerance seems to talk in circles.
    d. When the students sit on the edge of their chairs and shoot their hands into the air is a sure sign that they are excited about class.

11. **Which of the following sentences has a problem with the subject or the complement of the sentence?** I've underlined the adverb clauses (the ones that begin with subordinating conjunctions) to give you a hint. **(mixed/inc)**
    a. The students twisted in their seats <u>when Professor Flunkemoften told them that there was no Santa Claus.</u>
    b. <u>If Professor Flunkemoften keeps making fun of student beliefs</u> should justify his dismissal.
    c. <u>Because students should give up their past beliefs about grammar,</u> Professor Flunkemoften was exonerated.
    d. So Professor Flunkemoften still teaches <u>even though he may be abrupt, rude, and uncaring.</u>

12. **Which one of the following sentences does not have a faulty subject?** Or which one of the following does not have a problem with the subject, something in the subject part of the sentence that just shouldn't be a subject? **(mixed/inc)**
    a. Because state funding is based on head counts, enrollment is always important.
    b. Because the school increased its standards is the reason enrollment dropped.
    c. If the administrators had only thought ahead would have made the enrollment drop less severe.
    d. When schools raise standards is the chief cause of enrollment drop.

13. **Which one of the following sentences does not have a faulty complement?** In other words, which sentence does not have a problem with the construction after the **linking verb?** Remember? This case involves an adverb clause next to an <u>is</u> or <u>was</u>. **(mixed/inc). Also look at the clumsy construction of the sentences with errors. Could you streamline them?**
    a. Thus one way for enrollment to increase is if Professor Flunkemoften would quit teaching.
    b. Of course, the reason he won't resign is because of tenure.
    c. He won't resign because he has tenure.
    d. But the reason that tenure exists is because of academic freedom.

14. Now look at these sentences with linking verbs (which are like equal signs). The subject and the complement (the stuff after the linking verb) just aren't equal in meaning. **Which one of the following is the best? (mixed/inc)**
    a. Granting tenure is almost a sacred part of the university system.
    b. Getting tenure is years of writing and publishing.
    c. Working in academics is lots of work reading, writing, and studying, not just teaching.

15. What are you starting to figure out? Linking verbs, besides just being lifeless, cause problems. So can you try to find better verbs? Can you replace your linking verbs with better verbs? Below are some corrections. Notice the verbs. **Pick out the one that is _not_ correct. (mixed/inc, vb)**
    a. Getting tenure takes years of writing and publishing.
    b. Working in academics takes lots of work reading, writing, and studying, not just teaching.
    c. Getting tenure is revising, staying up late, praying, and cussing.

16. *That* signals a noun clause. *That* should follow certain verbs, or the sentence becomes unclear. With these verbs, we usually need a noun clause in the object slot; thus, the reader needs to see a *that*. Also be very wary of the *and*. Make sure that the sentence reports all that the speaker "said" or "knew." **Which one of the following sentences is clearest? (mixed/inc)**
    a. I think Professor Tolerance is the best teacher at Lame Duck University.
    b. Billy Drool knows that Professor Flunkemoften, deep down inside, likes students and he tries to help them.
    c. Meantime, Professor Flunkemoften told the class the girl who was the smartest student he had ever met was sweet Mary Sunshine.
    d. But Professor Flunkemoften did not know that Mary Sunshine was just paroled.

17. Any time that a student uses a coordinating conjunction *(and, but, so, for, nor, or, yet)*, she should be sure that the elements that the coordinating conjunction joins are equal in structure. The elements should be *parallel*. **Which <u>one</u> of the following sentences is correct? (//)**
    a. All professors in the English department must teach grammar in composition class, grade countless essays, and contribute to the university in some manner.
    b. Teaching, grading, and contributions to the school are thus a part of a professor's worth.
    c. Professor Tolerance says that teaching, grading, and student appreciation should determine a professor's worth.
    d. Professor Flunkemoften responded with the fact that students may not fully appreciate professors, the fact that students may base opinions on grades, and on statistics from *U.S. News and World Report*.

18. Try that again. Find the sentence that is parallel. **(//)**
    a. Students who have good study habits, self-discipline, and time management skills are sure to be successful.
    b. However, not reading, skipping classes, and bad attitudes contribute to failure.
    c. Listening, taking notes, and conferences with instructors help students.
    d. Successful students are good listeners, diligent note takers, and attend class often.

19. **Select the sentence that has <u>no</u> agreement error** (with the pronoun). Advertisers have already given in to this mistake. Look at billboards, listen to TV ads, and see if you can spot them using this mistake. The underlined words will give you some help. **(agr)**
    a. Every student deserves <u>their</u> right to protest <u>their</u> grade.
    b. Given market conditions, the economy, and supply and demand, <u>everyone</u> is not capable of achieving <u>her</u> desired career.
    c. <u>Each</u> student should formulate <u>their</u> own plan for success.
    d. However success depends on each person defining success for <u>theirselves</u>.

20. Do not use a *which* clause as an adverb. A clause beginning with *which* should only modify a noun, and then it should be the noun closest to it. **Which one of the following sentences is the clearest? (mixed, inc, ref)**
    a. Since he has tenure, which is an academic right and tradition, Professor Flunkemoften is fairly safe from students' complaints.
    b. In a show of sympathy with the students, Professor Tolerance said that she would give up tenure, which upset Professor Flunkemoften.
    c. Now, Professor Screwy is torn between giving up his tenure or not, which has given him shingles.
    d. So Professor Tolerance took her tenure back, which confused everyone.

21. Always make sure that *it* has an antecedent; do not use it as an expletive, just a word to fill the subject slot. In other words, be sure that *it*, a pronoun, stands for something definite. Don't just throw *it* into sentences. Also be very sure that *this* has a clear antecedent. One way to make sure is to put a summarizing noun after *this*. Sometimes, though, with a linking verb, you don't need a summarizing noun after *this* because the linking verb equates it with the complement. **Which one of the following is the best sentence? (ref)**
    a. Now that Professor Tolerance gave up tenure but took it back, this has caused all sorts of confusion.
    b. Professor Tolerance knows that her action has caused legal confusion. This legal situation is very unusual at Lame Duck University.
    c. This should be a lesson to everybody. It is important to hold on to tenure.
    d. It is important that, in this, there is no way to resolve it.

22. **Which of the following sentences is the clearest? (ref)**
    a. It is obvious that there is no need for further judgment in this.
    b. Obviously, judging this is taking too much time.
    c. This situation needs to be dismissed.
    d. No one knows where it all started.

23. **Which of the following sentences is clearest and most efficient? (ref)**
    a. Professor Flunkemoften now knows this to be true. It is important to fight for tenure.
    b. There are times that Professor Screwy just does not know what to do about it.
    c. Other times, Professor Screwy does know what to do about this.
    d. Professor Tolerance now believes that tenure is a nuisance. To her, it is an antiquated idea.

24. Pronouns should be in the proper case: nominative (subject), objective (object), or possessive (adjective). The real problem occurs with *who* and *whom*. Use *who* for subject case and *whom* for objective. Here is a tip that sometimes works. If a noun comes after the dreaded *W* word, then it should probably be *whom*. If a verb comes after the dreaded *W* word, then it should probably be *who*. **Which of the following is a correct sentence? (ca)**
    a. Professor Screwy doesn't know whom he should blame for the low grades in his classes.
    b. Billy Drool knows exactly whom is to blame.
    c. The blame, as always, belongs to Professor Flunkemoften, whom never taught the students in their first classes.
    d. Thus Billy Drool does not know who he should write about on the bathroom walls.

25. **Which <u>one</u> of the following is correct?** (ca)
    a. In order to cut college expenses, the administration forced Professors Flunkemoften and Tolerance into the same office. She and him have already threatened each other.
    b. His sitting right across from her irritated Professor Tolerance to abstraction.
    c. Professor Screwy knew that him and professor Tolerance would both suffer.
    d. Us students just didn't care.

26. Remember that possessive pronouns are adjectives. As such, they must have a clear antecedent before them. ***Look at the use of pronouns and possessives in the sentences below. Which is the best sentence?*** (ca, ref)
    a. In Professor Flunkemoften's classes, he makes fun of students' inabilities.
    b. In her classes, Professor Tolerance compliments those students who try.
    c. Professor Screwy, he just doesn't care about anything.
    d. The composition instructors just cannot agree on their classroom conduct.

27. Be aware of corporate or group nouns in subject and pronoun agreement. All of the following sentences are technically correct. ***But which one of the following sentences doesn't sound stupid—as though this mass is a single human entity?*** The LBH gives some differing advice, but see how you can write yourself out of the problem? (ref)
    a. So the English Department had a conference, so it could correct those who needed correction.
    b. As usual the tenure committee complained that it needed a pay raise.
    c. The chair dismissed the entire committee and told it to go home.
    d. The members of the committee are now in their own offices and not talking to each other.

28. *The Little Brown Handbook* says that "comparisons should be complete and logical" (397). Look at the following comparisons. ***Which one is both complete and logical?*** Look at the hints. **(mixed/inc)**
    a. Professor Flunkemoften likes Shakespearean sonnets better than Professor Tolerance.
    b. Professor Screwy loved Chaucer so much.
    c. Professor Tolerance loved Greek myth so much that she spent a summer in Greece in a goatherd's shack.
    d. Professor Flunkemoften compares his knowledge of Greek myth with Professor Tolerance.

29. **Which <u>one</u> of the following is grammatically correct and most efficiently written?**
    a. If Professor Tolerance doesn't get elected teacher of the year will make her the most depressed teacher of the year.
    b. If Professor Tolerance doesn't get elected teacher of the year, it will make her the most depressed teacher of the year.
    c. If Professor Tolerance doesn't get elected teacher of the year, this will make her depressed.
    d. If Professor Tolerance doesn't get elected teacher of the year, she will be very depressed.

30. *Which **one** of the following is correct and most efficiently written?*
    a. Professor Flunkemoften secretly knew that his teacher was better than her.
    b. Because Professor Tolerance hugs and kisses all of her students makes her popular.
    c. Professor Screwy liked hugs and kisses as much as Professor Tolerance liked them.
    d. The hugs and kisses irritated Professor Flunkemoften so much.

31. *Which **one** of the following is correct?*
    a. Professor Flunkemoften's smartest student is that girl standing by the BMW in the short skirt.
    b. Wearing a short skirt to class, the desk creaked and groaned when the smart girl sat down.
    c. Wearing a short skirt to class did not help Billy Drool at all.
    d. Success in college is wearing a short skirt.

Punctuation (see LBH, chapters 28 Comma, 29 Semicolon, 32 Other Marks)

32. When a writer joins two sentences, he may join them with which of the following methods?
    a. a comma
    b. a semicolon **or** a comma and a coordinating conjunction *(and, yet, but, so, or, nor, for)*
    c. a semicolon **and** a coordinating conjunction *(and, yet, but, so, or, nor, for)*
    d. a colon or dash

33. Look at the following sentence: "When a writer joins two sentences, he should join them with a comma and a coordinating conjunction." This sentence has a clause beginning with *When*. This clause comes before the sentence. The name for *When* is a subordinating conjunction. Subordinating conjunctions make adverb clauses. These are clauses, not prepositional phrases. **A Hint:** Think about the order that you expect a sentence to follow: subject, verb, object. Anything that disrupts this order, this flow, may need some sort of warning, some sort of punctuation, usually a comma. The LBH suggests that you ask if a clause is essential or not. Okay, try that too. ***Which of the following is not good advice or not always true about punctuating adverb clauses (those beginning with subordinating conjunctions: if, when, because, before, while, after etc.)***
    a. If the clause starts a sentence, put a comma after the clause (as in this sentence).
    b. Put commas, if the clause is in the middle of the sentence, around the clause (as in this sentence).
    c. <u>Always</u> put a comma between the end of the sentence and clause, when the clause comes after the sentence (as in this sentence).
    d. Use a comma or not when the clause comes after the sentence (as in this sentence), depending upon "essentiality," contradiction, and type or purpose of writing.

34. Below are groups of sentences. Some are joined with conjunctive adverbs *(however, evidently, moreover, nevertheless, accordingly, consequently, meanwhile, thus, otherwise)*. **Which one is punctuated correctly?**
    a. Slapping at his face and taking No-Doze, Billy Drool tried to stay awake for his classes; however, none of his tactics could overcome his boredom, so he always went to sleep.
    b. Billy never paused to consider why he went to sleep, however that question was the one that needed answering.
    c. Since everything was boring to Billy, consequently nothing was really exciting.
    d. Sleep or no sleep, Billy lived in a world of semi-consciousness, thus, he knew neither excitement or displeasure.

35. When a writer uses a colon, he should most typically have which of the following?
    a. a sentence on either side of the colon
    b. a sentence to the left of the colon; a list, an enumeration, a restatement of the sentence to its right
    c. a phrase or clause before it and a full sentence after it
    d. have a colon only in documentation

36. When a writer uses a semicolon, he should most typically have which of the following?
    a. a sentence on either side of the semicolon
    b. a sentence to the left of the semicolon; a list, an enumeration, a restatement of the sentence to its right
    c. a phrase or clause before it and a full sentence after it
    d. have a semicolon only in documentation

37. Restriction governs the punctuation of adjectives. If the adjective is vital to the sense of the sentence, if defining the noun is vital to meaning, then the adjective is restrictive (it is "essential," as LBH says) and has no commas around it. If it is not vital, if it doesn't "restrict" the meaning (if it is "non-essential," as LBH says), then it is non-restrictive and has commas around it. Generally, use *that* for restriction and *which* for non-restriction **Which one of the following sentences is correct? (Non-essential elements)**
    a. The action, that sealed Billy Drool's fate, was his putting a whoopee cushion in Professor Flunkemoften's chair.
    b. Putting the whoopee cushion, which sounded like a freight train, under Professor Flunkemoften's chair brought Billy Drool notoriety.
    c. But this notoriety which Billy surely didn't need started the proceedings to expel him.
    d. For Professor Flunkemoften who may seem ineffectual to many can be vengeful.

38. Which sentence means that all soldiers should get a raise?
    a. Soldiers who face combat should get a raise.
    b. Soldiers, who face combat, should get a raise.

39. Nouns that simply rename another noun, *appositives,* can also be restrictive or non-restrictive. See the previous sentence for an example. **Which of the following sentences is correct?** Read closely.
    a. Professor Flunkemoften's third book, *Demeaning the Demanding Student,* was a very popular work twenty years ago.
    b. However, since the publication of Harold Clark's rebuttal *Demanding from the Demeaning Student* educationalists have lost interest in Professor Flunkemoften's book.
    c. Professor Screwy's, *Demanding Less but Getting More,* a rebuttal of Clark's rebuttal, is now standard reading in composition pedagogy.
    d. However, Professor Tolerance, long recognized as a promising scholar, has just published an overview of the debate *Demeaning More, Demanding Less, Getting By.* Many scholars expect it to be the last word in the field, at least for the next two months.

40. **Which one of the following is punctuated correctly?**
    a. Billy Drool defended himself inadequately in front of the Dean and the Vice President, his argument that his whoopee cushion was an educational tool just was not convincing.
    b. The Dean made three distinct points: that students are held accountable for their actions, that whoopee cushions are indeed distracting, and that Billy Drool did not seem vicious but rather unconcerned.
    c. Billy's rebuttal was: that Professor Flunkemoften was no more educational than the whoopee cushion and that no one could realistically think that Lame Duck University students should be held accountable.
    d. Once the Dean and the Vice President presented their verdict; that Billy should be expelled, Billy wept.

41. **Which one of the following sentences is punctuated correctly?**
    a. Surprisingly, Professor Flunkemoften begged for Billy Drool's reinstatement at Lame Duck University, for beneath his fussy exterior; Professor Flunkemoften liked students like Billy, the ones who barely tried.
    b. While Billy was grateful, while administrators were surprised, in fact causing them to question their own judgment; Billy and the administrators both agreed that he would be better served at a community college.
    c. So, Billy had people to say goodbye to, first on his list was Professor Flunkemoften.
    d. Billy just didn't know what to say to Professor Flunkemoften this weird man, who had defended him.

42. **Which one of the following sentences is punctuated the best?**
    a. (Parenthetically speaking) parentheses can sometimes take the place of commas if they clarify the sentence.
    b. A dash—adds more emphasis to a sentence.
    c. Professor Flunkemoften's habit of visiting expelled students (a habit that mystified everybody on the faculty), finally did not help Billy Drool.
    d. Billy Drool told Professor Flunkemoften about his reasoning: that he just did not want to attend a place that didn't share his sense of humor.

43. ***Which one of the following is punctuated the best?***
    a. Anyone who cannot sympathize with Billy is someone whom Professor Flunkemoften does not want to know.
    b. Anyone, who cannot sympathize with Billy, is someone, whom Professor Flunke-moften does not want to know.
    c. For, Professor Flunkemoften does not care what the student has done, or whom he is, he believes that humor deserves a place at Lame Duck University.
    d. Professor Flunkemoften does not care what the student has done or whom he is, he believes that humor deserves a place at Lame Duck University.

44. ***Which one of the following is punctuated the best?***
    a. Since he was in the first grade, Professor Screwy has tried to protect whomever, he thought was right.
    b. However, according to Professor Screwy, the case with Billy Drool was a case against a student, who was clearly wrong.
    c. As the case evolved, Billy Drool was singled out, because he defied codes of conduct at Lame Duck University.
    d. Billy Drool, who had previously been scolded in high school because of his feeble at-tempts at humor, finally gave up on Lame Duck University.

45. ***Which one of the following is punctuated the best?***
    a. As influenced by the actions against Billy Drool, as the rules now stand, no students can: humiliate instructors, disrupt classes, or make disgusting sounds.
    b. Billy Drool has thus become the means to an administrative mandate, to a change in policy and to a different temperament at Lame Duck University.
    c. However this case turns out to have been a milestone in academic legislation.
    d. The President of Lame Duck University, who is a lawyer, has said that this case will go on—perhaps making it all the way to the state's Supreme Court.

46. ***Which <u>one</u> of the following sentences is punctuated the best?***
    a. The committee consisted of Mrs. Granny Smith, the apple maker, Mr. Sole, the shoe shiner, and Mr. Black, the coroner.
    b. The committee consisted of Mrs. Granny Smith (the apple maker), Mr. Sole (the shoe shiner), and Mr. Black (the coroner).
    c. The committee consisted of: Mrs. Granny Smith (the apple maker), Mr. Sole (the shoe shiner), and Mr. Black (the coroner).

47. ***Which one of the following sentences is punctuated correctly?***
    a. Joey Buffer had two jobs, one in the morning before class started, and one at night after all classes stopped.
    b. Joey Buffer had two jobs: one in the morning before class started, and one at night after all classes stopped.
    c. Joey Buffer had two jobs: one in the morning before class started and one at night after all classes stopped.
    d. Joey Buffer had two jobs, one in the morning before class started: and one at night after all classes stopped.

48. *Which one of the following sentences is punctuated the best?*
    a. Joey Buffer being conscientious always tried to read one chapter a night before he went to sleep.
    b. Being conscientious Joey Buffer always tried to read one chapter a night before he went to sleep.
    c. Joey Buffer being conscientious always tried to read one chapter a night, before he went to sleep.
    d. Joey Buffer, being conscientious, always tried to read one chapter a night before he went to sleep.

49. *Which one of the following sentences is written the most clearly and punctuated the best?*
    a. It is obvious that staying in class is dependent upon the care with which the student gives to study habits within the framework of class.
    b. The framework of class should set the parameters by which a student measures his ability at success in school.
    c. Therefore, the outcome to be reached is to secure more study time while producing valuable work in the context of out-of-class activities.
    d. Though students sometimes find going to school while holding a job difficult, they should always find the time to study.

50. *Which one of the following sentences is written the most clearly and punctuated the best?*
    a. The solution to Jack's problem with his lack of an attention span in class was given to him by Professor Screwy.
    b. Professor Screwy suggested a solution to Jack's wandering attention in class.
    c. Thus Joey Buffer knew that in order to succeed, it was imperative that he study harder and more often after class in the afternoons on his days off.
    d. Thus it is a fact known and proven to Joey Buffer that not paying attention is not conducive to the ongoing welfare of his studies.

Some Exercises on Style, one of the keys to As and Bs.
(for extra credit, practice, or substitution)

51. ***Coordination*** puts equal content into equal structures. So equal information should appear in equal sentences, clauses, phrases, or words. These structures should thus be ***parallel.*** In a sentence the most important information should be in the main clause, the dependent clause, or in the sentence itself. ***Subordination*** puts unequal structures in subordinate or dependent structures (non-sentences). Information that is of less importance should be in some sort of subordinate structure—a clause or phrase connected to the depend clause, the main clause, or the full sentence. So a sentence that consists of a main clause with another clause attached to it is a complex sentence. These complex sentences can thus show which information is most important. ***In which of the sentences below is the fact that the faculty members think that Professor Flunkemoften is a gentle soul emphasized while the fact that the students think him rude is de-emphasized?***
    a. The students always complained that Professor Flunkemoften was rude and inconsiderate. The faculty members however, thinking Professor Flunkemoften a gentle soul, would not believe the students.
    b. The students always complained that Professor Flunkemoften was rude and inconsiderate; the faculty members, however, thinking Professor Flunkemoften a gentle soul, would not believe the students.
    c. The students always complained that Professor Flunkemoften was rude and inconsiderate even though faculty members thought that he was a gentle soul.
    d. Although the students always complained that Professor Flunkemoften was rude and inconsiderate, faculty members thought that he was a gentle soul.

52. ***Now, look at the sentences below, and try to find the sentence in which the students' complaints are equal to the faculty members' knowledge.***
    a. The Faculty members thought that Professor Flunkemoften was a gentle soul even though the students thought that he was rude and inconsiderate.
    b. The students always complained that Professor Flunkemoften was rude and inconsiderate; the faculty members, however, thinking Professor Flunkemoften a gentle soul, would not believe the students.
    c. The students always complained that Professor Flunkemoften was rude and inconsiderate even though faculty members thought that he was a gentle soul.
    d. Although the students always complained that Professor Flunkemoften was rude and inconsiderate, faculty members thought that he was a gentle soul.

53. Now let's consider the order of information. A ***periodic sentence*** puts the important information last. Thus a reader does not fully know the meaning of the sentence until the period. ***Which sentence delays the information from being delivered?***
    a. The faculty members thought that Professor Flunkemoften was a gentle soul even though the students thought that he was rude and inconsiderate.
    b. The students always complained that Professor Flunkemoften was rude and inconsiderate; the faculty members, however, thinking Professor Flunkemoften a gentle soul, would not believe the students.
    c. The students always complained that Professor Flunkemoften was rude and inconsiderate even though faculty members thought that he was a gentle soul.
    d. Although the students always complained that Professor Flunkemoften was rude and inconsiderate, faculty members thought that he was a gentle soul.

54. A loose sentence puts the full sentence (the important information) first and the lesser information last). The effect is that the reader gets the important information right away and then gets some lesser information. Can you take a breather and figure out how structure can start to mean? Can you see how subordination and coordination determine what is the important information? Can you see how the placement of the subordinate information either gives the information right away or builds some suspense? See the choices that you have? *Which sentence gives the important information right away and then gives the secondary information afterwards?*
   a. The Faculty members thought that Professor Flunkemoften was a gentle soul even though the students thought that he was rude and inconsiderate.
   b. The students always complained that Professor Flunkemoften was rude and inconsiderate; the faculty members, however, thinking Professor Flunkemoften a gentle soul, would not believe the students.
   c. Although the faculty members thought that Professor Flunkemoften was a gentle soul, the students thought that he was rude and inconsiderate.
   d. Although the students always complained that Professor Flunkemoften was rude and inconsiderate, faculty members thought that he was a gentle soul.

QUOTES AND PARAPHRASES

No quote should stand alone. In other words, a sentence cannot be completely enclosed in quotation marks. In other words, avoid the following: . *"[full sentence]."* So the comments below describe three ways to use quotes.

1. The **informal quote** has a simple phrase introducing it. **Perrine says of Aristotle's notion of tragedy, "If the hero's fall is to arouse in us the emotions of pity and fear it must be a fall from a height" (1053).**
2. The **formal quote** has a full sentence introducing the quote. **Perrine's view of a tragic hero is the same as Aristotle's: "If the hero's fall is to arouse in us the emotions of pity and fear, it must be a fall from a height" (1053).**

Distance becomes important in a hero's fall: "If the hero's fall is to arouse in us the emotions of pity and fear, it must be a fall from a height" (Perrine 1053).

3. The **incorporated quote** "incorporates" the quote into the writer's sentence structure: **The "hero's fall" must be "from a height" to invoke a certain amount of fear and pity from the reader (Perrine 1053).**

When creating a tragic hero, the writer must evoke Aristotle's "emotions of pity and fear" by allowing the hero's fall to "be a fall from a height" (Perrine 1053).

4. Example of a "Works Cited" entry:

Perrine, Laurence, ed. *Literature: Structure, Sound, and Sense.* 4th ed. New York: Harcourt Brace Jovanovich, 1981.

5. **A paraphrase** is the writer's use of the <u>ideas</u> from a source. In order to avoid accidental plagiarism, a writer must sandwich the paraphrased material in between a lead in phrase (some mention of the author of the source or the source itself) and a page number. Later on, in a works cited page, the writer will alphabetically list his sources.

According to Perrine, the Aristotelian tragic hero is not an ordinary man. He is a great person, perhaps a prince or a king. Equally, his rank may simply be a symbol of his greatness. His greatness is found in him not in his power of office or noble blood. To make a successful tragic hero, the hero must fall from a high position in life (1053).
According to Perrine, an Aristotelian tragic hero is a man of greatness, outstanding qualities, nobler blood than others, and the possessor of extra-ordinary powers (1053).

WRITING ABOUT LITERATURE, FILM, OR MEDIA _____

1. Always write about literature in the present tense, not the past.
2. Do not simply tell what happens. You are interested in **how** "what happens" leads to the total meaning or theme of the story, poem, or drama. So, while you may want to give some plot summary in your introduction, you should not give plot summary in your main body unless you explain its thematic significance.
3. Develop a firm and narrowed thesis. Without a narrowed thesis, your entire essay will be ineffective. For instance, your thesis should contain a statement of the theme and the techniques used to establish this theme. You should not just say that the theme is enhanced. Explain the theme. Your subject segments should then follow to indicate how you will organize your essay. You should state these subject segments *after* the thesis, either in grammatically equal clauses, phrases, or words attached to the thesis or in *one* sentence following the thesis.
4. You should use a title to *indicate* your thesis. You should also include the title of the story in your title. Thus, a reader should be able to see what you are writing about and what your thesis will probably be when he reads your title. *Do not use the title of the work as the title of your essay!*
5. Stories and poems are put in quotes. Novels, long poems, and plays are underlined or italicized.
6. Make sure that your paragraphs are unified and coherent and that they contain some depth. Make sure that your topic sentence indicates to the reader exactly where he is at in the essay. To achieve unity, coherence, and depth, label the levels of generality in your paragraph. Combine sentences where possible to avoid choppiness.
7. Avoid the following grammar mistakes: Dangling Modifier, Faulty Subject, Faulty Complement, Reference (especially with *this, it, which, that, these*), Agreement with subject/verbs and pronouns/antecedent.
8. Avoid <u>it</u> and <u>there</u> as expletives. Avoid passive voice and linking verbs. Avoid Point of View errors. In other words, don't use "you" in a formal essay unless you mean whoever is reading your essay. Avoid writing imperative sentences like this one.
9. Make sure that you have no comma errors. Refer to the rules cited in this manual.
10. Pet peeves:
    a. Use *this* only as an adjective. Do not write, "This gives the report drama." Instead, write, "This technique gives the report drama."
    b. Do not use *you*. See above.
    c. Do not write, "In Wicker's report, *he* . . ." *He* has no antecedent; *Wicker's* is an adjective, not a noun. So instead write, "In his report, Wicker writes . . ."
    d. Do not use faulty complements: "is when," "is if," "is because."
11. All out-of-class essays must be typed.

Documentation:

1. You should refer to the text, to the stories themselves. Thus, **you should quote from the stories.** Long block quotes are rarely needed. Shorter quotes are much better. These quotes will prove points about your narrators or your settings. And, remember, when you quote, **you must introduce your quote.** A quote cannot stand alone. So introduce your quotes with formal, informal, and incorporated quotes. Quotes within quotes (quotation marks that appear with in your quote) should have single quote marks. Secondary sources, works

about your primary source, or the work that you are writing about, **must be documented** when you use them. You may use quotes or paraphrases, but either **must be cited correctly.**

2. **Use <u>only</u> formal, informal, and incorporated quotes.**

3. All paraphrases must have a mention of the author's name before the actual paraphrase and must end with a parenthetical citation of the page number.

4. Use three ellipsis for material that you skip that is all in one sentence. Use four ellipses if you go beyond at least one period. If you skip words and quote from two or more different sentences put four ellipses for the words that you skip.

5. If you quote from Hemingway, cite Hemingway in the text and again on the Works Cited page. You should not cite the editors from you textbook. For instance, you might write the following: The younger waiter says that "'an old man is a nasty thing'" (Hemingway 72). Note that I do not put the editors. Hemingway will also appear on the works cited page. Note how I treat quotation marks within quotation marks.

6. Be sure to look for bibliographical and biographical works in the reference section of the library; i.e., *The M.L.A. Bibliography, The Humanities Index, The General Index to Literature, Contemporary Authors.*

7. Be wary of the internet. It has very good information, but it also has some bad information. If you do use it, be sure to give a proper citation. However, with your library identification, you can access the Lamar electronic research data bases. *Academic Search* is a good one. See your handbook about documenting these sources.

8. **Do not ever plagiarize from any source! This is a crime. You will be prosecuted. You will be caught.**

FIGURATIVE LANGUAGE: ITS CARE AND USE

Students should read this section along with, right after, or right before my advice about denotation and connotation. See the discussion in the next section: "Essays on Education: Argumentation."

If students have followed this manual, they might have strengthened and toned their writing muscles enough to try spotting and then using figurative language. Student might want to make their writing buff.

Wait, before you stop reading, using figurative language is not necessarily writing poetry. The use of metaphor, symbol, allegory, and imagery is vital to all sorts of writing. In fact, technical writing depends upon metaphor. Think about your car. It has shoes, drums, diaphragms, chokes, and throttles. Circuitry has male and female plugs.

The use of figurative language, especially in technical writing, makes ideas and things more vivid. Look back at the section on grammar. I said that concrete nouns and active verbs make for good writing, that they make a sentence vivid. They do so because they create an image. We respond best to an image, which is a sensual appeal. I'll state that a different way. We respond first to what we can sense: taste, feel, see, hear, or smell. Thus we can sense images. Poetry tries to communicate primarily through imagery, so poetry is the most concrete and specific language that we have. Readers should first try to sense the poem. Poetry can teach the fiction writer, the technical writer, the wise manager a lot about communication. So using concrete nouns and active verbs is a start at writing poetry.

When writing anecdotal, description, narration essays—essays about personal experience—or any experience, students can start to build their writing muscles with vivid imagery. Look at some of the following essays. I particularly remember Elenora Market's description about waking after the bombing of her apartment to broken glass and finding her dog's bloody paw prints. You shuddered a bit didn't you? You acted emotionally. Elenora has trained, lifted, and increased the pounds. She can relax and flex a little. She can let others admire her work and effort. And we admire it the most when we don't seemingly see the writing, when it doesn't call attention to itself, when it seems effortless. Writing doesn't produce extravagant muscles, but toning.

However, when students turn to writing essays about ideas, concepts, or theory—as they will be asked to do in history, science, business, computer science, sociology, etc.—then active verbs become scarce. Then concrete nouns become scarce. Writing about the United States' foreign policy during the 1950s might not allow for active verbs and concrete nouns. But the rules still hold. The basic strengthening exercises are still important. One way to add imagery is to use concrete nouns and active verbs whenever possible. This practice first takes strain, then repetition, and then some heavy lifting.

But sometimes those verbs and nouns aren't there, so the writer should illustrate through modification. The writer should get specific through modification. The writer should start to create images in adverb and adjective constructions. Or, the writer should start to create metaphor through the illustrations that he creates. Look at the following sentence:

The Soviet Union, a wounded, starving tiger after World War II, clawed its way to being a superpower by the 1960s.

1. What does "clawed" suggest? That's right a tiger. Even without my putting "a wounded, starving tiger after World War II," a reader could see that "clawed" suggested a fierce cat.
2. This is a **submerged metaphor. Active verbs can readily create submerged metaphors.** But don't overdo this trend. As with any other figurative device, if used too much, it calls attention to itself. Using active verbs that give human qualities to inanimate things gets syrupy, cloying, overly sweet, bad for diabetics—creating what John Ruskin called the **pathetic fallacy.** Too much of this humanizing of inanimate objects is like taking steroids: the muscles show but don't look natural.
3. The appositive "a wounded, starving tiger" compares the Soviet Union to a tiger. It attaches an image to the Soviet Union. So it is acting as a metaphor.
4. Notice that these "metaphors" **illustrate** the Soviet Union. ****But they **prove** nothing about it. Let me repeat, they do not prove anything. Inductive method—the use of facts, figures, data, statistics, experiments, tests—proves. Deductive method—syllogistic reasoning—proves. Allegories and metaphors **illustrate** but prove nothing. To prove, a writer or thinker needs the nitty-gritty, the sweat, the hard work, and the hours in the gym lifting. The United States has made a lot of terrible policies and decisions based on analogies—the domino theory for Southeast Asia, America as a cowboy or a gunfighter as another—rather than relying upon facts, research, and intelligence. In reading and writing, the writer and the reader must wade through the research.

Here is a near cliché. A cliché usually starts out as an image or metaphor, but it gets used so much that it becomes meaningless. Avoid clichés. So now I'm going to use one.

In 1962, during the Cuban missile crisis, Kennedy and Khrushchev, representatives of two views of the Western world, *stood eyeball to eyeball, hands at their sides, about*

to draw. **After thirteen tense days, with U.S. military urging Kennedy to draw, Khrushchev** *blinked.* **Thus, the two men averted a catastrophic shoot out.**

1. This is a cliché because the metaphor of an old west shoot out for the Cuban missile crises has been used before.
2. Look at the submerged metaphors.
3. Are any of the metaphors mixed? That is, do I introduce any images that create a different metaphor?
4. Do you see how I extend the metaphor?
5. Does this metaphor work? I'm not sure it does. It is a cliché.
6. Does the passage have any modification that adds to the metaphor but does not add to the meaning?
7. Look at "blinked." This submerged metaphor almost mixes the metaphor. **Do not mix metaphors.** If you start an extended metaphor don't shift to another metaphor.

Look back over this essay. You might notice that I compare writing to weight lifting. I never say weight lifting, but I use **metonymy,** words closely associated with weightlifting, or **synecdoche,** words that are a part of weight lifting (see below). So I never name the figurative term (weightlifting). Did this extended metaphor help your understanding? Did it grow distracting? Did I use it too much? Did I mix any of it?

IMAGE, SYMBOL, METAPHOR

Below, I more fully define figurative terms and comment about them.

Image

At the basis of any figurative writing is the **image,** which is an appeal to one of the five senses: touch, taste, smell, sound, sight. Imagery starts with specifics. It starts with concrete nouns and active verbs (how many times have you heard this now?). With the sensual appeal comes an emotional response. With the sensual appeal comes a more vivid transfer of information through words. With sensual appeal, language transcends itself, as John Gardner says. Thus, with imagery, the reader goes through the words to a nearly direct experience. A person gains experience without having had the direct experience. A reader gets vicarious experience. His life gets larger without direct experience of the difficulties that he reads about. This vicarious experience is among the attributes that art provides.

Symbol

A **symbol** is not something that requires a decoder ring. It is not something that the writer or the reader makes up. It is something that the writer *creates* and the reader *discovers.* **A symbol is first and foremost an image. It never stops being an image.** However, through repetition, placement, context, and associations—an image gathers meaning beyond the literal. Throughout *The Great Gatsby,* Fitzgerald refers to the green light at the end of Daisy's pier. Jay Gatsby stares at the light from his mansion across the bay from Daisy's mansion's pier and pines for her. Fitzgerald mentions this light several times. At the end of the novel, he mentions that the original settlers, the Dutch sailors, were inspired beyond their imaginations by the "fresh green breast of the new *world.*" Fitzgerald then reminds us that their view was much like Gatsby's. Thus, through repetition (lots of reference to *green),* association (Gatsby and the sailors as well as associations throughout the novel), placement (at the end of the novel), and context (the longing in looking at green); the green light at the end of Daisy's dock becomes a symbol in Gatsby. The color green, through the same process, becomes symbolic. But the symbolic value of green is closely related to the literal color and to the light at the end of that pier. The more that we respond to the color and to the light at the end of pier, the richer its symbolic value becomes. So, the way to spot, use, or write about symbols is to pay close attention to the images.

Some Advice to Writers about Symbolism

Do not set out to create symbols. Intention usually spoils the symbols. Symbols come about when the writer looks at what he has written and sees what his consistent imagery suggests. Symbolism comes about in third, fourth, and fiftieth drafts.

Metaphor

1. A metaphor has:
    a. **a literal side,** the subject or term actually being discussed, and
    b. **a figurative side,** the illustration of the term.
2. The literal term is usually an abstraction and becomes clearer when the abstraction is compared to a more concrete or specific term.
3. Now, if you are ahead of this game (there's a metaphor), you know that an image is specific and concrete. So an image is the figurative side of a metaphor. If the writer literally says that the literal side "is like" the figurative side, then this is a **simile.**

Robert Burns says, **"my luv is like a red, red rose."**

Here, love is the abstract literal term. "Red, red, rose" is the more specific figurative term. The more we look at the specific figurative term, the more we know about love. Love is perfectly beautiful, like a rose. Love is perfectly symmetrical, like a rose. Love is red, like a rose. Thus love is hot, like a rose. Love has thorns. . . . So that simple metaphoric comparison shows us about love and adds complexity to it. However, don't use that line above. So many people have used it so many times that it has become a **cliché.** Remember cliché?

4. The literal side of the metaphor can be **named or implied.** The figurative side of the metaphor can be named or implied. Two ways to imply are:
    a. **synecdoche** (implying by appealing to a part of the whole), and
    b. **metonymy** (implying by appealing to something closely associated with the term.

In my extended metaphor about writing being like weight lifting, I named writing (the literal term), but I use things closely associated with weightlifting or a part of weight lifting—"toned," "buff," "muscles," "strengthen," "lift"—to imply the figurative side of my metaphor. **Notice that these associative terms or parts for the whole are concrete nouns, active verbs, or adjectives.**

In his classic poem the "Love Song of J. Alfred Prufrock," T. S. Eliot has the following famous lines:

I should have been a pair of ragged claws
Scuttling across the floor of silent seas.

In these lines, Prufrock, the narrator, compares himself to a crab. How do I know this? Eliot writes "ragged claws," a part for the whole, synecdoche. Then he writes, "scuttling across the floor of silent seas," something associated with a crab, metonymy. So Prufrock sees himself as a crab. So? Crabs are scavengers, living off what floats to the bottom of the sea. So Prurfrock sees himself as a crab. Crabs don't really think; they are all instinct. Crabs move backwards. Crabs are disgusting. You get the idea.

Figurative Language Abbreviated
1. Try to be as specific as possible. Use concrete nouns and active verbs.
2. If the content robs you of concrete nouns, use modification to add specificity and illustration.
3. Use similes, submerged metaphors (being careful of cuteness and triteness), extended metaphors, and implied metaphors to illustrate, explain, and clarify.
4. Remember that illustration is not proof.
5. Use symbols sparingly. If you do use them, let them arise out of your writing, in the second or third or fourth draft.

Some Closing Advice
Much of what you have read in this manual is simplistic and formulistic. But, as with any skill, with writing, first you must master formula before you can move on to form. The hope of this manual is to scoot you toward form. This manual, English composition courses, and sophomore literature courses will not make you a complete writer. If you wish to pursue business, science, engineering, or math, you should write sentences, paragraphs, and essays that are efficient, precise, and clear. You will need to know other formulas and forms. If you wish to become a writer yourself, if you wish to write in the liberal or fine arts, then besides efficiency, precision, and clarity, your writing should have eloquence and grace—and maybe even irony and humor. Thus, no matter what your intentions, to match your writing to your vocation and your desires, you should take other writing courses.

Technical Writing can immensely help business, engineering, and science majors. Lamar offers English 3310—Technical Writing.

Advanced Writing can help with academic writing. Lamar offers English 3326—Advanced Exposition.

Creative Writing courses can help not only with writing fiction, non-fiction, poetry, and other types of writing but more importantly with reading and understanding writing. Creative Writing students, perhaps most important, can recognize when writing is trying to cheat, seduce, or harm them. Lamar offers poetry, fiction, and creative non-fiction in English 3350 and 4345. And the Communications Department offers a course in screenwriting.

The University Press always needs good writers to cover stories. Through hands on training with the UP and through courses in the communication department, Lamar offers Communication 2372—Editing and Copyreading, and Communication 3330 Advanced Journalistic Writing. The Communication Department also offers 3385—TV Writing and Performing.

Section 2

Essays for Composition I

FORWARD

Students in my classes during seven years at Odessa College and my many years at Lamar University have written these essays. Some of these essays have come from other instructors at Lamar University, most notably from our Longman essay award winners and nominees. I give the names of students for some essays; for others, I do not. I have edited some of these essays; for others, I have not. I encourage students to read ahead for two reasons: first, to see what expectations lie before them, and second, to appreciate the progress, hard work, and grace that these students have achieved in their writing.

I have added some minor editorial changes in parts of the essays, and some still contain errors. However, they are all A or B essays, and they all exhibit exceptional organization, punctuation, grammar, and thought. You should use them as models or examples for your own writing. I will insist that you copy their basic organization, and you may want to imitate their style or punctuation. However, do not copy their ideas or their content, for such action is plagiarism and warrants very severe punishment.

ANECDOTAL ESSAYS: DESCRIPTION & NARRATION

Most textbooks discuss description and narration. From fifth grade on through college, I was terribly confused by the terms *description, descriptive,* and *narration.* My teachers told me that my writing was supposed to be "descriptive." Yet they also told me to write "description" and "narration." Now, I think that the two rhetorical modes, Description and Narration, are very close together and almost self-evident in any writing. All nouns in our language describe something that we see in Newtonian terms as a fixed spatial object. All verbs are motions. Thus any sentence is both narration and description; that is, it occupies space and designates some time.

On one hand, *Descriptive,* the term that English teachers always told me that my writing should be, as I see it, is a term that teachers use to describe a quality in writing. This quality is specificity. I've already discussed some of these descriptive techniques in the opening sections on language and grammar. Writers should use concrete nouns and active verbs if they are to write "descriptive" essays. They should then move on to modification and then maybe even to figurative language.

On the other hand, *Description,* as a rhetorical mode, is thinking about and organizing an essay spatially. Since Description, as a rhetorical mode, often forces a writer to concentrate most fully on this descriptive quality, it is arguably the most important and should appear as a part of almost any essay.

Narration seeks to organize an essay around chronology. So *Description* and *Narration* simply describe spatial and chronological organization.

However, given the nature of our language and the way we use it, narration, like any other rhetorical mode, must have description to be effective. So, all essays need some description, some spatial specificity. But, while essays incorporate narrative elements, not all essays need have narration. Our language and our vision is such that we see, feel, and think mostly in spatial terms.

So, I'll restate my point, *Description,* as a rhetorical mode, arranges an essay or a paragraph or some other section of writing according to space. It will have transitions like *over, beyond, across, under, over, etc.* Narration, conversely, organizes an essay or a section of writing according to time. It will have transitions like *after, before, during, while, meanwhile, three months later.*

Description as a rhetorical mode is vital to all writing—even narration—because it is descriptive. Description emphasizes place, which we can more thoroughly sense with touch, taste, sight, sound, and smell. Appeals to these five senses, or imagery, "show" as opposed to "tell." Every writer knows the cliché that a writer should "show" and not "tell." Showing is the key to good writing, then.

Narration is not as vital as description. So, even if an essay is narration, it should slow down and concentrate on a few spaces.

In narration, many students write like kids describing an exciting movie. The description comes back as all time: and then, and then, and then, and then. There is no detail, no showing, no senses, the writing just jumps from one time to another. So a narrative essay may be organized around a series of times, but then each time ought to slow down, stop, and *describe* some spaces.

The following essays are combinations of narration and description. Notice how the basic organization is on time—memory. But the writers/narrators stop at different points in time/memory to concentrate on space and appeal to the senses. Notice that the writers appeal not just to sight but also to the other senses.

And notice too that the thesis statements in most of these essays are almost redundant. The writers' uses of sensual appeal, of imagery, **show** the reader the essays' points, the theses. Thus description and narration, used to show personal experience, are vital to the personal essay. The personal essay, as it grows more sophisticated, is a vital part of literature. It is one type of creative non-fiction.

EXEMPLIFICATION

Exemplification always seemed obvious to me. It is simply the practice of giving examples. The basic essay organization that you studied calls for examples. Christensen's subordinate structures called for examples.

The essays below have examples. But these examples are personal (and thus anecdotal) and from memory. They are organized around space or time. Thus, they are description or narration.

If you have an essay assigned in which you have to prove a point or discuss something that you read, watched, or heard (nonfiction, fiction, poetry, music, TV, movie), then you would want to give examples to prove your thesis. You will have to provide examples to prove your topic sentence. Your examples might come from personal experience, but your examples might also come from evidence outside of your personal experience. Perhaps, if you are writing about how the symbolism in a story illustrates its theme (a common assignment in Composition II), you would pull examples of imagery or character or plot from that story. These examples from the story might take the form of narration or description—or any of the other modes.

I'll try to explain my point in a different way. I labeled this section as *"Anecdotal Essays."* By *anecdotal,* I mean that the essays come from personal experience. These types of essays will depend upon the use of *I*. The *I* will narrate, tell a story that will depend upon narration and description. The emotion, the power, and the point being made depend upon the attention to imagery (or *spatial arrangement,* or *description*).

But if the anecdotal writer turns her attention to a subject outside of her own experience, then she will need examples. The examples that she uses can take the form of description or narration. These description or narration examples can be from personal experience but more than likely from other sources. The *I* will probably disappear because the essay is not about an *I*.

Personal essays will use description and narration. Exemplification, as a process, might use personal or observed narration and description as examples. So, as I hope that you might sense from this section, I think that Description, Narration, and Exemplification ought to be studied together and that Description and Exemplification will be in all essays. So while the essays that immediately follow are narration and description, the essays in the other sections will have examples of their theses or topic sentences. These examples will use other rhetorical modes to supply the details.

NOTE ON AN ASSIGNMENT

The next two paragraphs are the results of an assignment that I would give.

1. I would ask students to write a paragraph about a really scary or weird or funny incident. Concentrate on "showing," on just getting down one sense, sight probably, but,
2. Then we would rewrite.
3. Then I would ask them to write another paragraph about the same incident or shortly before or after but to concentrate on another sense than sight: smell, feel, sound, taste.
4. Then we would rewrite.
5. Then I would ask them to write another scene combining senses that took place some time later or took place from a different location.
6. Thus space, time, or sense would determine the arrangement of the paragraphs and the organization in them. The essays would be narrative or description essays.
7. Then students would try to turn these paragraphs into a tight five-paragraph essay.

MEMORIES OF EARLY CHILDHOOD—DAVID CHASTEEN

As I grow older, entering what must be considered my "adult" years, I often find myself reminiscing about my childhood. For the most part, the memories wash through my mind with no set pattern, mixed like colors on a painter's palette. Occasionally, however, they form a coherent picture in my mind, and it seems almost as if I am living them again. Among my fondest memories are the vivid recollections of my earliest days in grammar school. I lived close enough to the school to walk, and my daily walks would take me through a neighborhood park, past the town bakery, and through a dark pedestrian tunnel that ran under a busy street.

The neighborhood in which I lived was bordered by a large park, and everyday my walks would take me through it. Following the sidewalk out of my block, I had to cross a small creek which acted as natural boundary for the park. I would pause there every morning, stand on the rickety wooden bridge, and stare into the crystal water, looking for tadpoles among the growth of green moss. As I entered the park, the tall trees seemed to welcome me; their limbs extended like outstretched arms. In the fall, the broad maple leaves would be riotous colors of red and orange, and I would often pause and play among the piles of leaves that the park workers had raked and left to pick up. Continuing through the park, I would often pause and play on the playground equipment until I knew that if I stayed longer, I would be late for school.

After leaving the park, I entered what would be called the business district of the town. Within this area, my walks always took me past the bakery. It was a large building; an imposing structure rising—so it seemed to my young eyes—to touch the sky. The smell of the bakery, however, stayed fresh in my mind all these years. The scent of fresh baked bread would greet me many blocks before the bakery came into view, and it would draw me toward it like an invisible guiding hand. As I got closer, the smells became more distinct: the dry dustiness of wheat flour. Walking alongside the building, I smelled the tangy earthiness of the baker's yeast, smelling to my young mind of the primordial earth. The temptation to sit on the curb and revel in the smells was strong, but my conscience pushed me along my way.

As I emerged from the business area, there lay only one more obstacle between me and the school: a dark pedestrian tunnel. The school, standing on the other side of a busy thoroughfare, had for many years feared for the safety of students walking to school. The city, somewhere in the past, had taken note of this concern and had constructed a tunnel that ran under the street. However, it was poorly constructed. Descending the stairs was as frightening to me as a descent into hell. The tunnel was a dark place, dank and smelling of a tomb, with few lights to illuminate the way. It always seemed to be damp, and older children told stories of rats as long as their arms that lived in the confines of the tunnel. Finally, the light of the exit became visible, and I would run to it, ascending the stairs into the daylight once again.

Perhaps, as the years progress, these memories will dull and my feeble mind will forget the vividness of the colors and the heights of emotion that they would stir within my soul. Possibly, in the twilight of my days, they will become part of the collage of half remembered experiences stored somewhere back in the far reaches of my mind. But, for as long as I can recall these fond memories, I will revel in the happiness of those times and the walks to school: the park, the bakery, and the tunnel.

MEMORIES OF AN INTRIGUING PLACE: PERKINS SCHOOL—EDITH A. STARKS

The quiet school seemed almost out of place in its immediate surroundings: heavily trafficked Beacon Street, Watertown Square, and eventually, a few miles away, the huge, never-sleeping city of Boston. I could tell little of what lay beyond the black, wrought-iron fence that separated Perkins School for the Blind from Beacon Street. There were many trees directly behind the fence that hindered me from viewing the campus. On many occasions, I had noticed the unpretentious green and white sign that hung near the entrance to the school and bore the school's name. A growing interest in the blind and a strong curiosity about the well-known school made me want, in some way, to become associated with the school. I contacted the volunteer program director to learn what types of volunteers he could use and later came one evening a week to read to one of the high school students. I was fascinated by the school and looked forward to my weekly visits; furthermore, the orderliness of the campus with its romantic older buildings, the serenity and overwhelming feel of the place and the intriguing students themselves seemed to pull me into the *world* of Perkins School.

The buildings on the campus were scattered here and there among neatly clipped shrubs, relaxed as a napping cat in the afternoon sunshine. The variety of buildings included dormitories, cottages, and various activity and instructional buildings. Modern, reddish brick structures with skylights and slanted roofs contrasted sharply with some of the older, grayish buildings such as the Howe Building. The Howe Building, probably the oldest one on the campus, contained several stories and had a high tower that could be seen from several miles away. The lobby of the Howe Building included the expected chairs and end tables, but it also contained a mammoth globe that was about waist-high to me. Continents, mountain regions, and ocean floors were raised on the face of the globe so that it could be "read" by skilled, eager fingers. The building contained long, echoing corridors with high ceilings. On the back wall of the auditorium, which was off the main hallway, hung a large photographic reproduction of Helen Keller and her teacher, Anne Sullivan, who both had attended the school.

The school seemed to project certain feelings of calmness, serenity, and constancy. I enjoyed my trips to Perkins although I never spent quite as much time there as I desired. My visits to the school were almost always in the afternoon. At that time of the day the campus was fairly quiet. From a pond almost hidden by trees might come the gentle sound of water washing upon the banks and the staccato noise of birds calling to one another as they played in the fading sunlight. Many sidewalks laced in and out between the resolute buildings. As I left my car and walked from the parking lot to the Howe Building, I could often hear the hesitant and shuffled steps of the students making their way to classrooms, the snack shop, and other destinations.

The Howe Building lobby and main hallway, silent and musty smelling as an old library, were the normal places where I would meet the student for whom I would read. Steps on the corridor floors were loud and echoing and often the student could recognize the approaching person by the sound of his steps. After calling out my name and receiving an affirmative reply, the student would usually smile and take off with a confident step in the direction of our classroom. One of my students seemed to enjoy the fact that I had a little trouble keeping up with her quick pace. Admiration for these blind students came quickly—but not pity. Indeed, they desired no pity. The students' snack shop was located at the far west end of the Howe Building. Here, the students seemed to relax the most. They shyly made conversation with members of the opposite sex. Their jokes came easily and boisterous laughter sometimes filled the air mingling with the pungent odor of the cook's grease.

My interest in the blind and curiosity about the school itself caused me to venture beyond the wrought-iron fence where the orderliness of the campus' building, the serenity and feel of the place, and the students themselves seemed to draw me into the intriguing *world* of Perkins School. My thoughts of Perkins School are bittersweet but fond memories—of a place somewhat out of step with its surroundings where relationships are built with different tools.

ONE NIGHT IN THE WAR—ELEONORA MARKET

Born in Yugoslavia, I spent 20 years of my life in my hometown, Belgrade. Living there was not always easy: economic sanctions and political conflicts with most of the other countries of the world. Last spring, the troubles of my youth culminated with the most unpleasant experience of my life: a war. I lived in constant jeopardy for months; my days were monotone, completely meaningless, and I pondered on survival only. Attacks followed one another all day around giving me barely enough time to hearten myself for the next one. I quickly developed a phobic fear of night since it kept on bringing the scariest, longest, and loudest assaults. I clearly remember the night of my parents' anniversary; I felt nothing but fear, heard nothing but sirens and detonations, from dusk through the night until dawn.

As the darkness was settling in and the birds were finishing their lullabies my fear grew rapidly. I rushed down the black streets to get home before the attack started. There were only a few people in the streets, and I could hear their footsteps as well as mine. The stomping noise of rubber boots, rhythmic knocking of high heels and whisper-like sound of tennis shoes were mixing to form a strange melody in the city as quiet as a city of ghosts. Merely some 50 feet away from my apartment, I found myself out of breath when that piercing sound of the air raid siren interrupted this orchestra of shoes. The siren's shivering sound was only 60 seconds long, but to me it seemed like an eternity every time it went off. It alternated high and low frequencies every 20 seconds like an old, dilapidated record player. Listening to it, I felt as if I were surrounded by a herd of wolves doing the long, throaty howl. I stumbled and almost fell as I walked into the apartment to find my sister and my parents sitting around the dining table, waiting on me so we could all eat together.

Another long, dangerous night was just starting, and I was petrified. I was just about to take the first spoonful of fresh homemade soup when the whole building started shaking, and unnatural light flashed as a loud blast spread around through the air. I jumped up to the window, and my eyes were blinded by reddish mushroom looking light that lit up the neighborhood. The light suddenly changed into the fire, which then gave out huge amounts of heat. Smoke and dust were flying in the air; I had to close the windows in order to keep pollutants out. However, the smell of burning wood invaded our home and settled down in our furniture and our clothes.

Meanwhile, my sister ran up the stairs to the eighth floor that was actually a terrace on the top of the building. She saw the fire coming from the corner of two busy streets in downtown Belgrade. Smoke was shaping into a big cloud and breathing became hard for her. Ashes were high in the air, attacking her eyes and lungs. Nevertheless, she stayed out there staring at the settling dust. Like an ancient ruin, what was left of the big Army Headquarters building appeared in front of her eyes. She said good-bye to the building that she always walked by on her way to school and decided to come back to join us in our horror. The night continued in the same manner; whistles of projectiles and airplanes flying over kept us all awake in spite of our sleepiness.

The first wave of the strike finished, I tried to enjoy delicious chocolate cake with my family. During these few serene moments, we smiled and completely forgot about the peril that will follow. My mother was telling a story about their honeymoon trip to the Islands of Grand Canary. Her voice assimilated with the one coming from the television show as I daydreamed I was walking barefooted along sandy beaches that seemed to touch the sky at the horizon. But the feeling of safety did not last long; shrill noise of three projectiles flying toward their targets announced the second wave of the attack. Knowing that I was safe only after the explosions, I remained stock-still until three consequent blasts ripped my ears. The power went off and I felt lost in the dark while I tried to find my way around the house as if I were in a cavern. Before I could even adjust to walking through the darkness, the floor shook harder and faster than after the detonations, and I found myself on the ground, with books landing on the top of me. "What more is there to happen?" I wondered if this were an earthquake. As soon as I got up, I lied back down on the couch trying to catch my breath and slow down the rhythm of my heart.

Morning sneaked up on me as I was dozing off in my dad's lap. He held me close, whispering into my ear that everything would be all right. I looked deep into his green, naïve eyes trying to find a ray of hope. Instead, a tear came rolling down his wrinkled cheek, and I knew at that moment he felt as lost as I did. I looked around and saw my mom picking up pieces of her favorite Chinese vase that broke during the night. One of our two curious little dogs tried to help her and cut its paw; he walked around the house leaving bloody paw prints on the floor. Happy to see everybody was alive and well, I sighed with a relief and got up to clean the ground behind my pet.

From the Sunset throughout the night until the Sunrise, I tried to justify the death and devastation caused by the war. Never in my life had I imagined to find myself encircled by bombs, ruins, and blood. This intervention was approved to save lives, but instead it brought about even worse atrocities, leaving more people homeless and hopeless. How can killing by ones stop killing by the others? I still can't seem to find the reasons for any war or any hatred among people. Nevertheless, I hope to see humankind peaceful and tolerant in the centuries yet to follow.

REFUGE AT THE WATER CANAL—LORENA HERNANDEZ

(2006 Longman Award Winner for Composition I, Lamar University)

After driving down winding roads and seemingly endless dirt trails, we finally arrive at my grandmother's quaint house in a small town in Mexico. The family unloads bags of groceries in preparation for our traditional family cookout. As the men make their way to the smoking barbeque pit, the women gather inside the house over the hot gas stove, gossiping and laughing hysterically at the most inane jokes. In the midst of all the commotion, I look out the kitchen window toward a place of memories and great significance. A refuge for my wandering thoughts and from my daily stresses, the water canal behind the house still serves as my hideaway.

The walk to the canal allows me to view my surroundings from a perspective that is untainted by the urban city life of car exhaust and crowded areas. As I drag, my fingers across the metal gate, the clamor of the women's clanging pots and pans and men's loud laughter begins to fade away. Tiny gravel rocks jump and pop like firecrackers beneath my feet as I tread the familiar path. The path connects me to the world of my early childhood, for now, all grown up, I rarely come to visit. Like an old picture that has decayed over time, the natural landscape presents no bursts of color nor vibrant shots of life like those seen in glossy tourist brochures touting paradise vacations. To the white-collar businessman and the modern soccer mom, the area seems a waste of property, but to the wide-eyed child, it was the home of imagination and childhood games. The trees that line the path to the irrigation canal lie in a sea of overgrown grass whose color has been sucked up by the sun. The colorless branches of the trees dip low as if, over time, the thin layer of dry leaves have weighed their fragile am-is down. Further down the walkway stands a rundown concrete building, a massive structure where the town's justice issues were once handled. Now, humiliated by time, it shrinks away and blends in with the background. Its white, glossy paint has cracked in several places, unveiling a rough facade, and the royal blue letters that once read "Caseta XVII" have been chipped away by time. Past the building, looking back. I see my reflection in the cracked window and, for a brief moment, see people hustle in and out the once busy doors. As I approach the canal, the sun scorches the hair on my arms and its heat penetrates my skin. I make my way up the small hill, stepping on sparse little plants that have been powdered by the very dirt they grow in.

From the top of the hill, the rough, undulating terrain stretches far into the distance where it bumps into the horizon. The glowing evening sun descends into the earth and illuminates the canal with a burnt copper tint and casts soft shadows on those objects hiding from its rays. A rusted iron railing, whose orange paint has deteriorated over the years, lines one edge of the sturdy bridge that runs across the canal. Opposite the railing on the bridge stands the massive mechanism of three large iron wheels that control the water for irrigation of the fields. Rough in texture and hot to the touch due to the sun's heat, the wheels seem to have been untouched by other's hands for years. The wide canal runs, like a winding snake, into the distance. On both banks, small thorny shrubs, not even one foot high, line the edge of the canal. Bunches of sunflowers appear sparingly among the shrubs. Sitting on the ledge of the bridge with my feet dangling into the canal trench, I watch as a large dust storm emerges in the far distance and drags itself across the horizon, possibly indicating a speeding, rickety truck making its rounds in this remote neighborhood. On the left side of the canal, a lonesome brown cow grazes, quietly trying to nourish its skeletal frame. Unaffected by the new visitor, the sickly cow never flinches or looks away from the small patch of green. Small pebbles plunge down to the empty canal as I stand up, but there is no splash, for today there is no water.

I descend into the canal down a concrete slope on one side of the canal. The dry heat has absorbed every drop of water, leaving only an empty, desolate trench where water sometimes runs. With every step I take, a new footprint appears upon the dry, crumbling mud. The dry canal bottom has cracked in several places and now looks like plates of broken tile. Covered with shrubs and thorny bushes, the walls of the canal ascend steeply on both sides, allowing little view of the ground level terrain. Standing in the center of the canal, I feel like an ant enclosed in a long box with only the lid left open. The arid atmosphere enfolds my body and fills my nose with an earthly aroma. My peaceful thoughts are momentarily interrupted as a dark brown snake slithers by and hides within the cool comfort of a dark crevice. The nocturnal insects, invisible to the eye, begin to fill the evening air with the melody of nature's music. I close my eyes and imagine the past; I can almost see the murky water splash as I and other neighborhood children refresh ourselves with a swim. But the childish laughter fades away as I come back to reality and night slowly closes in.

I make my way back to the house, and the canal is left behind, frozen in time, unchanged by the hands of civilization. A place for my lingering thoughts, for my unbound imaginings, and for my escape from daily life, the water canal behind my grandmother's house serves as my secret refuge.

CONTRAST/COMPARISON ESSAYS

Everything is alike but different from everything else. So to say that A is like B only different is essentially to say nothing. Looking at the similarities and differences of two objects, people, books, or so forth will not produce a specific or interesting essay. So a writer must narrow a contrast/comparison essay. A writer should choose two things to contrast or compare. Then, a writer should choose a means or criteria to compare them. The writer should then apply the terms or criteria to A and then B.

Say a writer has three terms or criteria: 1, 2, and 3. He should apply all of them to A and then to B. So this system or thinking would imply that the resulting essay would have a thesis in which the writer states the criteria or means of comparison and then have two subject segments A and B. Thus this essay's main body would be organized **subject by subject.** First with A1, then A2, and then A3. Second, this essay would have B1, B2, and B3.

An alternative order would be a **point by point comparison.** So this essay would have A and B in the thesis and then list 1, 2, and 3 as the subject segments. Thus this organization would be 1A and then 1B, 2A, and 2B, and then 3A and 3B.

Generally, an essay that seeks to convince us that one subject is better than another, say that B is better than A, should be a point by point contrast/comparison essay. This method is also a way of choosing. If you want to choose between two cars, you might make list of attributes: price, comfort, gas mileage. Then you would rate car A and then car B according to price, comfort, and gas mileage. So to make a choice, you ought to use this method.

An essay that seeks to show us a clear picture of the two subjects—without a judgment or assessment—would be a subject by subject essay. However, you might also find yourself simply exemplifying or illustrating, without choosing, using the point by point method.

CONFORM TO UNIFORMS—KATHERINE LETHERMON

(Notice how Katerine Lethermon uses contrast and compare (especially the point by point method) to "prove" that requiring school uniforms is a better practice than allowing students to wear what they choose).

"I can't afford those high prices!" "They're too much of a hassle!" "They're so ugly!" "When it comes to what they wear, I want my children to have freedom of choice!" These are the arguments of many parents and students when they think of mandatory uniforms in public schools. Currently, uniforms are required in multiple public elementary schools, but standardized dress has not successfully been imposed in intermediate or high schools. Because the benefits of uniforms in schools significantly outweigh the few criticisms against them, uniforms should be implemented in all public schools.

A common argument among parents against the institution of school uniforms is that they "cost too much money." On the contrary, according to the *Daily News Journal,* the average parent spends $350 to $500 dollars each semester on back-to-school clothes for their children. Children always want the newest and most stylish clothes. They see the models and celebrities wearing these expensive clothing in magazines, and they feel that they can't possibly go to school unless they own them, too. On the other hand, uniform shirts, shorts, and pants would cost a parent $5.88, $9.88, and $10.88 respectively at Wal-Mart. At these costs, a parent could purchase school uniforms for one week, including a winter jacket costing $14.88, for well under $110. Even if parents consider replacing torn, worn out, and outgrown clothing, this low price of school uniforms makes the choice clear that spending $110 for one year is better than spending at least $350 for only one semester. Until money begins to grow on trees, implementing school uniforms in public schools is the smartest and most economical choice.

The belief that uniforms are "too much of a hassle" is also an argument of parents who oppose the implementation of school uniforms. As children stress to keep up with the latest trends and fashions, uniforms actually eliminate this hassle. A child begins his or her school shopping before school starts. Typically, the child enters the store and heads straight for the racks of clothing with the most appealing, and sadly, the most expensive, apparel. The child whines and complains until his or her parent purchases the over-priced, trendy clothes. However, as the child gets dressed for school the next morning, the real "hassle" begins for parents. Each morning before school, children spend an excess amount of time fumbling through drawers and closets, searching for "the perfect outfit." This desperate search usually ends with the child complaining, once again, to his or her parent that he or she "has nothing to wear!" This true form of "hassle" could easily be avoided by the implementation of uniforms. Children would know exactly what they were buying at the stores and what it was that they were to put on in the morning. In order to avoid the "hassle" that parents fear, the implementation of uniforms is a simple solution.

Parents are not the only ones who argue against uniforms. Students often argue that uniforms are "too ugly." However, if everyone in the entire school wore the same uniforms, school would be a place that didn't focus on how everyone dressed, but instead, students would be more focused on learning. If Sally, whose Mom and Dad are both lawyers for a major law firm, and Joe, whose single mother works double shifts at a local diner, wore the same affordable, although considered slightly "ugly," uniforms to school, they would be looked at as equals. Students like Joe, who would normally be made fun of because he can't afford the clothing at the top of the trend charts, would be able to dress the same as the other children. In turn, he would be able to hold his head high while at school, and he could learn and play comfortably like the other children. The implementation of uniforms would erase social divides and allow all students an equal opportunity to learn in a comfortable, care-free environment. Also, as children advance in age and promote to middle school and high school, the clothing that their classmates wear can become distractive. If uniforms were implemented, girls wearing shirts or skirts that were too revealing or boys wearing baggy pants that start around the knee area wouldn't be such a recurrent and distracting problem. School is supposed to be a place where students can easily learn. Learning without social divides and opposite-sex distractions are far more important than the fact that some students may consider uniforms "ugly."

More important than ease of shopping and dressing, erasing social divides, or even creating a better learning environment, is the fact that uniforms better insure the safety of students while in school. Many parents who combat the idea of their children being forced to wear uniforms would argue that it "takes away the child's right to choose what they want to wear." However, these same parents would readily agree that more important than the right to choose what they wear is the in-surance of their children's safety. Uniforms are defined as "a distinctive outfit intended to identify those who wear it as members of a specific group." In the same manner, students in uniforms can be easily identified as members of the school. As such, an outsider, whether there to harm the students or not, can easily be spotted. Especially in high schools, where the students are older and more developed, sexual predators, robbers, or even simply parents, can easily be mistaken for students. The implementation of uniforms could easily prevent this mistake. The right to attend school in a safe environment is more important than the student's right to decide his or her own outfit.

Despite the trivial arguments from parents and students, the implementation of uniforms in public schools would produce phenomenal results. It is easy to agree that saving money, avoiding hassles, maximizing learning, and insuring safety are all factors that make opposing arguments such as "too ugly," "too expensive," "too much hassle" and "too little freedom" insignificant. In order to have and be the best, people must conform to decisions and rules that are somewhat dis-tasteful. To gain the benefits associated with wearing uniforms, parents and students must be will-ing to conform to uniforms.

EARLY WAR ADVANTAGES OF THE NORTH

(Below is an example of a contrast comparison essay in a history course. The student's assignment was to take notes from a particular course and turn them into an essay.)

Many Historians think that the American Civil War is the most important even in the history of the United States. Most colleges require two history courses: one leading up to the war and then another lead away from it. So students entering college ought to know something about the war.

When the guns started at Fort Sumner, neither the North nor the South was prepared for a war at home. In 1860, the U.S. Army had 16,367 officers and men. Most of these soldiers were sta-tioned at remote outposts on the Western frontier. Within these thin ranks, soldiers were divided according to loyalties to their regional "homes." Thus, the army didn't have much feeling of unity. In fact, when the war started, thousands of officers and enlisted men resigned from the U.S. army to join the Confederate Army. Both loyalty and the perception of victory motivated these soldiers. Perhaps these soldiers who switched sides and the South itself should have more closely examined the advantages that the North had. These advantages would eventually give the North victory:

The Union had a larger population and thus more available manpower. The Union consisted of twenty-three Northern states and seven territories, containing 22 million people, arrayed against eleven Southern states with 9,105,000 people—of which 3,654,000 were Negro slaves whose value to the Southern cause was questionable. 1,556,000 men eventually served in the Federal army. However with a primarily agricultural economy and rural population, the South had no more then 900,000 who fought for the Confederacy. The Southern armies' numbers peaked in 1863 then declined sharply thereafter. But, the Federal forces continued to grow in size until the very end of the war. So, by the end of the war, the Union had 800,000 troops, and the South had only 200,000. Thus, the confederates after four years of battle and loss were outnumber by 4 to 1.

The North could sustain these numbers because of its economic security. The North's natural resources ranged from Midwestern dairy products, to New England manufacturing. The Union had 110,000 manufacturing plants and 1,300,00 industrial workers. The Confederacy had only 18,000 manufacturing plants and 110,000 skilled workers. New York alone produced four times as much value as the entire South.

The North had experience governing. The South only had hope for an experiment. The two respective presidents illustrates the clear advantage of governmental experience and knowledge in the North. Abraham Lincoln, the Union president, and Jefferson Davis, the Confederate president; both concentrated too much on military matters and not civil matters. In a sense, however, both were forced to do so until each had obtained generals of proven ability. The South had talented officers behind them from the beginning, chiefly General Robert E. Lee, a West Point graduate. However, Lincoln went through a series of generals until he found the tough modern theorists, Ulysses S. Grant. But once he had a leader, and even before choosing Grant, Lincoln concentrating on maintaining his government. However, Davis, the former Secretary of State, stubbornly concentrated on military affairs at the expense of civil matters. Thus, the Confederate government—without experience, tradition, or real leaders—without a strong president, remained weak throughout the war.

The North, thus, should have won quickly, but the South had some luck. First, the South fought defensive war. Protecting itself from "northern aggression" required less men for the South and gave the South a psychological advantage and some patriotic fervor. The South's propagandist were able to portray the federal forces as oppressors of a free people. With the psychological advantage and defensive position the South's only hope was to defeat the Federal armies in battle or two or fight them to a stalemate. The South could also hope for European help. The Union actually had a harder job because it had just one option. The Union Army could restore the Union only through conquest of the South. Those early war advantages, in the end, allowed the Union to do exactly that—crush the South.

Because the North possessed a large reservoir of manpower, economic superiority, and an established government, the Federal forces were able to defeat the Confederacy. Robert E. Lee surrendered to Ulysses S. Grant bringing about the conclusion of one of the worst internal conflicts in American History.

CLASSIFICATION AND DIVISION ESSAYS

Writers always use classification and division before they write. In selecting a topic, in choosing a thesis, and in writing subject segments, a writer narrows his topic or groups bits of information under certain labels. Thus, the very nature of the basic essay organization calls for classification and division. In fact, if a student writes a thesis with subject segments, as I mention in Basic Essay Organization, then that student has divided his thesis into two or three categories. If that student wishes to narrow that essay, then he might make one subject segment the thesis and then divide that new thesis into two or three categories. So this whole process of division works for narrowing a topic.

In thinking about classification and division or in writing about classification and division, a writer should establish "mutually exclusive categories." The levels, compartments, definitions of those categories should exclude other categories, so that an item can appear in only one category. This mutual exclusivity is hard to maintain.

THE STEPS IN THE CIVILIZATION OF MAN

(This may be a Process Essay rather than a classification/division essay. I'm not sure. Again, this student simply turned some class notes into an essay).

Anthropologists believe that man has lived on earth for about one million years, but documentation in the form of written records does not exist before 5,000 B.C. So our age calls this pre-writing age "prehistory." To find out about our pre-historical ancestors, humans are dependent upon archaeologists. Early humans may not have been able to talk or write, but they were not without intelligence. These early homo sapiens made crude tools and weapons. They communicated with gestures and grunts. They hunted and lived in groups, made fire, and created art and crafts. But these humans were nomadic. They had to constantly move to find enough to eat. Rarely could more than a dozen people stay together for more than a few days at a time.

The advent toward a true civilization came when early humans figured out how to stay in larger groups and thus become less dependent upon available good. With larger groups of people living together, humans developed specialized skills—particularly in regard to tools. With specialized skills comes civilization and eventually a written record.

Scientists trace the development of according to tool making. Since early men made their tools out of stone, the entire prehistoric period (approximately 995,000 years) is called the Stone Age. The Stone Age has three main periods: the Old Stone Age (the Paleolithic period), the Middle Stone Age (Mesolithic period), and the New Stone Age (Neolithic period). Man's records of himself began in The Bronze Age, about 3000 B.C., when people began to smelt and forge their tools. An increase in technology began in the Iron Age, about 1100 B.C., and continues to today.

The Old Stone Age began about a million years ago and ended about 8,000 B.C. and corresponds to the Ice Age. At this time, "men" lived in Europe, Africa, and Asia. Later in the Old Stone Age, around 15,000 B.C., men crossed the land bridge connecting Asia and America. In present day, when we say "cave men," we are talking about these peoples. Three types of tools characterize these peoples. "Pebble tools" are oval, smooth stones. "Choppers" are heavy scrapers with the sides tapered down. And "hand axes" are almond-shaped rocks pointed at one end. Cave men attached these carved rocks to wooden handles or shafts to make crude spears, hatchets, axes, or shovels. With their tools, Old Stone Age people lived in small groups, hunted, seared their meat in fires, and wore sewn animal skins. The cave men also had art. Using four colors—white (from clay), black (from charcoal), and red and yellow (from iron ore), which they mixed with animals fats, these people made a sort of crayon, which they used to decorate their caves. This is the art that modern archaeologists have found in France, Spain, and Italy.

The Middle Stone Age began about 10,000 B.C. and lasted about 2,000 years in some parts of the world and longer in others. These people used tiny flints attached to wooden shafts or bones. Thus, they developed more sophisticated spears and bows and arrows. They needed these new hunting tools because the Ice Age was receding. Instead of large slower animals, these people hunted faster, small animals: deer, dogs, and boars. Additionally forests replaced the open plains. Hunting was tougher, so man adapted, and civilizations developed more fully.

The change in hunting and its new difficulty, made The New Stone Age, about 8000 B.C. It lasted until people could make their own "stones" and smelt metals about 3000 B.C. Men ground and polished their tools instead of chipping them in order to kill the faster, smaller game. More important, in the New Stone Age, people learned to grow crops and domesticate animals. Besides advancing beyond nomadic hunting to more sedentary farming and herding, these stored food for the winter and times of famine. With accumulation and storage came settlements. "Neolithic Man" moved out of his cave and made himself a house with rock slabs. He made fences to protect his newly domesticated animals. And Neolitic man developed new crafts: basketry, weaving, and pottery. Man invented the wheel, lever, and wedge and thus made bigger and better shelters. He built animal traps and fishing nets. He also must have begun to wonder about himself within the world, for Religion, chiefly naturalistic beliefs centered on the seasons, begun. Rituals built around seasons or occasions, such as rain or drought, developed. Men who lived long enough tracked the circular seasons and developed rudimentary calendars. These people began to speak to each other in simple languages and began to use rocks to count. Our word "calculate" comes from the Latin word "calculus" meaning "pebble." When Homo sapiens emerged form the Stone Age, he was a fully realized human being. He could think and reason. He could compute and communicate. He was indeed us.

With the same mental and emotional capacities as us, these peoples developed "communities." Not just Egypt, Mesopotamia, Babylonia, and ancient Persia developed, but the Inca, Aztec, and Mayan Indian civilizations developed on other continents in Central and South America. Because the western world considers itself more important and because the western world has been excavating longer, we know more about the peoples who inhabited the areas around the Mediterranean.

Most scholars agree that "civilization" began with writing. The first writing appeared around 5,000 B.C. as symbols written in wet clay. Again, need and technology advanced civilization. The Egyptians "paper" was "papyrus," a reed that was woven into thin sheets that could be preserved. With transportable and preserve able writing, the Egyptians kept records: taxes, transactions, history, and religion. The Egyptians could observe, record, and calculate. They applied these skills to their celestial observations and perfected a calendar with 12 months, each with 30 days, with five additional holidays, to make up the 365 day year. Like the Babylonians, the Egyptians developed laws and governing bodies to govern their keen sense of community and society. With advanced smelting techniques these societies made bronze, and with their jewelry, tools, and art objects named their age.

The next great metallurgic advance led to the Iron Age, which began about 1100 B.C. Iron was cheap and plentiful metal. Craftsmen and weapons makers abandoned bronze for the more readily available iron. With their new smelting techniques, they made stronger and more sophisticated tools and weapons. With these physical and technological advancements; The Iron Age was the development of vast empires. With them came international trade, and thus the production of coins, and then of course, credit and business procedures. As trade developed, so did personal wealth and all that personal wealth creates. Additionally, scribes became teachers, so schools furthered advanced and spread mathematics and writing. Societies needed and supported scientists, teachers, and artists. Vast civilizations prospered in Egypt, the Middle East, India, and China. The milder the climate and the abundance of water played an important role in whether a civilization failed or prospered.

As historians and archaeologists have shown, the progress from a pre-historical time to a historical time is accompanied by need and adaptation. In developing from the old, to the middle and new stone ages, to the Bronze Age, and then to the Iron Age, man has shown that civilization depends mostly upon writing in order to preserve ideas. But writing is dependent upon technological and social growth. Man must have the need and means to write. And essentially, he must live in larger more well-defined societies. Civilization, then, is related to our awareness of and our ability to communicate with each other, with those both in and out of our own groups.

DEFINITION _____

Definitions usually start as a classic sentence (or dictionary type definitions) and then expand to a paragraph or an essay or shrink to a non-restrictive phrase, clause, or appositive. I'll go slower.

A sentence definition consists of a *term,* a linking verb, a *class,* and *differentia* or *distinguishing characteristics.* The *term* is the thing to be defined. It should be the subject of the sentence. **Since a linking verb is like an equal sign and equates the subject with the subject predicate, it links** the *term,* which is the subject, to a group or classification, *the class,* which is the subject complement. The *differentia* further distinguishes the *term* from the *class.* It specifies the *class.* The *differentia* is thus some kind of adjective phrase or clause that modifies the class. **The key to a good sentence definition is to narrow the *class* as much as possible so that you don't have so much to distinguish.**

Look back at what I am trying to do. I am trying to define *definition.* Let me try to put it into a sentence.

A definition is a rhetorical tool in the form of sentence, a modifier, an essay, a paragraph, or a part of a paragraph that equates a term with a class and then distinguishes the term within that class.

Whew, that was hard. I'll try something simpler.

Term   linking verb   class   differentia
    (the linking verb is an equal sign)
A wrench   is   a thing   used to connect things.

This example above a rotten definition.
    I'll try to fix it.

A wrench   is   a tool used to fasten.

This is a better definition. The class is narrowed a little, but it has no differentia.

Term   class   differentia
**A wrench is a small hand held tool used to tighten, loosen, or attach nuts, bolts, or
    screws to grooved connections.**

This definition is overstated but better.
    I'll try again with something else.

**A media projector is an audio, video, or digital *projector* that *projects* a moving or still
    image and accompanying sound from a DVD, VCR, or computer onto a screen.**

Okay so far, so good, but this definition is rather circular. By **circular,** I mean that I use the term itself in the class and the differentia. A writer cannot use a term to define itself. Look back at the wretched first definition of a wrench. So I'll try again.

**A media projector transfers and enlarges moving or still images and their accompa-
    nying sounds from a DVD, VCR, or computer onto a screen.**

Look, look, look, I think that I did better, but I did so by using an active verb. So verbs can still do a lot of your heavy lifting (see, I made a metaphor; see figurative language).

Expanded Definition: For a complex term a writer may need to expand her definition. So she could elaborate on the class or, more likely, the differentia. So, recall Christensen. Suppose that a classic definition is a topic sentence. Label it a 1. Now, what could be a 2? What could make up the content of the rest of the paragraph? A writer could write more sentences specifying the differentia or further describing the distinguishing characteristics. Of course to further define, the writer may use description, narration, process, or any of the other following rhetorical modes. **The point here is that in good writing these modes are rarely distinct and separate.** Look, I've sort of written a sentence definition.

Of course, a writer may want to quickly define something. In that case, often, a writer can simply pull out the verb, use the term in a sentence, and then use the class and the differentia in an adjective clause, phrase, or appositive.

term

Lincoln did not deliver the *Emancipation Proclamation, the legislation that finally made slavery illegal,* until the union had a clear cut victory at Gettysburg.

term

After initial skepticism, most police welcomed *the concealed weapons permit, a law passed by the Texas legislature allowing citizens of Texas to inconspicuously carry firearms.*

So how does a writer decide if she needs a sentence, condensed, or expanded definition? She probably decides in revising or rewriting the initial draft. Now think about the rhetorical points that started this manual. Content might determine the length of some definitions. But more likely, audience and purpose will determine what the writer condenses or expands.

Now, as meager proof, I offer David Cherry's essay. I am perplexed as to whether to count Dave Cherry's essay as classification, or definition, or cause and effect. He uses elements of all three as well as process. He started out writing a process essay. This was the result.

Part of the problem is that writers use all the modes that we have discussed together. See why, as Christensen claims, a writer does not set out to create a particular essay but that an essay simply is the result of his thought?

SURVIVAL OF THE FITTEST—BY DAVID CHERRY

(David Cherry manages medical claims on injured workers with local governmental agencies. He has two girls with his wife Leslie, to whom he has been married for twenty-five years. He says that he still regards his education as the best thing that he ever did for himself. Bracketed comments are mine.)

The earth was inhabited by a wide variety of animals long before man evolved. These creatures ranged in size from the unseen, to the largest mammals that ever lived on the earth. The largest of these ancestors have long since disappeared and have been replaced with more compact versions better suited to survive changing world conditions. The most compact living creatures today include the animal class of *Insectia.* Insects live in our world by the hundreds of millions, outnumbering man by a thousand to one. They are, by far, largest class of animals. They have been on the earth longer than man, and with natural or man-made disasters threatening man's existence, insects will probably survive the demise of humans. Insects are moving rapidly on a path to outlast man through better achieved efficiency in breeding, eating, and adaptation.

[Notice definition, example, induction, analogy] In nature, Species needs determine their breeding. Insects have variously adapted their breeding. Not only can insects reproduce in vast numbers, but in many cases, insects can decide upon the sex of the young larvae (immature insects) produced. Ant beds, often containing thousands of workers, their sexes determined by the need of the colony, often come into existence by the egg-laying ability of a single Queen. In order to replenish the sperm supply needed for the next egg laying season, wasps decide sex of the new larvae (immature insects) and produce mates only in the fall,. In a season, the female wasp may have as many as twenty thousand young. For example, if future generations of a single female fly were allowed to reproduce for a year with no mortality rate, her offspring would cover the earth's surface ten feet deep. So insects adaptation of their vast breeding ability to their hazardous environments protects them as a species.

[Notice definition, classification, process in next two paragraphs.] To maintain the numbers, insects have developed two methods to consume foods. Chewing insects have gained a notorious reputation among homeowners and farmers. Grasshoppers have laid waste to entire crops, stripping crops of leaves. Caterpillars, also tireless chewers, eat leaves layer by layer until the leaf disappears. Then, they effortlessly move to the next green meal. Termites have ruined entire houses by chewing wood to a pulp. They then digest this pulp. Another familiar chewer, the Praying Mantis, simply chews and devours whatever insect happens to come within its reach.

Those insects deciding not to chew their meals drain their host of fluids. By using a hollow tube attached to their mouth parts, these insects penetrate vegetation, animals, and even humans. Mosquitoes seek warm blood and obtain their meals by "biting" the host and "sucking" however much blood needed. Rose gardens know no mercy from the tiny, sap sucking Aphids, deriving their meal from the stems of the plants. The noisy Cicada actually draws fluid from his perch in the treetops, and spiders have learned to save their meals, not draining the victim when caught, but saving the catch until it is needed, thus showing insects' abilities to further their needs in eating.

[Notice classification and cause and effect.] More impressive than insects' eating and reproducing, however, is their uncanny ability to dominate their surroundings. All insects originated as simple ground dwellers, living in cracks in the earth and crevices along fallen trees. Food and shelter became scare with the insect's reproducing, so eventually, some insects moved underground. To preserve the water in their armor-clad bodies, ants went underground to control the humidity of their housing. Long, small earthworms left the marshes for the rich minerals found in the soil, evolving into permanent underground dwellers.

Through millions of years of evolution, insects came to dominate the water. Many species live their lives in or on the water. Breathing by way of a pocket of air under their encased wings, water beetles are capable of staying under the water's surface. Aquatic insects skim the surface of the water. These buoyant creatures patrol the waters looking for other insects trapped on the surface, and larger skimmers are able to catch small minnow along the shoreline.

When insects also adapted to winged flight, the dominance of their surroundings was completed, and again insects had opened new avenues for survival. Flight enabled insects to evade attackers, as grasshoppers flee when disturbed. Flight also gave insects an avenue of attack, such as a Giant Robber Fly capturing its prey in mid-air. Some airborne insects use flying to cover greater areas in search of food or housing, flying hundreds of miles in a single day. Whatever advantages flight offered, insects have perfected.

So, by being able to ensure the individual species, take advantage of available foodstuffs, and conquering all their surroundings, insects fear no reduction in future generations. Mankind would do so well to ensure his future by learning all the facts about insects.

WHITE TRASH—NO RESPECT—PEGGY NASH

White trash gets no respect. I don't mean trailer trash or good ole boys with mullet haircuts or the big haired women that Bill Clinton targeted during his days as governor of Arkansas. I mean the racial epithet, "White Trash." Other racial slurs get all the press. Newscasters, politicians of local, state and national position, educators of every stripe have all lost their jobs and their prestige for uttering the wrong epithet in the wrong place at the wrong time. One politician used the perfectly acceptable adjective "niggardly" and felt the scorn of the nation until he apologized for using a word with an unfortunate combination of vowels and consonants that reminded the politically correct of the ultimate racial cut. However, "White Trash" can be thrown out there any old time in its entirety—no "W or WT word" required to lessen its effects. Thus I have often wondered about the images that come to mind when the words "White Trash" are spoken. I know what comes to my mind. I wonder if the person saying these words really understands the meaning or the effect those words have on others. This term may generate a few good laughs for comedians or other people who use invective to feel better about themselves at someone else's expense. A closer look tells us that the term is obviously a racial epithet. "Trash" is something that no one wants and is thrown away. "White," of course, refers to the race of the persons being denigrated. Thus, the term is pejorative despite its origin and common use because it can still hurt people.

The term first came into common use during the 1830s. Slaves of upper-class Southerners used it against poor whites. Today, people use the term, across the United States not only in the South, Appalachia, and Midwest, but on the East and West Coasts as well. In an attempt to further the image of being "cool," people on the West Coast use the abbreviation PWT. In addition, White Trash has become part of the arts. In literature, the novels *Poor White* and *To Kill a Mockingbird* deal with the subject, and in music the heavy metal group White Trash and Everlast's album *White Trash Beautiful* do the same. Edgar Winters has an album called *Edgar Winter's White Trash* and an entire genre of rock music is known proudly as *White Trash Rock*.

In recent years, some people say the phrase has softened. Along with the so-called softening comes the capitalization of the "White Trash" life style. Sales of cookbooks, television programs, and films that deal with the topic make huge amounts of money for marketers. People say that the phrase "White Trash" was provoked by the "confusion of racial identities and stereotypes." The origins may come from a racially segregated past, but the term places more emphasis on the word "trash" than on the racial reference to "white." Just as some people use the word "Nigger" to make themselves feel better about their social status, some others use the phrase "White Trash" for the same reason.

I have first hand experience on the subject. I was born into and raised in what would easily qualify as a "White Trash" environment. I lived in a house that was dilapidated, but it kept the family dry when it rained and kept us warm during the winter. My front yard had no grass to speak of and that was good because it would never have been mowed. While we always had a couple of old cars, my parents never owned a new vehicle during their entire lives. The vehicles were old and seemed to always be in need of repair. Of course, they were parked in the front yard as there was no garage. I did not have running water in my house until I was fourteen years old. The family took cold water baths in a number three wash tub in the middle of the winter. We would heat water in a pot on the stove, turn on the oven for heat, and seal the doors with a towel so we could be a little warmer. My father would sleep on the front porch with a mosquito net over the bed during the spring and summer. I had a tree house in the front yard because that was the only tree. Strips of wood nailed to the tree formed a ladder. Here was my refuge. I could escape the mundane routine of the day and watch the world go by far below. Everyone that drove past my house could see how we lived, and it made me feel exposed in a way that embarrassed me. The directions to my home included the phrase, "Turn off the paved road."

I was born into this lifestyle, and like most people, I did not have a choice in the matter. People who find themselves in this situation do the best they can with what they have. The majority are hard-working, God fearing, and decent folks. The problem they face with little money, little education, and little opportunity for earning a living is too difficult for most people to imagine. But, the biggest difficulty that they face is their no win situation. "White Trash" earn minimum wage, perhaps a little more. Because of their meager income, they do not qualify for government assistance, and most are too proud to accept it. They believe the American dream is attainable, but it very rarely happens, and then only to others. The only thing they are guilty of is not acting the way the rest of society thinks they should.

So even though people and the media use the term casually, it still carries a sting. The term "White Trash" earns no respect. And those who utter it suffer no loss of respect.

CAUSE AND EFFECT

Besides being a way to organize writing, cause and effect is a way of thinking. The fault in logic occurs when a writer or thinker assumes that simply because an occurrence preceded an event that it caused it. This is called *post hoc* reasoning. Editorial cartoons often use faulty reasoning about cause and effect for humor. Also editorials base a lot of their arguments on cause and effect.

Cause and effect arguments either **look back** at causes or **look forward** and anticipate effects. Cause and effect arguments can take a present good or bad condition, and then try to look back in time at what caused this condition. For instance, global warming is accepted as true. It is an effect. So scientists look back for its cause. On the other hand, cause and effect arguments can take a present condition and then forecast or predict what its effects will be. For instance, scientists take global warming as a cause and then debate about what the effects of global warming will be. Louisiana and most of Texas will be under water. We will all be boiling. We will all be freezing. So a good cause and effect argument looks back or predicts.

If the causes seem simple or apparent, then the arguments will probably be simplistic or wrong. The world needs no more of these arguments. We have enough public relations people, advertisers, politicians, self-promoters, con men, and terrorists. Simple causes and effects are the standard means of argument for people trying to manipulate you. A writer or thinker should look beyond the apparent causes.

1. Good thinkers and writers should not just look for **one cause,** for one villain or good guy, but should look for **multiple causes.**
2. Good writers and thinkers must look for **remote** or **distant** causes—not the most apparent cause or causes.
3. Good writers and thinkers question and research.
4. Good writers and thinkers should also look for a **causal chain:** a chain of occurrences that lead to the outcome.

Students should also be wary about the difference between the words *affect* and *effect.* Most dictionaries will point out their usage.

THE EFFECTS OF THE WAR IN SERBIA IN 1999—ELEONORA MARKET

Many centuries ago, Serbia was one of the most dominant monarchies in Europe. Situated in the South-East of the continent, Serbia was always considered to be the crossroads and the heart of a big multinational environment that was Europe. For many centuries, Serbs have been a very proud, rich, and cultured people who were constantly seeking improvements in economics, politics, science and society. Once the communist party took over the country after World War II, Serbia's role and status in the world had greatly changed, and the country finally reached the humiliating point at which Serbs stand today: opposed to the whole world. Consequences are severe, yet absurd, affecting all of the main actors: Slobodan Milosevic, United States of America, and Serb people.

Slobodan Milosevic, the president of Serbia, and the members of his Socialist Party should stand trial for their war crimes. As the sole commander in chief, he has forcefully drafted more than 100,000 people and pushed them into the conflict in which they did not want to participate. Some 10,000 of the new soldiers died for a cause they never believed in; most of them were still young boys who had just graduated from high school, and they never had a chance to make something out of their lives. The survivors wake up from night mares telling their stories of horror—they were drugged and forced to devastate Albanian villages. When they invaded the villages, soldiers took anything of value from the households and broke everything else they laid their hands on. Afterwards, draftees burned the houses and killed innocent people of different nationalities.

While Mr. Milosevic believed that he would gain more supporters among the extreme nationalists in Serbia, who think of themselves as "heavenly" people who are always right, he actually endangered his leadership, and his presidency was severely rocked. Although most of the people were scared to speak against him during the conflict because they knew he had control of the armed forces, once the military went back to their barracks, the public began to express its opinion more freely. The opposition parties are now coming together to form a united "Movement for changes"; its members are calling for the resignations, and they are gathering thousands of people on the daily rallies that are taking place across the country.

On the other hand, the United States of America led the NATO alliance into the same ridiculous conflict. After many years of isolation politics towards Serbia, Great Britain, France, Germany, US and 15 other countries have decided to break their own rules and invade one sovereign country. NATO policy distinctly states that no sovereign country can be attacked unless that country had previously attacked one of the NATO pact members. European countries have never before undertaken a similar action, and this precedent clearly shows that the United States is taking up a leading role in the world.

This is not the first time US government interfered with internal affairs of other nations. Interventions, such as the ones in Korea, Vietnam, Iraq or Bosnia, have become the recognized method of dealing with foreign affairs. And while the US administration claims the victories in all of those cases, very little was ever accomplished. For instance, in the Vietnam War, a total of 46,397 Americans lost their lives in combat and as many as 306,653 U.S. military personnel were wounded in battle. The United States spent an officially acknowledged 138.9 billion dollars, but still destroyed the economies of both parts of Vietnam. After the fall of Vietnam, Americans were perceived in the rest of Asia as an insufficiently reliable military and political partner. Another 50 years will have to pass before historians can look back on the war in Serbia without dispositions; time will tell how successful this war was or was not.

Serbs are probably in the worst position right now. NATO troops have largely demolished Serbia and they left it up to its inhabitants to clean up the mess. Although most of the population did not want to be a part of the conflict to begin with, it is understandable that they will do all it takes to rebuilt their homeland. And while the Serb government is only worried about how to find a way to stay in power (and steal some more money); and the United States has returned to minding their own business, Serbs realize that they have been manipulated by both sides. It was never a question of justice and honesty as Serbs claimed. It was never an effort to make the world a better place for our children as the other side liked to look at it. It was only a big, political game of chess, and Serbs were the pawns.

I find it hard to tell what kind of a future Serbia is looking forward to, but it doesn't look too bright. The government has taken over the Universities, and this new school system makes it very hard for young, smart students to attend corrupt schools. Since most of the population is very poor, scholars cannot expect their parents to pay their way through higher education abroad. Science cannot advance in constrains; the new ideas have to be born in the free, open-minded society. The black market is taking over the economy and the lack of goods is resulting in an exponentially increasing inflation. Employees are desperate since they haven't been paid in months, and most of them cannot even afford the essential food for their families. Still, they are afraid of changes, because they think that situation could get worse, since it has been gradually going downhill—for the last 55 years.

Serbs, the United States, and Slobodan Milosevic, the diva of the show, have taken their masks off of their faces when the curtains came down. They have all smiled one last time for the audience before they left the stage. Now, back to the usual everyday lives. Serb population is the only side that is faced with displeasing outcome. I try to look back without prejudice and summarize the effects of the war, and I always come up with the same answer: there are no winners in the wars. We have all lost, whether we want to admit or not. Being in the US and living a normal life now, after years of chaos, does not make me a winner either. I have left my family and my friends in Serbia, and I will never again be able to spend as much time with them as I would like to. We can only risk and we can make choices, try hard enough and look forward to seeing the results of our efforts. My choice was life in an open-minded society, full of opportunities that one scientist-to-be needs. I chose love and liberty.

THE TECHNOLOGY TRAP

[cause and effect—causal chain]

College education, as opposed to vocational training, is supposed to provide a student with the ability to think, communicate, evaluate or calculate and with a certain breadth and depth of knowledge and cultural awareness. Focusing on these attributes, a college education should develop students' values and beliefs, not simply make employees. With these intimidating and rather abstract expectations, most students step into college straight out of high school with few of their own values. Instead, they believe what they have been told to believe by church, state, family, or peers. So students may not see much coherence in a college's core curriculum. Though students' may believe that they know what they want to major, they can not possibly know what they will spend their lives doing. But a student can not realistically know his future nor his major without trying college on for size. This trying-on-for-size takes trial and error.

However, the moment students set foot on campus or even sign up for a college, they gets pressured from the college, their parents, the state of Texas, and society itself to choose a career and a major. Soon the student is out of time and loan money. Many people, including a lot of students, blame education for this dilemma and point an accusing finger at the educational system. But the cause is not education (though it may be the most readily apparent cause). The real culprit is technology, the cold industrial boom. Rather than equating education with knowledge in the arts and sciences—as in the past, today society equates education with vocational or technological skill. So in American's eyes education equals technology. And technology and our expectations for it and of it, not education, brainwashes the students of today with the promise of higher salaries and a more secure and admired job, resulting in the fact that technology has come between students and their value judgments.

When meeting the pressure to choose a major, many students base their choice not on what they like or admire but on money. Because technology is always advancing, and by definition leaving older technology behind, new, cutting-edge technologists are rare. The rarity and the desire for the new, not only disposes of the old technologists, but rewards the new technologists. Society, parents, and state legislatures look at universities and colleges to fulfill the demands of society, and in fact, would punish higher education for ignoring society's technological needs. Therefore, education has a legal and financial "obligation" to produce what society needs. Students, still not having developed ethics, values, and judgments, still not fully educated, jump into this channel and follow the flow into technology.

Besides big salaries, prestige attracts many students. Not knowing his own mind, a student may want the respect, earned or not, that accompanies a certain job. Once again, technology, with a sincere promise of a certain amount of prestige, lures students into technological majors. But prestige is no good without a job. A student graduating with a degree in engineering is much more likely to find a job than a student graduating with a degree in physics or chemistry, subjects that that engineering degree may be based on. Careers, not knowledge, not fields of study, and career opportunities now lie in technology. Education, therefore, promotes and advertises more technical training opportunities (due to the demand of society), and the student is lured into the technological trap.

With the siren call of high salary, prestige, and security, technology woos students—even those without the scientific or math background. Without know what they like, what they believe, how they should vote, what tickles their fancy and their minds, students study technology. So students with dwindling core courses, with declining hours for the major, with more hours require in the technological major, students neglect themselves, their culture, and their society to get technological skill. By the time a student makes her value decisions, she may have misplaced, non-existent, or vocational values. In between the student and his value is a technological wedge. In the end, society and culture are hurt the worst.

Colleges and Universities should break the hold that technology and the romance surrounding it have on them. The promise of money and admiration continue to fill our society with technical experts who have ignored the study that could have given them values and worth. Technology is filled with experts who are estranged from their own ideas, beliefs, and values. Yet technology continues to grow. And our values seem stagnant.

PROCESS DESCRIPTION ESSAYS

Many textbooks and teachers equate process descriptions and instructions. They say that instructions are a type of process description. I like to keep the two separate.

Instructions (or more appropriately, a set of instructions) enable a person to perform a particular task. They are written so that the person may put the instructions next to him and then build the birdcage or load the mousetrap. Since, like narration, they move through time, they should be organized according to chronology; thus instructions are organized according to the steps involved. They may have seventy-six subject segments. Each of these steps should receive its own emphasis and importance, usually in the form of a complete sentence.

Obviously, the instructions about how to connect a wing to a DC-10 will have many complex steps and precautions. For complex instructions then, the writer should break the steps into sections or into major and minor steps. Instructions usually take topography into account and accordingly use spacing and numbering to accentuate the steps.

Often then, instructions are no more than a collection of sentences. The introduction might be a short process description to tell the performer the theory behind his performance. It might describe the machine at rest and in motion. It might also list the tools needed or the ingredients. It might also give a short overview of the instructions.

Instructions, or more correctly a set of instructions, if a series of sentences, are usually short simple sentences. These sentences have as their subject "you" since they directly address the individual about to perform the task. Often, though, a writer will need to warn the person performing the instructions. So, before the simple sentence, the writer might put an adverbial clause. Passive voice is deadly to a set of instructions. And the writer of a set of instructions must be very careful in his selection of good active verbs. See why?

Process description rather than *process* or *process analysis* best labels this rhetorical mode, for this mode seeks to describe actions. Like narration, it is a description that moves through time rather than occupies space (oh my, back to the principles of Narration and Description). As such, like instructions, a process description should be organized chronologically, or as nearly as possible. **But, unlike instructions, which enable a person to perform something, process description enables a person to understand a process without necessarily being able to perform it.** Can you then see that process descriptions tackle much tougher, more abstract subjects than instructions, and that process descriptions require a more sophisticated audience? I want the surgeon who operates on me to have read process descriptions rather than a set of instructions.

Since process descriptions again emphasize action, they should have good verbs. But, many times, this process or the verb becomes the subject of your entire essay. So gerunds become good tools to help a writer with his process description. Sometimes though, especially in scientific reports, a researcher or writer simply won't know the cause of something. Modern physics tells us that this is not a causal world. So, if the researcher cannot find a proper gerund, he might use passive voice. This is really the only rhetorical mode that might require passive voice.

A WRITING METHOD—(AN ABBREVIATED ESSAY)

(process description)

When writing an essay, the writer should use the method of "streamlining." "Streamlining" merely means trimming down and improving an essay so that it is smooth and coherent. The method makes essays "streamlined," yet as informative as possible. This practice makes the essay more interesting, prevents some usage of unimportant facts, keeps the writer from rambling and losing his main theme, and leaves less of a margin for many types of errors. By preferring subordinate clauses to coordinate sentences, by preferring phrases to subordinate clauses, and by preferring a few descriptive words to phrases, a writer can "streamline" his sentences, therefore streamlining his essay.

Many times inexperienced writers try to combine separate but related ideas by using a coordinating conjunction, therefore, turning two independent clauses (sentences) into coordinating sentences. An example of coordinating sentences is:

Karen enjoys using computers, and she enjoys drafting on a computer.

The above sentence is two separate sentences (ideas) which are related and, therefore, joined by the coordinating conjunction "and." To better show the relationship between these two ideas, a writer should prefer to use a subordinate clause rather than create a coordinate sentence. To do this, a writer must choose the idea that he wants to subordinate and then change one of the independent clauses into a subordinate clause.

For example:

Karen, who enjoys using computers, enjoys drafting on one.

The subordinate clause is *who enjoys using computers,* and the main clause is *Karen enjoys drafting on one.* In this way, a writer gives the important information that Karen likes computers and enjoys drafting on computers in only one sentence. But a reader still finds out the same information that she did in the coordinating sentence.

However, the sentence can be reduced even more. To further "streamline" the sentence, a writer should prefer the phrase to the clause.

For example:

Enjoying computers, Karen likes drafting on one.

Once again, the reader gets the same information as before, but in the briefer, yet just as informative, sentence. By using a participle phrase rather than a subordinate clause, I have minimized my margin for error further, still provided the same information, and kept the reader's interest by not rambling on. However, the sentence can be trimmed down even further.

A writer may choose to "streamline" his sentences as much as he possibly can but still have the sentences remain as informative as possible. The writer can do this trimming by preferring the word to the phrase. In other words, a phrase can be replaced by just a few modifying words.

For example:

Karen, a computer buff, enjoys drafting on computers.

I have managed to streamline the original coordinating sentences into a very brief yet informative sentence. The reader still gets the same information as before but more quickly.

By using this method of preferring the subordinate clause to the coordinate sentence, by preferring the phrase to the subordinate clause, and by preferring the word to the phrase, a writer is able to develop more informative sentences. He may choose to develop several independent but related ideas (sentences) into one sentence by using modifying words, phrases, and clauses, with the end result being a better paper and a reduction in the margin for error.

CONFESSIONS OF A NOMINAL CHRISTIAN—PRINCE WILLIAMS

[Notice that this essay ends with a question. Many essays classified as creative non-fiction do just that. Also, as with much creative non-fiction, this essay implies as much as it states. And note too, that I'm not sure how to classify this essay. It could be a definition essay, a process essay, or a narrative essay]

To state that I believe God exists would not be entirely correct; more accurately, I am unwilling to believe He does not exist. I agree with Christian principles in theory, and I would like to think the Bible cannot err; however, Christianity influences only the fewest of my actions. One of my friends describes me as a "nominal Christian": better than some, worse than many, but in any case virtually indistinguishable in lifestyle from a nonbeliever. That is who I am now. However, nearly a decade ago, I supported strong religious devotion and acted passionately against the nominal Christians I presently so resemble.

During my teenage years, I was heavily involved in a medium-sized nondenominational Church. I worked in the offices, played the piano, and weekly attended the youth services. Such was my routine for many years, and in that time, I did not question anything; yet as I grew older and more aware. I increasingly discovered that the members of the Youth group, for all their vocal support of the Christian lifestyle, lived at tremendous odds to it. Most of them were no different from anyone outside their faith. They watched and discussed the same music, movies, and television programs as anyone else. They indulged in as much swearing, drinking, and pre-marital sex as anyone else. They were as unaccepting as anyone else, preaching love but only reaching out to likable persons, just as anyone else. They were nominal Christians practicing nominal Christianity: while they certainly acted no worse than their secular peers, they just as certainly acted no better.

If the youths' actions did not distinguish them from non-Christians, neither did their thinking. Devoid of the supernatural, their religious beliefs were tantamount to secular self-help: they preached psychology, not power. They overcame difficulties through positive thinking and psychology, through effort accompanied by a few meaningless prayers—meaningless because the youth decided that any outcome, regardless of what they asked, was God's will. Rather than an instrument of change, they made prayer little more than a few moments' relaxing meditation.

If Christianity offered nothing more than a way to approach life positively, could not Buddhism. Taoism, or any other "—ism" provide the same? What made the difference? Was fear of hell the only reason to subscribe to Christianity? The lives of the youth provoked me to these questions, and I do not believe I wondered alone, for those who left the youth group over the years did so with such disillusionment that they forsook any functional form of Christianity.

The church youth were indistinguishable from secular youth, but I could not have been more different. I never swore. I did not smoke or drink. I refused to try drugs. I did not watch "PG-13" movies, let alone "R." More than that, however, I fervently believed in a God of the present tense, a God of "is doing" rather than "has done," a God currently interested in knowing His people, not a God who previously dabbled in humanity but now would prefer we handle things ourselves. The nominal Christians and I contrasted sharply.

More and more, I realized I was no longer willing to weekly surround myself with everything Christianity should not be. I knew I must leave my church. However, I also knew I could not do that until I had shared with the church leadership what I believed to be the ultimate failures of the youth ministry. I had to tell them they were losing an entire generation.

Because I expressed myself most clearly on paper, I composed a letter to show my views. I described the typical church service, its lack of godliness, and its excess of psychology. I revealed what I knew of the two-facedness that characterized the youth, I explained they showed a veneer of virtue at services, but proved outside of church that the ministry made no real impact on their lives. I stated that, without supernatural power, Christianity was no better than any other religion and worse than many. I declared the heart of Christianity was Christ. Talking with Him, and most importantly, hearing Him talk back was more important than depending upon guidance from the latest vaguely religious book on the power of positive thinking. I said all this, and I believed it strongly. I felt I had never written anything more important.

As I left the last service I attended at this church. I handed copies of my letter to the pastors and the youth leaders. I did not know what reaction this might cause, but I was ready to be vilified. When the senior pastor of the church called my house a few days later, however, he surprised me by humbly vowing a spiritual change in the youth ministry. I waited with eagerness to see this new beginning, yet I soon discovered no such change would occur, for the church staff ultimately dismissed my letter as pessimistic and me as theologically twisted. To them, my ideas were ridiculous and contrary to contemporary Christian wisdom. That I expected Christians to hear clearly from God, to experience the supernatural, and to live unlike others proved, in their minds, that I had completely misunderstood and distorted Christianity. Such were the opinions of my fellow Christians as I left that church and that stage of my life forever.

Seven years later, I am now the antithesis of whom I was. Christian beliefs languish somewhere in the back of my mind while, often in the company of those disillusioned former churchgoers that once so saddened me, I indulge in doing all I once so passionately decried. Ironically, I subscribe wholesale to nominal Christianity. So, in a way, my church instruction worked. Despite my earlier protests, I am what I abhorred. And whether my life now proves that I was then correct in thinking my church could produce only nominal Christians, whether my life now proves that my church was right to pronounce me a religious lunatic who could come to no good end, or whether my present attitude proves that we must inevitably make compromises and become nominal Christians, I cannot say.

ARGUMENTATION

The following essays combine rhetorical modes and manipulate the language very well. Most of these essays use logic or reasoning also. Reasoning requires the use of induction or deduction. Unlike some books and teachers, I classify cause and effect as a logical process as well as a rhetorical mode because it abides by certain rules of logic. Therefore, it can create and prove an argument. Notice then, how these essays use induction, deduction, cause and effect, classification, definition, and process to prove their points. Notice too, the descriptive quality in them. Particularly look at how these essays use submerged and extended metaphors in their description of abstractions. Remember, these metaphors illustrate, not prove. Look back at some of the previous essays. They too argue.

A Note on Induction and Deduction
Induction is the scientific method. It is the gathering of data to make a hypothesis. It uses statistics, experiments, and data. A lab report is inductive.

Deduction is syllogistic reasoning. It usually used the induction to make a hypothesis. Then, it comes up with a hypothesis that we assume to be true or widely accept to be true. It puts the two hypothesis or assumptions together. The two together make a third statement that must be true. So if 1 is true, and 2 is true, then 3 must be true. That previous sentence shows the classic design of a syllogism.

For example, Thomas Jefferson bases "the Declaration of Independence" on deduction, on a syllogism. He says that we have "self-evident truths." These "self-evident truths" are thus *a priori* assumptions, ideas or assumptions that we all assume to be true. Thus self-evident truths, or a priori assumptions, need no proof. One of these self-evident assumptions is that all people deserve and seek certain "inalienable rights." He then states the next obvious fact. 1) If a government takes away the inalienable rights of its citizens, then the citizens have the right to break away from the government. This is the **major premise.** 2) He next states that Great Britain has denied the American colonies' citizens certain rights. This is the **minor premise.** Jefferson needs proof for this fact. Even the colonists did not all accept this fact. He needs data and proof. He needs induction. So he uses more emphatic words. He uses connotation. He grows more flowery and passionate, but he also lists facts about Great Britain, its actions against the colonies, or King George. This listing takes a while. It is mostly a series of "He"s directed against King George. After several paragraphs of facts,

Jefferson states the third assumption of his syllogism, the one that is now obvious, given the a priori assumption and the inductively proven second assumption: that the colonies ought to break away from Britain. This is the **conclusion.**

I've been criminally brief. You should find a good textbook to further explain these terms.

A Note on Connotation and Denotation, Euphemism, Jargon, Cant, and Clichés

I have left out diction completely. But I should mention **connotation** and **denotation.** I discuss these terms here because people use connotation so often in making arguments. *Denotation* is the dictionary meaning of the word. *Connotation* is the emotion or the judgment or the assumption we make beyond the literal meaning.

For example, I have been bald most of my life. Someone who likes me might say that I have *thinning* hair. Someone who wants to make fun of me might say that I have *a chrome dome.* Years ago, people might have called me a *skin head,* but that term has taken on a whole different meaning because of the associations or the connotations that we now give to it.

For example, who wants to be *fat?* Wouldn't you rather be *plump, hefty, stout, full-figured?*

For example, years ago, I got my *college loans* from the U.S. Department of Health, Education, and Welfare. People applauded me. When I got some food stamps from the same U.S. Department, people said that I was a lazy *welfare bum.* So facts have connotations.

You can probably see the ethics here. As with metaphor and analogy, connotation can not prove anything. It can only illustrate. So name calling and using suggestive names or phrases or even derogatory names proves nothing. It is unethical. Yet think of all the times you hear and read connotation being used to "prove." The facts, induction, deduction, syllogisms, and data prove. So use connotation to support the facts. Jefferson uses connotation in "The Declaration of the Independence." But he supports his connotation, his name-calling, with facts. Most good editorials in newspapers work this way also.

Now we are getting into **euphemism.** These are words with more pleasing connotations used to change our opinion of what they name. Sometimes euphemism uses pleasant connotations to hide unpleasant facts. We no longer have *used cars.* We have *pre-owned cars.* Sending more troops in is called a *surge.* The U.S. military leaders called the Grenada Invasion a *"pre-dawn vertical insertion."* (What is on their minds? The movie *Dr. Strangelove* comes to mind.) People *pass away* rather than *die.* We have *full-figured* shops.

Another type of word usage that attempts to prove through connotation is **cant.** This is a political language that uses the emotions and associations given to words in order to convince people toward a certain action. This is not a valid or ethical way to prove a point or to think. When you hear cant, hold on to your pocket book.

A type of language that is bereft of emotion and that confuses the average reader if not all readers is **jargon.** Jargon is a type of language or the type of words that a field, a major, or a profession uses. Only professionals in that field know those terms (and sometimes I doubt that they really know those terms). So when someone writes for a regular, non-professional audience and uses jargon, then that writer is being purposefully confusing. You can find plenty of examples of jargon and cant all around you.

Read your insurance statement or your phone bill. Can you make sense of these? Look for the deliberately vague language. Look for the jargon. Look for the specialized terms. This is writing without emotion, writing meant to confuse.

Finally, the world is full of **clichés.** These are words or phrases that may have once been vital, but through overuse they have just lost any real meaning. Your instructor can help you distinguish between these words. You should basically avoid jargon, cant, and cliché. Use these words only if audience or purpose might demand their use. Below is a list of clichés, jargon, cant, and euphemisms.

People use the following as adjectives and rely upon connation to say that a person or idea is good or bad: *Liberal, Conservative, Christian, family-oriented, atheist.* Here are some more:

Student Learning Outcomes	*Underachiever*	*Unilateral*
The American People	*Bleeding-heart liberal*	*Punitive Paradigm*
Vast right wing conspiracy	*Purge*	
Text (instead of book)	*Children are our future*	
The modern world of today	*Vocationally, mentally, or otherwise "challenged"*	
Discourse analysis	*Prompt* (as in a written assignment)	
Fuzzy-headed intellectual	*Common Sense*	*Common man*
Horse sense	*I take pen in hand*	*It is with deep regret*
Passed away	*Freedom Fighters*	*American values*
Family values	*Sunshine Patriot*	*Infidels*
Nay-sayers	*non-believers*	

EDUCATION AND CRITICAL THINKING

[classification & division, definition, deduction]

Most students enter college thinking that the purpose of college is essentially to give them a high paying job. While salary is connected to education in most surveys, making money is not the only reason to go to college. In fact most colleges don't claim to teach a student to make money. According to various sources, including the Lamar University core curriculum philosophy statement in the Lamar catalog, the purpose of a general education is to make students aware of their culture, to develop students' senses of ethics or right and wrong, to teach students to communicate more effectively. However, colleges almost always claim to teach students critical thinking. But colleges rely upon different departments to teach what makes up critical thinking. To become good thinkers students should develop their logical, abstracting, and discovering abilities, and they should do so in a variety of courses.

Critical thinking is not just the ability to analyze just art. Thought should be logical. Since the Greeks, we've understood logic to be reasoning, understanding, deducing, or inferring to arrive at a conclusion. Thus, logic is exercise for the mind. A logical thinker puts facts together clearly and reaches a conclusion that is based upon those facts. This is pure induction or scientific method. As a thinker grows and practices induction, he can use more complex facts and thus come to more astute conclusions. Once the thinker has induction down, he should also start exercising deduction. Deduction is the ability to put two conclusions together to come up with a third. Together induction and deduction make up logic. And thus logic indicates an individual's capacity for thinking.

But logic isn't all that a student needs to fully exercise his critical thinking. The good thinker must also be able to take abstract ideas and associate them with more concrete objects. Abstractions are general concepts such as love, happiness, and freedom. We may *know* what these concepts are, but the good thinker *sees* these abstractions around her. This type of thinking is the type that poets and artist do. It is also the type of thinking that the physicist or scientist uses when he figures out the theories in the natural world, or sees theory take form in the natural world.

Critical thinking also implies the ability to actively seek new knowledge. Thought as a thing done is not as important as thinking. The thinking muscle should constant work. So a well-conditioned thinker is able to grow and learn more. This ability to discover not only makes for an aware person but a better employee—and perhaps might make a person more money. So, ironically, by teaching thinking, colleges by their very nature might be *giving students the ability* to find a good job as opposed to *training* those students for a job.

Now, as any senior student can see, the core curriculum or basic academic foundations or the course that all students have to take attempt to teach these attributes of thinking.

Math, science, and technical courses rely on logic. Most college students are required to take at least one math course, and mathematics classes teach logic through the use of syllogisms, which are the basis for deduction. A basic algebraic principle is that if a=b and b=c then a=c. Once students learn this association in math, they can apply it to their academic and vocational worlds. And hopefully, with this basis, students will progress to more complex problems: more facts and longer threads of deduction. Computer science classes teach students to write programs, and a good computer program must be extremely logical. Computer programs consist of small, orderly steps that lead to the completion of a task. Without each step in place, the task doesn't work. And of course, any science lab relies on induction.

Students must deal with abstractions in almost all of their courses. In English, the students see how great poets use imagery, metaphor, and symbol to find the abstract in the concrete. For example, in "Do Not Go Gentle into That Good Night," Dylan Thomas compares death to night. He wrote, "Do not go gentle into that good night,/Old age should burn and rave at close of day;/Rage, rage against the dying of the light." Furthermore, literature classes and other classes with their writing assignments force students to write about abstractions. In such cases, students must write papers about an abstract subject and practice using imagery and metaphors himself.

State and Federal Government political science classes study the United States Constitution. The Constitution is a broad, abstract document, and the courts have interpreted it often. As students study these interpretations, they learn how the abstract terms of the Constitution can be applied to daily life. For example, Amendment VIII states that no "cruel and unusual punishment" shall be inflicted. This clause means that no American citizen who breaks the law can be punished more harshly than the deed merits; for instance, a man who breaks the speed limit cannot be interred for life.

Perhaps most important, a university education encourages students to actively seek new knowledge. This desire for discovery is not instilled in any particular course. Instead, the desire occurs in the process, especially when the student becomes interested in a field or an idea. Perhaps colleges can't so much *teach* discover as to *prepare* students for it. Colleges should make students want to learn more. In science, perhaps in just learning about past technological and scientific advances, students yearn for further growth. Students have plenty to discover and further explore: solar energy, space exploration, and medicine.

Students can also learn to discover in areas such as World History or Literature. The French Revolution might fire interest in a student's mind, so he will try to learn all he can about that subject or France or other revolutions, and so on. Likewise, a student may be fascinated by poetry and try to read and discover all the poetry he can. Or a student may even attempt to write poetry. Thus, if a student gains interest in any subject, he has learned "discovery."

Finally, despite the assumptions about what colleges should do, colleges should emphasize the one thing that all colleges agree should accompany college education: critical thinking. To encourage the development of critically thinking individuals, colleges should teaches students to think logically, to handle abstractions, and to seek new knowledge. The basic or core curricula at colleges thus pushes students in this direction. So a college's mission is not to gain money but to gain thought.

SAME-SEX MARRIAGE: A PROPOSAL FOR DEBATE—RICHARD MCCUE

(2005 Longman Award Winner for Composition I, Lamar University)

The debate over the legalization and social acceptance of same sex marriage dates back hundreds of years. According to William N. Eskridge, Jr., the western world never accepted these marriages as either legal or moral; however, other cultures have accepted them in various configurations since the thirteenth century (16). The issue became controversial when members of the gay community pressed their desire to have these marriages recognized as legal. On May 18, 1970, Richard John Baker and James Michael McConnell petitioned the State of Minnesota for a marriage license after they were joined in a quiet religious ceremony in their church. The controversy arose on May 22, 1970, when Gerald Nelson, Clerk of the Hennepin County District Court, denied their petition because they were of the same sex. Nelson based his decision on the fact that same sex marriage is illegal in the state of Minnesota. The petitioners, Baker and McConnell, carried their battle to the Supreme Court of Minnesota and received a negative ruling in 1971. These proceedings became the beginning, but by no means the end of the Constitutional challenges presented in the various states by gay and lesbian partners (Eskridge 48). Generally, people support same-sex marriages because they believe that discrimination in any form is no longer acceptable in society. Generally, people oppose same-sex unions because they it is a personal affront to the values and traditional family structure that are a strong part of their history and their cud lure. This opposition is supported in a newspaper article from *The Beaumont Enterprise*. Kevin J. Dwyer points out that John Gray has won legal custody of his two nephews. His custody is jointly shared with his sister Ursula, the mother of the children. The boys, ages five and seven, live with Gray and his "lover," Paul Burch, for the preceding twenty-one months. Gray testified that living in the home with their natural parents, the children were exposed to other individuals with felony drug convictions on their record (A1). Gay marriage should be legal because it will afford legal protection to the partners, it will provide equality for all citizens gay or not, and it will provide benefits currently reserved for heterosexual couples only.

First, gay marriage should be legal because it will afford legal protection to the partners. Dwight J. Penas argues that the cost of denying marital status to the partners becomes enormous. This denial exposes them to discrimination from employers, discrimination from landlords, and discrimination from institutions offering services and facilities to the public. He continues to note that unmarried couples, regardless of their sex, face discrimination in housing, banning them from spousal benefits from worker's compensation laws, special tax treatment and Social Security benefits (152). Mary Bonauto asserts that marriage is a relationship, similar to the relationship of a "family." No one dares challenge the right to be by a spouse's side if a couple is legally married. The word marriage, of itself, becomes a protection marriage. Married couples can take for granted rights of hospital visitation, security for their children, and rights of inheritance. Additionally, gay and lesbian families can protect themselves in limited ways by creating wills, health-care proxies, and co-parent adoptions; however, this does not come even close to giving the peace of mind that the simple ceremony of marriage guarantees (739). Scott Bidstrup notes that married couples are not required to testify against one another in a court of law. Gay partners lack this protection under the law (28). The opposition would assert that gay marriage should not afford legal protection to the partners because they believe that legal protection is only for those couples married in the sense of a marriage between one man and one woman. Gay and lesbian couples allowed the legal ceremony of marriage would truly be equal participants with the rest of society in the protections afforded under the law.

Secondly, gay marriage should be legal because legalization will afford equality for all citizens, gay or not. Richard D. Mohr claims that limiting homosexual couples' civil unions, reported as separate but equal to heterosexual marriage, serves only to degrade the gay men and lesbian women. The lack of legal marriage accessibility to the gay couple strikes directly at the issue of their dignity. Their dignity is at stake because of the denial of their equality (34). In an interview with Mary Bonauto, author Jo Ann Citron asked her to respond directly to the issue of dispensing with the commonplace idea of marriage and making marriage simply a contract between two people. Her response was that it would only work if there were no repercussions or if it did not convey any stigma or disrespect. Bonauto's position is that a place will be reached where the government no longer denies equal rights to gay couples. She believes this issue will be resolved in the near future (18). Evan Wolfson discusses still another parallel when he compares the direct relationship between the struggles for equality fought by those that supported interracial marriage and those that support same-sex marriage. The language used today relative to same-sex couples is eerily familiar to those who remember the language used to oppose interracial marriage (32). He insists that the denial to gay couples of their freedom and their equality is based only on the choice they make regarding whom they love (Wolfson 35). Yuval Merin references *Identity and the Case for Gay Rights* in which David Richard discusses the similarities between the three minority groups: racial minorities, women, and homosexuals, as they struggle for equality. The battles fought by civil rights advocates and women's rights advocates have paved the way for the fight now at hand in the gay community (43). The opposition would assert that gay marriage should not afford equality for all citizens because equality is already at hand. Equality is an innate right, which allows all Americans, gay or not, the dignity and freedom supposedly guaranteed in the constitution.

Finally, gay marriage should be legal because it will divide benefits currently reserved for heterosexual couples only. Walter Isaacson reports that a Domestic-partnership Benefits Commission, recently established by the City Council in Washington, is to explore the feasibility of extending benefits to the partners of municipal workers (102). An employee derives as much as 40% of his remuneration from a fringe benefits package. The denial of fringe benefits to the gay couple while allotting them without question to the married couple is direct discrimination (Isaacson 101). Jonathan Goldberg-Hiller reveals that labor, in both private and public contract negotiations, supports the expansion of benefits to include gay and lesbian partners (115). He points out that Fourteen years after going officially on the record in support of gay and lesbian civil rights, the American Federation of Labor national leadership appointed a "constituency group" among its membership. The purpose of the group was to promote mutual understanding of gay rights and labor issues (Goldberg-Hiller 5). Workplace benefits of same sex partners usually do not measure up to the benefits of heterosexual partners. Even the Internal Revenue Service does not recognize or qualify same sex partners' benefits unless they meet the criteria as a dependent (Merin 199). Jeff Barge divulges many law firms have begun to include benefits packages for same sex domestic partners. Recruitment of law school graduates many times turns on the firm's policy relative to domestic partner benefits (34). Todd Henneman discusses the fact that benefits follow the couple into death. Inheritance rights are put in place to assure that, even if the deceased spouse has not left a will, the surviving spouse will inherit. This benefit is just another that is not available to the same sex partners (3). The opposition would assert gay couples do not deserve the same benefits as heterosexual couples because they are not married. Benefits available to gay partners, if they are indeed married, in and of themselves give strong reason in favor of the continuing quest for the legalization of gay marriage.

To reiterate, gay marriage should be legal because it will afford legal protection to the partners, equality to all citizens gay or not and benefits currently reserved for heterosexual couples only. Marriage is a dynamic institution. The reason for marriage throughout history has changed but includes such considerations as money, consolidation of property, power, and politics (Merin 6). The day that same sex marriage becomes legal is the day that all citizens can be proud to be Americans. Today, the inclusion of love in a marriage influences the couple more than at any other time in history. The debate over the legalization and social acceptance of same sex marriage will no doubt continue as civilization progresses through the twenty-first century.

Works Cited

Barge, Jeff. "More Firms Offer Benefits for Gay Couples." *ABA Journal* 81.6 (1995): 34–35. *Academic Search Premier*. Ebscohost. Mary and John Gray Lib., Beaumont. 28 Oct. 2004.

Bidstrup, Scott. "Arguments against Gay Marriage Are Baseless." *Roleff* 23–29.

Bonauto, Mary. "Should Gay Marriage Be Legally Recognized?" *CQ Researcher* 13.30 (2003): 739–45. *Academic Search Premier*. Ebscohost. Mary and John Gray Lib., Beaumont. 26 Oct. 2004.

Citron, Jo Ann. "Goodridge Takes Effect: Now What?" *Gay & Lesbian Review Worldwide* 11 (2004): 14–18. *Academic Search Premier*. Ebscohost. Mary and John Gray Lib., Beaumont. 31 Oct. 2004.

Dwyer, Kevin J. "Another Local Case Spotlights Gay Right: Man Wins Custody of Nephews in Orange Case." *Beaumont Enterprise* 04 Sept. 2003: Al, A4.

Eskridge, William N., Jr. The Case for Same-Sex Marriage: From Sexual Liberty to Civilized Commitment. New York: FP, 1996.

Goldberg-Hiller, Jonathan. *The Limits to Union: Same-Sex Marriage and the Politics of Civil Rights*. Ann Arbor: U of Michigan P, 2002.

Henneman, Todd. "Marry Me and Save." *Advocate* 30 Mar. 2004: 34–35. *Academic Search Premier*. Ebscohost. Mary and John Gray Lib., Beaumont. 28 Oct. 2004.

Isaacson, Walter. "Should Gays Have Marriage Rights?: On Two Coasts, The Growing Debate Produces Two Different Answers." *Time* 20 Nov. 1989: 101–02.

Merin, Yuval. *Equality for Same-Sex Couples: The Legal Recognition of Gay Partnerships in Europe and the United States*. Chicago: U of Chicago P, 2002.

Mohr, Richard D. "Equal Dignity under the Law." *Gay & Lesbian Review* 11 (2004): 30–35. Academic Search Premier. Ebscohost. Mary and John Gray Lib., Beaumont. 31 Oct. 2004.

Penas, Dwight J. "Bless the Tie That Binds: A Puritan-Covenant Case for Same-Sex Marriage." *Same-Sex Marriage*. Ed. Robert M. Baird and Stewart E. Rosenbaum. Amherst: Prometheus, 1997. 146–63.

Roleff, Tamara L., ed. *Opposing Viewpoints: Gay Marriage*. San Diego: Greenhaven, 1998.

Wolfson, Evan. "Lesbians and Gay Men Should Fight for the Freedom to Marry." *Roleff* 30–40.

MRS. AND MRS. SMITH—ALYSSA FINCHER

(2007 Longman Award Winner for Composition I, Lamar University)

Throughout the United States, the government prevents thousands of couples from marrying because of an important part of their identity, gender. But on the twelfth of February, 2004, the mayor of San Francisco changed this for many couples by legalizing same-sex marriages in that city. Sean Cahill states that because of this landmark event, anti-gay activists went into overdrive, and between 2004 and 2006 state legislators put nearly two dozen anti-gay marriage proposals on ballots to be voted on by the public (99). Generally, people support same-sex marriage because they believe that not allowing same-sex marriage violates human rights. Generally, people do not support same-sex marriage because they believe that marriage is a union between one man and one woman. According to Alison Beck, on February 12,-2004, she received a breathless phone call from her partner of nine years, Huong, urging her to rush to city hall. The mayor of their city, San Francisco, had legalized same-sex civil marriages. Alison hurriedly put shoes on their seventeen month old son, Theryn, and made it to city hall only ten minutes before closing time (50). After waiting in line and taking a number, Alison and Huong exchanged vows in an impromptu wedding ceremony with no wedding dresses and no flowers; they could not risk waiting until the next day for fear that there would be an injunction by morning. Sadly, on August 12, 2004, after six months of being married and six months of being told that their family and others like it destroyed the sanctity of marriage and the fabric of society, the California Supreme Court invalidated Alison and Huong's marriage license (Beck 51). Society should allow same-sex marriage because not allowing same-sex marriage discriminates, violates human civil rights, and prohibits the state from receiving the benefits from same sex couples.

Same-sex marriage should be legal because prohibiting same-sex marriage discriminates on basis of gender similarly to the way not allowing mixed-race marriages discriminates on basis of race. William N. Eskridge explains that opponents of both types of unions (mixed-race and same-sex) cite "natural law" as a reason for bans. Opponents of mixed-race marriage argue that marriage should promote racial purity, and those who protest same-sex marriage believe that marriage's purpose is procreation (154). The similarities can be further shown by comparing the United States Supreme Court case Loving versus Virginia and the Hawaii Supreme Court case Baehr versus Lewin. The Hawaii Supreme Court declared it racial discrimination to allow marriage between a black man and a black woman, but prohibit marriage between a white man and black woman, where only the race of one person differed. Similarly, Baher ruled legalizing marriage between a man and a woman, but not a woman and a woman, where only the gender of **one** individual differed, is gender discrimination (Eskridge 162). One should also consider that seventeen state constitutions specifically bar legislation that discriminates on the basis of sex (Eskridge 163). The opposition would assert that making gay marriage illegal does not discriminate because marriage, by definition, is a union between one man and one woman. This argument is invalid because society-has altered the nature of marriage throughout time to better fit society's needs such as when Congress legalized interracial marriages.

Another reason to consider legalization of same-sex marriages is that not allowing same-sex marriages violates one's civil rights. The first amendment declares that "Congress shall make no law respecting an establishment of religion." Restricting marriage to the Judeo—Christian definition of a union between one man and one woman is unconstitutional because it gives preference to those religious views. The first amendment also states that Congress cannot make any legislation that hinders "the free exercise" of any religion. When one bears in mind that numerous religions sanctify same-sex marriages, it becomes clear that not legalizing these unions obstructs the exercise of said religions. In addition, the fourteenth amendment decrees that the state cannot "deny to any person within its jurisdiction the equal protection of the laws." Placing a ban on same-sex unions withholds the protections that accompany marital status. Further, the first section of the Declaration of Independence describes three "unalienable rights" "life, liberty, and the pursuit of happiness." Not recognizing same-sex marriages interferes with same-sex couples' happiness by making them perceive themselves as inferior. The opposition would assert that banning same-sex marriage does not infringe on civil rights because as Chuck Colbert recounts, Amendments to state constitutions will be voted on by the public (14). This argument is invalid because in the past many bans ratified by the public on interracial marriage have been struck down by the Supreme Court because of unconstitutionality proving that America is not a "pure democracy" (Colbert 14).

Lastly, prohibiting same-sex marriages hinders the state from receiving benefits that accompany married couples residing in its jurisdiction. Strasser mentions that the state benefits from married couples because marital partners will provide for each other, if necessary, reducing the need for state assistance (34). In addition, the state has an interest in ensuring that children are raised in a stable environment, allowing same-sex marriages would stabilize families with same-sex parents (Strasser 35). Another social benefit would be a reduced amount of sexually transmitted diseases due to increased monogamous practices (35). One must also consider that the state has an interest in ensuring the orderly dissolution of relationships, such as divorce. If same-sex couples were legally bound to each other, then, if the relationship ended, the assets would be distributed fairly, and ideally, after the relationship has ended, the state would not have to expend funds to support one or both of the individuals involved (Strasser 35). Also, the state has an interest in promoting good mental and physical health, and therefore promoting productivity; Marilyn Elias remarks that not allowing same-sex couples to legally wed applies much strain on their mental and physical health (1). The opposition would assert that the state does not benefit from same-sex couples because these couples do not have children to raise. This is untrue because Katha Pollitt insists that at least one million children in the United States, including adopted children, children from previous marriages, and children produced within the same-sex relationship, live in same-sex households (12).

As previously stated, not granting same sex couples the right to marry discriminates on basis of gender, violates their rights, and prevents the state from receiving benefits that accompany married couples residing in its authority. Fortunately, the quest to legalize same-sex marriages is progressing. Timothy Stewart-Winter articulates that in 1953, in response to a magazine article predicting what the world might be like if same-sex marriages were allowed, one reader said that speculating such changes was equivalent to saying what if one day we all woke up and became giants (33), but C. E. Tygart reports that forty-nine years later, as of 2002, twenty-six percent of adults surveyed supported gay marriage and forty-two percent supported domestic partnerships (20).

WORKS CITED

Beck, Alison. "Taking the Long View: Reflections on the Road to Marriage Equality." *Berkeley Journal of Gender, Law, and Justice* 20 (2005): 50–55. *Academic Search Premier.* Ebscohost. Mary and John Gray Lib., Beaumont. 14 Oct. 2006.

Bill of Rights.

Cahill, Sean. *Same-Sex Marriage in the United States: Focus on the Facts.* Lanham: Lexington, 2004.

Colbert, Chuck. "Clergy Duel as Lawmakers Delay Gay Marriage Vote." *National Catholic Reporter* 11 Aug. 2006: 14. *Academic Search Premier.* Ebscohost. Mary and John Gray Lib., Beaumont. 14 Oct. 2006.

Declaration of Independence.

Elias, Marilyn. "Psychologists to Endorse Gay Marriage." *USA Today* 29 July 2004: Ia. *Academic Search Premier.* Ebscohost. Mary and John Gray Lib., Beaumont. 23 Oct. 2006.

Pollitt, Katha. "No Presents, Please." *Nation* 14 Aug. 2006: 12. *Academic Search Premier.* Ebscohost. Mary and John Gray Lib., Beaumont. 14 Oct. 2006.

Stewart-Winter, Timothy. "What Was Same-Sex Marriage?" *Gay and Lesbian Review Worldwide* 13.1 (2006): 33–35. *Academic Search Premier.* Ebscohost. Mary and John Gray Lib., Beaumont. 14 Oct. 2006.

Strasser, Mark. "The State Interests in Recognizing Same-Sex Marriage." *Marriage and Same-Sex Unions: A Debate.* Ed. Lynn D. Wardle. Westport: Praeger, 2003.

Tygart, C. E. "Legal Rights to Homosexuals into the Areas of Domestic Partnerships and Marriages: Public Support and Genetic Causation Attribution." *Educational Research Quarterly* 25.3 (2002):20–28. *Academic Search Premier.* Ebscohost. Mary and John Gray Lib., Beaumont. 14 Oct. 2006.

U.S. Constitution.

FINAL THOUGHTS ABOUT RHETORICAL MODES & PROCESS _____

If you have noticed, as I state in "Rationale for this Manual," I have left out the invention part of rhetoric to primarily look at arrangement and style. Some folks call invention "pre-writing." So I have left it out too. But I think that I have given some hints to help you with invention or pre-writing.

I think that the rhetorical modes and Christensen's methods can be used for pre-writing. As I said when discussing Christensen, if you can write one sentence, then using Christensen, you can start adding sentences. **Or,** you can pick a subject and think about how you might want to express it. Thus you might consider whether you want to write contrast and compare, process, cause and effect, or some other rhetorical mode. As I state, these rhetorical modes are as much ways of thinking or ways of planning as ways of writing. They are really most important for thinking about your topic and for planning your essay. You should also consider the persona, audience, and purpose—not just the content.

However the actual process of putting fingers to keyboards (I highly encourage composing on the computer) makes writing messy. The mind to finger to screen transfer smudges and changes the essay. The rhetorical methods are skewed. A writer mixes them. She uses one then another. Dave Cherry's essay comes to mind. I watched him go through several drafts.

As you may have noted in "A Hint at Process" at the start of this manual, I emphasize that good writing takes drafts and stages. So you think, maybe using rhetorical modes to help you think, and you have an essay in mind. Then, you compose, using Christensen to suggest what to write and where to take your writing. Perhaps, during the actual composing, you even forgot about what rhetorical mode you were using. So you have a mess of words on your screen. Now you need to shape what you have written. You can reapply Christensen to see that everything is subordinate or coordinate. You can impose a rhetorical mode (or two, or three; see Cherry) onto this mess. Fight the mess. Cut and paste and rewrite and revise. It is a shape shifter. You must be Prometheus and wrestle it until it holds still in a final shape.

Once you have it in some kind of shape, you must worry that writing into complete form. That is right, *worry*. You must neurotically check for words. Look for denotation and connotation. Adjust it. Could you add a metaphor to illustrate? Have you perhaps, heavens be, created a symbol? Worry some more. Does the style that you have used match the persona, purpose, and audience? How will those rhetorical considerations influence this draft?

Now you have your essay tuned up. Now be insistent. Be a Nazi. Look at the punctuation. Look at the grammar. Run grammar checks. Reread. Run grammar checks again.

So, as you can see, I advocate what works for you. But you can't know what works for you until you try a variety of methods. And trying isn't just writing at the last minute. It isn't just "writing it down." It is fighting, wrestling, worrying, being gentle to yourself, being a Nazi to yourself, being your best friend, being your worst enemy. Maybe after your struggle, it is ready to turn in. Maybe after several fights, after several psychological somersaults, after you've turned in several essays, you can confidently claim to be a writer. And then, maybe, you can refine yourself and your craft by completing another writing course.

Composition II—
Essays About Literature, Film, and Popular Culture

Section 3

Most of these essays have research. Some do not. For some, I lost the works cited page. None of these are meticulously researched. However, they are literary, film, or cultural analyses with some research or reference to support the point. Students might note that many times the primary source (the work being discussed) is from the student textbook. This practice is fine. Also, because of space restraints, I did not put Works Cited on a separate page. And the Works Cited Pages are single rather than double spaced. These essays, as with the ones in the first section, have had little or no editing. Also, the documentation for online or electronic sources has changed since these essays were written.

A FULL PACK: THE HEAVY PLOT IN "THE THINGS THEY CARRIED"—JEREMY BRISTER

(Notice how this essay follows the basic five paragraph format)

Tim O'Brien's "The Things They Carried" gives the reader meaningful insight of the burdens leaders in combat face as they attempt to separate personal emotions from obligation to duty. O'Brien's use of exposition helps the reader better understand how the conflict builds up and why the main character's resolution is of utmost necessity. An exploration into the plot reveals the author's personal feelings about the burdens war plays on soldiers.

The story is unique in that O'Brien uses an exposition paragraph to introduce each stage of the plot. Each exposition builds on what the soldiers carry and increases in complexity as the story unfolds. The story begins with an exposition introducing Lieutenant Jimmy Cross, the platoon leader, and mentions letters—from a girl he is fond of back home—that he carries in his rucksack. The opening exposition also introduces other members of the platoon, the personal gear they carry, and some essential items that every man carries, such as can openers, comic books, and extra socks. Although very descriptive, all of the items the characters carry, in this stage of the plot, are simple, material items. By the last exposition of the story, the author has built an extensive packing list of material items and has also introduced complex emotions that—to the soldiers—have physical weight that must be carried. O'Brien depicts this weight in the final exposition, "They carried all the emotional baggage of men who might die. Grief, terror, love, longing—these were intangibles, but the intangibles had their own mass and specific gravity, they had tangible weight" (677). The use of several expositions throughout the story helps to create a better understanding of the conflict and resolution.

The conflict between Jimmy Cross's personal emotion and sense of duty to his platoon is exemplified throughout the plot. The author makes the conflict evident by subtly changing the topic to refocus on Lieutenant Cross and his wondering thoughts of Martha. For example, "Almost everyone humped photographs. In his wallet, Lieutenant Cross carried two photographs of

117

Martha" (O'Brien 669), at which time the author goes into detail about these two photos and Jimmy Cross's thoughts of each, without explaining other pictures carried by other soldiers of the platoon. O'Brien makes the conflict more obvious in other parts of the plot by having Jimmy Cross address the issue and recognize that he is having a problem. An evident example of the conflict arises after Tom Lavender's death while Lieutenant Cross sits in his foxhole. "He felt shame. He hated himself. He had loved Martha more than his men, and as a consequence Lavender was now dead, and this was something he would have to carry like a stone in his stomach for the rest of the war" (O'Brien 675). The conflict the Lieutenant faces and the emotion he reveals about this conflict builds throughout the story and grows from very simple and unmeaning in the beginning to important and in need of resolution at the end.

O'Brien reveals the resolution—soon after the climax—with Jimmy Cross burning the letters and pictures of Martha to symbolize the separation of his personal emotions from his obligation to lead his platoon. The author gives a strong resolution as Jimmy Cross decides to drop all thoughts of personal nature and pursue a more disciplined attitude with his troops as a top priority. "Henceforth, when he thought about Martha, it would be only to think that she belonged elsewhere. He would shut down the daydreams. This was not Mount Sebastian, it was another world, where there were no pretty poems or midterm exams, a place where men died because of carelessness and gross stupidity" (O'Brien 679). O'Brien depicts the separation of personal emotion and obligation to duty as something very important to Jimmy Cross and the resolution is fitting to accomplish this task.

O'Brien, a combat veteran, uses his personal experience of war to exemplify the weight of physical and emotional baggage carried by soldiers and the importance of separation between personal emotions and obligation to duty for combat leaders. As a veteran and combat leader myself (I was a scout during Operation Iraqi Freedom in 2003), I feel O'Brien reveals an important point with an intriguing story. "They died so as not to die of embarrassment" (O'Brien 678).

Works Cited

O'Brien, Tim. "The Things They Carried." *Literature: An Introduction to Fiction, Poetry, and Drama.* Ed. X. J. Kennedy and Dan Gioa. 9th ed. New York: Pearson/Longman, 2005. 667–680.

CONTINUITY OF THE WESTERN HERO—DAVID CHERRY

Genre films are defined as films that "belong to a particular group of films that are extremely similar in their subject matter . . ." (Sobchack, Sobchack 223). So although these films are alike in content, the films are left with room to expand and show individualism on the part of the director. Two directors who used their freedom for expression were Sam Peckinpah and John Ford. In Sam Peckinpah's *The Wild Bunch* (1969), Peckinpah uses slow motion to "heighten, lyricize, and magnify the moment of making by his use of the landscape in which the film was staged to help set the tone for his movies and interact with his characters. Although their uses of filming techniques were highly individualized, the two directors still followed the genre pattern in presenting the western hero.

The western hero in any movie has always tried to find his place in society. This search would usually set the pace and tone for a western movie. Depending on the circumstances directly involving a particular hero, the viewer would see a film based on the hero's experiences. The protagonist had to live up to a code of ethics which included, "he never shot a man in the back or drew first, and . . . never kills a man merely for sport." (Sobchack, Sobchack 257). He also had to invariably overcome his own obstacles in life only to then be shut out from society or die trying.

These characteristics are shown in both Ford and Peckinpah heroes for their westerns. Ford introduces us to Ethan Edwards (John Wayne) in *The Searchers* (1956), Ford's film which he himself has referred to as "the tragedy of a loner" (Soloman 44). Sam Peckinpah then produces Pike Bishop (William Holden) in *The Wild Bunch* (1969) whom, although part of a gang, asserts himself as the film's hero. Through these two heroes, Ethan and Pike, we see the maintaining of the western hero icon by their superiority of those around them and their inability to fit into the society they live in.

Both Ethan and Pike show superiority in several ways to enforce the dominance of the men around them. By always laughing at someone else's expense, we see how they believe themselves above the rest. For example, Ethan is continually laughing when someone is being put down. In a scene from *The Searchers* (1956), Ethan is laughing at an Indian squaw mistakenly married to his cohort, Martin. The squaw does no wrong in her mind, but Ethan, through racism, continually puts her down and even kicks her. All the while, Ethan also laughs at Martin, who is innocent to the ways of the world which landed him in his position. Pike also finds humor when others are down. When the bunch is robbed of their gold by the railroad, who replaced the gold with worthless washers, Pike laughs at the brothers Gorch who try to leave the gang because they feel cheated. Another scene from the *The Wild Bunch* (1969) shows Pike laughing at the brother who got an empty whiskey bottle after the rest had their fill. Pike again laughs at the same character when he announces engagement to a Mexican whore. At the end of both movies, the heroes seem to only find humor in others misfortunes.

Of course, the fact that Ethan and Pike are the heroes again asserts their superiority over those around them. Not once do we find Ethan not getting his way in the film. He abuses the Captain Reverend Samuel Clayton on many occasions. Once Ethan tells the Captain Reverend that "I don't believe in surrenders" when the captain asks why Ethan still carries his sword form the losing side of the Civil War. So, here Ethan uses his superior and critical nature to put himself "one-up" from those around him. Pike also uses his unnerving nature to take command of his bunch. Pike repeatedly uses his excuse of keeping the gang together to actually maintain his place as a leader. As *The Wild Bunch* (1969) progresses, we witness Pike's unethical moral values in action against the very men whom he must control to keep his supremacy. Once when a member is wounded in a gun fight and becomes unable to stay with the group moving at Pike's pace, Pike simply shoots the injured man. In another example of Pike's lessening concern for his gang, Pike leaves an old friend behind instead of risking his men and his throne to save him. Again, through the portrayal of Ethan and Pike's psychopathic nature, they retain their superiority through the leadership they keep over others.

Another category of the western hero icon developed by Ethan and Pike falls into not being accepted into the society they live in. Both heroes never gain the acceptance they want during the films. Ethan may want to rejoin the world of normalcy around him, but he is constantly the opposite of what he should be. Ethan is rarely seen indoors, for example, and when the viewer does see him leaving his outdoor environment, Ethan disrupts the household he enters. When Ethan first arrives at his brother's wife. These feelings for Martha are unacceptable and make those aware of them uncomfortable. Ethan also goes indoors later in the film, and his presence results in the disruption of a wedding. For these reasons, Ethan seems comfortable only when he is outside, outside of society. Pike fares even worse in his attempts to go indoors. Of the few times that he is seen indoors during the film, the results are disastrous. The first time inside, he and his gang are committing a crime against society. Later, we see him go inside only to have a frustrating experience with a young prostitute, so he immediately retreats outside where he again becomes comfortable as leader. Pike's death eventually occurs while in the confines of an inn. During this scene, we witness his demise, contributed to by Mexican soldiers rushing outdoors form their safe confines within.

Therefore, we can see Ethan and Pike's inability to handle the home settings and the women in them, plus their warped sense of superiority of those exposed to them, reinforcing the acceptable characterizations of the western hero. By this comparison of two different westerns, we recognize the ability of directors for their following of set genre rules and still providing varied films to insure movie goers a never ending source of enjoyment.

WORKS CITED

Sobchack, Thomas, Vivien C. Sobchack. *An Introduction to Film.* Boston: Little, Brown and Company, 1987.

ref:*The Wild Bunch.* Producer Sam Peckinpah. 1969.

Mast, Gerald. *A Short History of the Movies.* New York: MacMillan Publishing Company, 1986.

The Searchers. Producer John Ford. 1956.

Soloman, Stanley J. *Beyond Formula.* New York: Harcourt Bruce Jovanovich, Inc., 1976.

O'CONNOR'S REDEMPTIVE SYMBOLISM—ANA CAMACHO, NOW ANA MILLER

(Ana Miller received her B.A. and M.A. at the University of Texas of the Permian Basin. After teaching in Odessa, Texas elementary schools, she is now a reading professional at the University of Texas of the Permian Basin.)

Flannery O'Connor's fiction radiates her staunch belief in spiritual reality which emerged from her inherent Catholic orthodoxy. According to Kathleen Feeley, the unknown was as real to O'Connor as the visible universe, and reality did not lead to mystery, it included it. In order to make the mystery of man's Redemption easily perceptible in fiction, Flannery O'Connor grounded her work in spiritual reality (5). Due to this pervasive spiritual reality, O'Connor recognized a human tendency to repudiate the truth that many of life's offensive circumstances are a result of self-imposed and self-destructive attitudes. As Dorothy McFarland says, "O'Connor's characters do not have anything like an inborn knowledge of human limitations, in fact, most of her characters suffer from a refusal of such knowledge" (2–3). The acknowledgement of this truth about life can ultimately open the door to divine redemption. In "Greenleaf," O'Connor lays the groundwork for Mrs. May's constant repudiation and eventual revelation of truth, and, through the use of symbolism, the Greenleaf bull comes to represent the medium by which Mrs. May experiences divine redemption.

Mrs. May, the central character in "Greenleaf," suffers from a series of obvious character defects; the most notable of which is her obsessive concern with her personal possessions, an acute sense of her own superiority, and her reflection of spiritual commitment. First, Mrs. May's excessive devotion to her worldly possessions has been the driving force in her life. She has spent her life fighting to make her farm a productive enterprise and a solid inheritance to leave to her two sons, Wesley and Scofield. Both sons are single, over thirty years of age, and still exist under their mother's roof. Neither of them takes any kind of interest in the maintenance of Mrs. May's farm. Wesley speaks for both of them as he insolently tells his mother: "I wouldn't milk a cow to save your soul from hell" (O'Connor 229). Mrs. May's sons' indifference and repugnance toward her and her farm, exemplify one agonizing aspect of her life which she views as unwarranted. Mrs. May manifests this feeling when she tells her sons, "O.T. and E.T. are fine boys . . . they ought to have been my sons" (O'Connor 229). Mrs. May is unable to acknowledge the truth that Wesley and Scofield are the products of her materialistic priorities and her aloof upbringing.

Another of Mrs. May's character flaws is her veritable sense of superiority, especially in regards to the Greenleaf family, which "she scorns as obvious white trash" (Walters 137). Mrs. May seems to relish her conception that the Greenleafs are in a much lower social class than herself.

However, this conception is challenged by the Greenleaf boys' gradual elevation up the social ladder, much to Mrs. May's dismay. She clearly states her fear and disgust at such a change in order. She thinks out loud; "And in twenty years do you know what those people will be? Society," (O'Connor 227). Much of Mrs. May's time and energy are consumed with her futile preoccupation that one day the Greenleafs may be her equals, and the Greenleaf boys' time and energy are consumed with the sole purpose of achieving their goals in life. As Dorothy Walters comments, "The Greenleaf boys are in the ascendant because they possess the vitality and imagination which have disappeared from the respectable class" (138–139). Nonetheless, Mrs. May looks upon the Greenleaf ascendance as a surreptitious conspiracy to reach and surpass her own social status. Here again, Mrs. May is oblivious to the truth that her self-imposed superiority is merely a figment of her desire to keep the Greenleafs under her oppressive rule.

Last of all, Mrs. May's rejection of spiritual commitment is perhaps the result of her refusal to acknowledge the truth that the "wrong" in her life, is an accruement of the "wrong" in her attitudes and beliefs. She cannot make a spiritual commitment since spiritually and true religion do not exist within her life's dogma. Mrs. May's view of herself in regards to religion is summed up in the following statement: "She was a good Christian woman with a large respect for religion, though she did not believe any of it was true" (226). There is no room in her mind for belief; therefore, there is no room in her soul for spirituality.

It is important to keep in mind that Mrs. May's "lifelong dedication to blinding pride" has built up such a high wall of self-righteousness that she can no longer see outside of herself (Walters 140). Throughout her life, Mrs. May does not attempt to reach out in charity, humility, or spirituality; consequently, reflecting any spiritual commitment. This vain attitude toward life permeates into her attitude toward death. As she contemplates the possibility of her death, she believes she will allow death to occur only when, "she is good and ready" (O'Connor 229).

Mrs. May's vain and solitary existence has been a series of intensive attempts to convince herself that she is not responsible for the inadequacies that surround her, and the emptiness that suffuses her. Mrs. May's relentless resistance to the truth has been a self-defeating process of alienation. In view of her unredeeming qualities, she would seem to be a most unlikely candidate for the transcendence of a divine redemption.

Yet, through the symbolic use of the Greenleaf bull, Mrs. May is given an opportunity to acknowledge the truth about her life, and even more important, an opportunity to savor the grace of redemption. Symbolically, the bull first appears as a god, standing in the, "east . . . silvered in the moonlight," and listening, "like some patient god come down to woo her" (O'Connor 222). The bull is crowned with a wreath of hedge, which Kathleen Feeley explains as, "an imagery which suggests the God-man Christ, at the hour of His passion and death" (95). This symbolic imagery serves as a foreshadowing of Mrs. May's own impending passion and death, culminating with a redemptive encounter with God and His mercy.

Mrs. May's death is again foreshadowed in a scene which links the charging bull with the unseen action of grace. One day as Mrs. May walks through her property, she is startled by "a sound so piercing that she felt as if some violent unleashed force had broken out of the ground and was charging toward her" (O'Connor 225–226). Mrs. May discovers that the "sound" was Mrs. Greenleaf's spiritual pleas as she indulged in her "prayer healing" (O'Connor 226). The "violent unleashed force" is portrayed as a charging bull, which becomes a symbol of the force of grace, and Mrs. May feels this "force" through Mrs. Greenleaf's obvious faith in the power of grace (O'Connor 226). At this point, Mrs. May quickly subdues this "force," which she cannot understand (O'Connor 226).

The actual circumstances that lead to Mrs. May's death and redemption are instigated by the Greenleaf bull. When Mrs. May realizes that the Greenleaf boys are not going to come for their bull, she adamantly informs Mr. Greenleaf that, "We're going to shoot that bull" (O'Connor 237).

Mrs. May follows Mr. Greenleaf and the bull into a pasture. Eventually, she looks out across the pasture, and sees "a violent black streak" bounding toward her, yet she makes to attempt to flee, as if she has decided to submit to this force, which is rushing to claim her (O'Connor 238). As one of the bull's horns pierces Mrs. May's heart, her face exhibits the look "of a person whose sight has been suddenly restored, but who finds the light unbearable" (O'Connor 238). Perhaps, Mrs. May has acknowledged and even understood the truth about her life, as a result of an instantaneous illumination of grace; but this enlightenment is too much for her to bear, so she rejects it. However, in the last line of the story, Mrs. May gives in to this enlightenment and allows divine redemption to embrace her, as the mysterious "last discovery" unfolds God's ultimate mercy (O'Connor 238). According to Dorothy McFarland, the convergence with the bull and he symbolizes, brings Mrs. May to an overwhelming illumination of grace and redemption (50).

In "Greenleaf," Flannery O'Connor utilizes her spiritual reality to create a self-righteous and spiritually hollow Mrs. May, who is logically unaware of her need to acknowledge the truth about her life and who is spiritually unaware of her need to experience redemption. Through the intricate weaving of symbolism, O'Connor reveals the significant role that the Greenleaf bull plays in Mrs. May's "final discovery" of God's mercy (O'Connor 238). Dorothy McFarland elaborates: "A major premise of O'Connor's thinking is that the realm of the Holy interpenetrates this world and affects it. It is the working of this mystery that she was most concerned with demonstrating in her fiction" (1).

Works Cited

Feeley, Kathleen Sr. S.S.N.D. *Flannery O'Connor: Voice of the Peacock.* New Brunswick: Rutgers University Press, 1972.

McFarland, Dorothy Tuck. *Flannery O'Connor.* New York: Frederick Ungar Publishing Company, 1976.

O'Connor, Flannery. "Greenleaf." *Literature: Structure, Sound, and Sense.* Ed. Laurence Perrine. New York: Harcourt Brace Jovanovich, 1983.

Walters, Dorothy. *Flannery O'Connor.* New York: Twayne Publishers, Inc., 1973.

SYMBOLISM AND ALLEGORY IN "RAPPACCINI'S DAUGHTER"—REBECCA PLEASANT

(2005 Longman Award Winner for Composition II, Lamar University

In "Rappaccini's Daughter," Nathaniel Hawthorne interprets Christian themes and their impact on men and women. The tale touches on several beliefs within the faith including the idea of a creator, free will of Man, and punishment for sins. A diverse range of images produces this effect. The setting expresses an artificial, manmade world, with frightful alterations to God's plan. Characters reflect prominent figures from the Bible story. Enlightenment and spiritual darkness set the tone, as well as the impact of sin upon the world and its inhabitants. By presenting aspects of daily life and their relation to Christian ethics, the story's purpose seems one of morality and correct judgment. The use of symbols in setting, character development, and tone convey the message. Biblical symbolism constructs an allegorical tale.

First, the reader experiences an idyllic garden comparable to the Garden of Eden. The narrator questions "Was this garden, then, the Eden of the present world?" (291). The garden possesses similarities of structure to Eden in that it contains a fountain and a beautiful, dominant shrub. Don Parry Norford contends that the fountain compares to the Tree of Life as the sustenance of all existence, whereas the shrub corresponds to the Tree of Knowledge representing awareness (177). The garden casts a hypnotic spell over all who enter it, in the same manner of Eden. This forbidden world appeals to the curiosity of onlookers. Temptation reigns supreme with wildly captivating plants, musical bubbling of water from the font, and exotic aromas which the vegetation emits. However, something awry abounds here. The unsightly, crumbling fountain sustains a garden bastardized by hybrid mixtures. Exceedingly beautiful, these variations among the fauna appear in opposition to those in nature, suggestive of paradise after the fall of Man, according to Joe Davis (7). Similarly, John N. Miller notes the corruption of the garden (29).

Second, the character roles resemble iconic figures in the Bible. Dr. Rappaccini, although irreparably flawed, presents as the Creator image. His earthly garden and daughter spring from his scientific endeavors. As noted by Leonard A. Podis, Rappaccini's obsession with generating life comes to fruition in his production of Beatrice and transformation of Giovanni (247). Rappaccini seeks to demonstrate his scientific expertise in tangible forms, surpassing all others in his field. His formation of Beatrice first alludes to the reversal of order compared to Eden's inhabitants. By securing Giovanni as Adam for Rappaccini's Eve, Hawthorne suggests that Rappaccini's power exists in an unholy realm. He places more importance on the maternal image, in contrast to Christian ideals of men as leaders. Furthermore, Rappaccini does not possess omniscient command of his creations. His inability to withstand physical contact with some of his plants demonstrates his limited authority. Therefore, Rappaccini may be viewed as a false god. Baglioni appears akin to the Serpent of the Garden of Good and Evil. His assertions to Giovanni serve as irresistible temptation. Samuel Coale alleges that Baglioni embodies ego and skepticism (60). Like the evil snake, he seeks to thwart God by damaging his children. Baglioni obsessively desires Rappaccini's position and diligently pursues attaining this goal. Similarly, the snake seeks to reduce God's dominant state and plots a downfall. By appealing directly to Giovanni as "Adam" instead of Beatrice as "Eve," Baglioni's character reverses the order of Biblical reference. Giovanni's likeness to Adam seems truer in form. Gillian Brown contends that Giovanni blames Beatrice for his misfortune and entrapment in Rappaccini's plan (95). Much like Adam, Giovanni refuses to reflect on his own shortcomings and permits manipulation from others. He also suffers from the inability to perceive evidence before him, instead choosing to adopt Baglioni's message as gospel. His first encounters with Beatrice leave him in bewilderment. Even the young woman's reassurances confuse Giovanni. Just as Adam rebukes Eve, Giovanni dispels Beatrice's assertions of her innocence. Ultimately, Giovanni's indecision leads to the demise of his only possible earthly mate. Beatrice resembles Eve in her naivete and willingness to appease the male influences around her. Nancy Bunge points to Beatrice's childlike qualities and purity of heart (70). She attends to her father's whims without question. Beatrice desperately depends on Giovanni's daily visits similar to a child who waits for a playmate. The only evil apparent in her character results from Rappaccini's making. So, like Eve, Beatrice's actions reflect domination by male influences.

Thirdly, the creatures within the garden represent innocent victims bearing the consequences of Man's sinful nature. Rappaccini's deeds affect every aspect of life in his provisional world. Beatrice's body exudes botanical toxins as a result of Rappaccini's science. Her impact on the lizard and winged insect demonstrates the wicked effects of altering nature. Even Beatrice acknowledges guilt by blessing the tiny martyrs. Giovanni witnesses these encounters and begins to view her as dreadful and repulsive. Baglioni promotes Giovanni's suspicions by telling of Rappaccini's experimentation on animals with deadly poisons. Baglioni stresses that Rappaccini does not value the sanctity of life in any creature, not even his own daughter. After his breath kills a spider, Giovanni experiences horror at his transformation to a poison being yet refuses to dwell on the deed. Instead, he focuses only on resolving Beatrice's defect. Rappaccini's sins foreshadow his ultimate recompense. He reveals his primary intentions to the young lovers. Rappaccini's injustices against the blameless result in destruction of his most sacred creation.

Furthermore, the effects of the Sun and moon note the Heavenly Father's hand in mankind's actions. In Genesis, God creates light and distinguishes it from darkness. By pronouncing light as good, it becomes a metaphor for a desirable state. Rappaccini's false world displays its heavenly light in Beatrice's beautiful countenance. Giovanni basks in the light from this human Sun, yet the nightfall causes him to doubt its wholesomeness. The moonlight beaming upon the garden dims his recollections. The total darkness of sleep brings terrible dreams to him as well. Alfred J. Kloeckner contends that the story fixates on darkness (335). Light and dark may suggest varying stages of consciousness. Edward H. Rosenberry recalls Giovanni's apparent confusion at dusk (41). Giovanni waxes and wanes between illuminative and shadowy aspects of a future life with Beatrice. The struggle between cognitive decisions and imaginings reflects the human dilemma (Norford 185).

Next, scientific experimentation typifies human nature's desire to rebel against the Creator. Jeannine Dobbs surmises that social views in the Victorian era stand in opposition to this exploration as an effrontery to God (429). Eberhard Alsen guesses that Rappaccini seeks domination as lord of a manufactured universe (431). Baglioni fears Rappaccini's advances and seeks to halt them. Unbeknownst to Giovanni, Baglioni and Rappaccini share a rivalry, equally wishing to control this new field of study. By heightening Giovanni's suspicions, Baglioni creates the catalyst for Rappaccini's destruction. In this way, Baglioni manipulates as despicably as Rappaccini. The unfortunate Beatrice suffers betwixt these destructive forces. She suffers as a laboratory specimen in this competition between scientists. In any society, experimentation with poisons on a person defies common sense. This unholy contest defies God's commandments and appeals to a sense of prudent judgment in all persons.

Lastly, the poison and antidote typify a contrast between good and evil aspects of mortal beings. Margaret Hallissy proposes an analogy between poison and sin, especially the association of females embodying the sexual downfall of males (231). Hallissy further implicates Victorian ideas viewing sexuality as toxic (234). Giovanni and Beatrice feel a mutually strong physical attraction. Nineteenth century ideals dictate marriage in resolving possible enticement to sin. Like the plants in the garden, Beatrice and Giovanni display powerfully noxious traits and their souls must undergo cleansing. However, Beatrice's pureness of spirit serves as her personal antidote (Hallissy 237). Since she displays true goodness, the antidote overwhelms her system. Richard Brenzo evidences the antidote's effect on Beatrice as further proof of Baglioni's evil intention (163). Baglioni uses Beatrice as a test subject, then blames her death on Rappaccini. This displacement of guilt from the sinner mimics human nature to refuse responsibility for actions. Adam tries the same course when God confronts him. Morton L. Ross presents Giovanni's all too human failings as Man's lot in life (345). Giovanni's blind pursuit of purging Beatrice's stain causes him to negate his own ugliness. He does not realize his own depravity until Beatrice verbalizes it. Interestingly enough, Giovanni's problems still exist after Beatrice's death, leaving the reader to suppose that Giovanni will bear responsibility indefinitely.

In conclusion, symbolism creates a dual atmosphere of reality and contrivance. A moral quest tantalizes with enigma and obscurity. The images of good and evil exist in each character and force the reader to analyze levels of representation. The setting draws on pastoral perfection in contrast to manufactured imitation. Although the Christian parallels abound, they inspire interpretation on an intimate level for each reader and serve as figurative examples. The attitude of the piece points toward personal responsibility at every turn. The desire to put an old lesson into a more modern context succeeds in its cautionary goal. As in Christian scripture, provoking God's justice usually proves dangerous, sometimes deadly. Comparisons with Biblical references assist in distinguishing character, developing setting, and establishing tone.

WORKS CITED

Alsen, Eberhard. "The Ambitious Experiment of Dr. Rappaccini." *American Literature: A Journal of Literary History, Criticism and Bibliography* 43 (1971): 430–31.

Brenzo, Richard. "Beatrice Rappaccini: A Victim of Male Love and Horror." *American Literature: A Journal of Literary History," Criticism, and Bibliography* 48 (1976): 152–64.

Brown, Gillian. "Hawthorne and Children in the Nineteenth Century: Daughters, Flowers, Stories." *A Historical Guide to Nathaniel Hawthorne.* Ed. Larry Reynolds. Oxford. Oxford UP, 2001. 79–108.

Bunge, Nancy. *Nathaniel Hawthorne: A Study of the Short Fiction.* New York: Twayne, 1993.

Coale, Samuel. *Mesmerism and Hawthorne: Mediums of American Romance.* Tuscaloosa: U of Alabama P, 1998.

Davis, Joe. The Myth of the Garden: Nathaniel Hawthorne's "Rappaccini's Daughter." *Studies in Literary Imagination* 2.1 (1969): 3–12.

Dobbs, Jeannine. "Hawthorne's Rappaccini and Father George Rapp." *American Literature: A Journal of Literary History, Criticism, and Bibliography* 43 (1971): 43031

Hallissy, Margaret. "Hawthorne's Venomous Beatrice." *Modern Language Studies* 19 (1982): 231–39.

Hawthorne, Nathaniel. "Rappaccini's Daughter." *The Compact Bedford Introduction to Literature: Reading, Thinking, and Writing.* Ed. Michael Meyer. 5th ed. Boston: Bedford/St. Martin's, 2000. 289–307.

IS IT REALLY WORTH THE PRICE: A LOOK INTO "YOUNG GOODMAN BROWN"—COLBY LISENBY

Many people argue that one act of indiscretion will never hurt anyone. The truth is that, many times, they use this as an excuse to "experiment" or "explore" a new area of freedom. One may use this excuse in the area of infidelity, drug use, or any other whim that may spark his or her imagination at the moment. Although this excuse may be true in some aspects, it stands to reason that no action is completely consequence free. There is always going to be price to pay. This price may tax the emotions, body, or mind, but, because of the very nature of the beast, the person who commits the act will pay. A good example of this reasoning is illustrated in Nathaniel Hawthorne's short story "Young Goodman Brown" which uses setting, point of view, symbol, and character, to support the theme of one night of sin can ruin a person's life.

To prove the given theme, Hawthorne uses the setting of the story to play an important role. To start, Hawthorne opens the work with a very crucial piece of information. He begins, "Young Goodman Brown [comes] forth, at sunset, into the streets of Salem village, but put[s] his head back, after crossing the threshold, to exchange a parting kiss with his young wife" (Hawthorne 584). This beginning is important because it gives a very conclusive time line from the beginning. The fact Goodman Brown is leaving at sunset says a lot for the very nature of the story. It also speaks of darkness about to set on Goodman Brown, both physically and spiritually. Generally, when one envisions crime, evil, or dirty deeds, the incident occurs under the cover of darkness. This gives insight into the deeds Brown is about to take part in, and, in turn, plays an important role in proving the theme. Along with setting the story at night, Hawthorne places his characters in a "forest, where no church [gathers], nor solitary Christian [prays]" (Hawthorne 589). This speaks of a completely new and uncharted wilderness. The very presence of new territory offers Brown an invitation to explore, and, as the reader finds out at the end of the story, the curiosity of this one incident drives Brown into becoming "[a] stern, a sad, a darkly meditative, . . . [and] desperate man" (Hawthorne 594).

The next element Hawthorne uses to prove one night of sin can ruin a person's life is point of view. Hawthorne uses the limited point of view in "Young Goodman Brown." This point of view is characterized by the use of a narrator who uses the third person language and is able to tell Goodman Brown's thoughts. A good example of this use of point of view is given in paragraph forty-five when Goodman Brown sees his minister and the deacon from his church traveling the same path on which Brown is traveling; at this point Brown questions inwardly, "Whither, then, could these holy men be journeying, so deep into the heathen wilderness? Young Goodman Brown [catches] hold of a tree for support, being ready to sink down on the ground, faint and overburdened with heavy sickness of his heart. He [looks] up to the sky, doubting whether there [is] really a Heaven above him" (Hawthorne 589). This helps prove the theme because readers are able to know only what is happening in the thoughts of Goodman Brown. Readers, from 1835 and onward, will never hear what Faith, Brown's wife, thinks, nor will they ever be able to hear what any other character thinks, and as a result they will be able to notice the change in Goodman Brown's thoughts from his hesitancy to leave at the beginning of the journey, to being so overburdened that he, eventually, gives in and willingly yields to the devil for just "one night" (Hawthorne 585). Limited point of view is important for "Young Goodman Brown" because it shows exactly how one act or night of sin changes Brown's way of thinking for the rest of his life.

While setting and point of view play a very vital part in proving the theme, Hawthorne uses symbol very liberally throughout "Young Goodman Brown" to drive the point home to the reader. In "Young Goodman Brown," many of the characters and elements of the setting have some sort of symbol attached to them. Some of the symbols are cultural. An example of a cultural symbol in "Young Goodman Brown" is the darkness. This darkness acts as a symbol of the evil which Goodman Brown is participating in throughout the story. This is important to help confirm the theme, for, at the end of the story, readers find out that this darkness, and Brown's questionable actions in it, cause him to become very introverted and miserable for the remainder of his life. Also, in "Young Goodman Brown," there are many contextual symbols. The most prominent of these contextual symbols would be Goodman Brown's wife who "[is] aptly named" Faith (Hawthorne 584). By giving Brown's wife the name Faith, Hawthorne personifies the attribute which her name implies. Also, this places faith very near to Goodman Brown. In paragraph seven of "Young Goodman Brown," Goodman Brown makes the comment to himself,

> What a wretch I am, to leave her on such an errand! She talks of dreams, too. [Methinks], as she [speaks], there [is] trouble in her face, as if a dream warn[s] her what work is to be done to-night. But, no, no! [It would] kill her to think it. Well; she's a blessed angel on earth; and after this one night, I'll cling to her skirts and follow her to heaven. (Hawthorne 585)

This reference to Faith could be interpreted as a clear reference to Brown's religion. In one sense, Goodman Brown is literally leaving his faith to go to a nocturnal Sabbath for "one night" (Hawthorne 585). This one blatant act of leaving faith for a few short hours demonstrates the effects of Brown's decision, and follows Goodman Brown to his grave; "for his dying hour was gloom" (Hawthorne 594).

Characterization, used in unison with setting, point of view, and symbol, plays an important role in proving the theme of Hawthorne's "Young Goodman Brown." The majority of the characters in the work are flat characters. They play a vital role in the story by remaining constant although everything in Brown's life is dramatically changing. Throughout the whole night and, in Faith's case, the remainder of Brown's life, the characters never change. Hawthorne uses this type of character to illustrate that no matter what Goodman Brown may partake in during his night of "enlightenment" that the people around him would never change their thoughts toward him, although Brown's life is in an utter turmoil. On the other hand, Goodman Brown is a very round character. When one first meets Goodman Brown, he speaks skeptically of venturing so deep into the forest without Faith. He makes comments such as, "Too Far, too far . . . I shall be the first of the name of Brown that ever t[akes] this path" (Hawthorne 586). By the middle to the end of the story, Goodman Brown changes his mind and comments, "Come devil! For to thee this world is given" (Hawthorne 590). This shows that this backwoods and secluded occurrence in which Brown takes part changes his very way of thinking for the remainder of his living days.

In the story of "Young Goodman Brown," Nathaniel Hawthorne clearly illustrates that, although one act of indiscretion may not kill an individual, it can certainly leave that person scarred both emotionally and psychologically for the remainder of his or her life. A good moral to the story could probably be that one should examine the consequence of his or her actions before he or she acts. Are the scars that he or she will have to endure really worth the few hours of pleasure? That is left for the reader to decide.

WORKS CITED

Hawthorne, Nathaniel. "Young Goodman Brown." *Literature: An Introduction to Fiction, Poetry, and Drama.* Ed. X. J. Kennedy and Dana Gioia. 9th ed. San Francisco: Longman, 2005. 584–94.

Sophomore Essays

The essays collected in this section are expansions of the essays, the topics, and the themes of essays written in composition. The reading also represents an expansion of the type of reading that students did in their second composition course. Students should note that some essays have research beyond the primary source and others do not. Individual instructors' assignments will vary.

Students at Lamar University or Odessa College wrote all of these essays. I am grateful to all of them. Students and instructors will note the sophistication in writing and thinking in these essays.

HAWTHORNE'S DIVERGENCE OF EMERSONIAN ROMANTICISM—ANA CAMACHO

Romanticism flourished during the mid 1800s due to the intense human desire to break loose from the bonds of societal and religious restrictions. The yearning for uncontrolled, sensual, and individualistic freedom from norms profoundly influenced Ralph Waldo Emerson's writing. According to Emerson, the Universe consisted of Nature and Self, and nothing was more vital then these two entities, with Nature being the more important of the two. Nature is the origin of a spiritual awakening called transcendence, and Self is the origin of individualism. Nathaniel Hawthorne utilizes these two Romantic Emersonian concepts of transcendence and individuality, in his short story, "The Artist of the Beautiful," to ultimately produce a Non-Romanticism conclusion.

According to Emersonian philosophy, Nature is wildly chaotic, perpetually changing, and highly individualistic; furthermore, Nature is the origin and means of transcendence. In order to initiate the Emersonian concept of transcendence, a person must embrace and absorb the rustic attributes of Nature; there after, the process of transcendence, which involves six distinct phases, can begin. The first phase is a sensual and perceptual rousing to the world's commodities. This elevated cognizance of sight, sound, touch, smell and taste results in a transition to the next stage, Beauty. During this phase of transcendence, the universe's commodities become a "delight in and for themselves", thus, a profound human appreciation of Nature's aesthetic attributes develops (Emerson 1015). The next phase, Language, incorporates symbols for material facts into symbols for natural facts, and natural facts into symbols for spiritual facts, ultimately resulting in Nature's permeation into the human concoction of words. In the fourth stage, Emerson regards Nature as the Discipline that encompasses all disciplines, and this Discipline of Nature merits devout and meticulous study. As each one of these first four phases progress, a person is gradually discarding the unnatural impediments that hinder the ascension into the world of ideals. This world of ideals is the fifth phase of transcendence in which a soul has shed the limitations of time, space, perception, sensuality, and even self. In this realm of ideals, only ideals can be trusted in order to focus on the one ultimate ideal of truth. Once this realm of ideals centers on the one conclusive ideal then the Oversoul emerges, and transcendence is experienced.

In "The Artist of the Beautiful," Hawthorne escorts the reader through Owen Warland's painful yet triumphant transcendence to the Oversoul. Owen, "the Artist", enters the phase of commodity "from the time that his little fingers could grasp a pen-knife" (Hawthorne 1171). He possesses an innate "delicate ingenuity" and heightened sensual awareness of Nature's commodities (Hawthorne 1171). Due to Owen's strong kinship with Nature, the transition into Beauty is practically involuntary; moreover, this phase of transcendence occupies much of Owen's life, since he continuously experiences a "passion for the Beautiful" (Hawthorne 1173). Owen's progression into the Language phase of transcendence occurs when Owen attempts to symbolize the natural idea of a butterfly as "the Beautiful". "The Beautiful" symbolizes not only a natural idea but also a spiritual idea that Owen cannot contain. The narrator offers insight into Owen's mind as he says," Owen Warland felt the impulse to give external reality to his ideas . . . But, would the Beautiful Idea ever be yielded to his hand, like the butterfly that symbolized it?" (Hawthorne 1175). Owen realizes his present inability to ascend into the realm of ideals where he would be able to create the symbol for "the Beautiful". The Discipline phase of transcendence has become almost second nature to Owen; incidentally, he is able to "lose himself in the contemplation of it" (Nature)(Hawthorne 1177). Owen not only studied Nature with reverence and devoutness, he also exhibited a desire "to imitate the beautiful movements of Nature" (Hawthorne 1171). Owen's overwhelming desire to become one with Nature culminates at the Discipline level of transcendence.

Owen approached this Discipline level of transcendence numerous times during his life, however, he had not been able to ascend past this stage into the realm of Idealism. Owen's inability to transcend any further stemmed from his inability to individualize himself to rise above the world's external criticisms and his own internal doubts. Owen is able to shield himself against most of the world's critics, and this ability is evidenced as he says, "I, too, will be strong in my own way. I will not yield to him!" (Hawthorne 1173). Unfortunately, Owen is unable to withstand negative comments from Annie, who is his heart's desire. Due to Owen's longing for Annie's love and respect, he mistakenly turns to her for affirmation; and when he receives mockery, instead, Owen confesses to her, "I yearned for sympathy-and thought-and fancied- and dreamed-that you might give it to me. It was not your fault, Annie—But you have ruined me!" (Hawthorne 1176).

Undoubtedly, Owen's existing self doubts were magnified by Annie's reflection. However, Owen is able to eventually overcome his better disappointment, and he also benefits from finally accepting the truth that Annie "had not been enlightened by the deep intelligence of love" (Hawthorne 1176). Between the time of Annie's reflection and Owen's final attempt at transcendence, Owen experiences extremes of defeat and self doubt, to the point that he seemingly reflects all, including Nature. Owen displays his exasperation as he exclaims, "I have thrown it all aside now . . . Now that I have acquired a little common sense, it makes me laugh to think of it " (Hawthorne 1179). Perhaps Owen searches for the words to convince himself that "the Beautiful" is no longer his heart's true desire.

Once Owen achieves transcendence, Hawthorne allows Owen to express his individuality by giving him a choice between the world of ideals and the world of reality. Owen chooses neither of the two and displays the strength of his individualism. Owen had struggled and succeeded in grasping the Emersonian individuality necessary to complete transcendence; yet, when he achieves this transcendence, Owen asserts his individuality by comparing the Ideal the Real, both of which he has experienced. Owen further asserts his individuality by choosing to balance the singularity of Idealism with the poignancy of Reality. Owen is able to accept this equilibrium because his "instant of solitary triumph" in accomplishing the creation of "the Beautiful" revealed to Owen that such a balance is indeed possible (Hawthorne 1180). This possibility emerged as Owen created "the Beautiful" and captured an ideal within the realm of Reality. Since Reality included Nature, the origin of ideals, Owen felt assured that his spirit could remain "in the enjoyment of the Reality" (Hawthorne 1184).

As the story ends, the reader is aware that the Romantic Emersonian concepts or transcendence and individualism have taken a turn away from Romanticism. The concepts themselves are still typically Emersonian, but the manner in which Hawthorne utilizes these concepts gives an appearance of Non-Romanticism. In regards to transcendence, Hawthorne takes the reader through Owen Warland's transcendence, much to the reader's expectations. The divergence occurs after Owen's ascent to the Oversoul, as Hawthorne entrusts Owen with two options: Idealism or Reality. The true Emersonian response would be Idealism, but Hawthorne leads the reader away from Romanticism by allowing Owen to balance the two conflicting worlds. This solution that Hawthorne formulates is distinctly contrary to Emersonian Romantic philosophy.

Similarly, Hawthorne converts the Romantic Emersonian concept of individualism, by bestowing Owen Warland with a unique, rather Un Romantic individuality. the fact that Hawthorne places obstacles for Owen to overcome during his transcendence, contributes to Owen's fortified individuality. When Owen creates "the Beautiful" and ascends to the Oversoul, the reader has anticipated Owen's success. However, the reader is not prepared to witness the extreme extent of Owen's individuality, as he displays his intention to strike a balance between Idealism and Reality.

Hawthorne, in "The Artist of the Beautiful," incorporates Emerson's Romantic concepts of transcendence and individualism, in a manner that would have certainly pleased Emerson himself. Nature and Self are at the center of the story, and the essence of transcendence is revealed. However, Hawthorne does not permit the story to end with this Romantic Emersonian quality, instead he craftily manipulates transcendence and individualism to produce a Non-Romantic conclusion, which ingeniously enhances the story's inherent Romanticism.

WORKS CITED

Emerson, Ralph Waldo. "Nature." *Anthology of American Literature, Volume I. Colonial Through Romantic.* Ed. George McMichael. New York: MacMillan Publishing Company, 1985.

Hawthorne, Nathaniel. "The Artist of the Beautiful." *Anthology of American Literature, Volume I. Colonial Through Romantic.* Ed. George McMichael. New York: MacMillan Publishing Company, 1985.

HUCK FINN: TWAIN'S OUTCAST AND HERO—STEPHANIE STAUDT

The Adventures of Huckleberry Finn, considered to be Mark Twain's masterpiece by a wide array of his fellow writers, is "the fountainhead of American colloquial prose" (Gottesman 1153). Began in 1876, it took Twain eight years to complete. With it, Twain displays his powerful style, capturing the images and local color of America, with an "incurable optimism and humor of the frontier" (Kesterson 41). In this novel Twain emphasizes the importance of character over plot, developing a unique form of irony through the distance between himself and the narrator, Huck Finn; whom he manipulates into saying what he wants, yet allows Huck to say it in his own words and style. Now, one is able to see the world through Huck's eyes, as it truly exits, in memory of details he remembers staying honest and true to himself. Huck as the narrator of the story is "passive and impassive, always the victim of events; and yet, in his acceptance of his world and what it does to him and others . . . he is more aware than any other person in it" (Kesterson 64). He possesses a vision and is very liberal minded, not being able to see things imaginatively. Huck is a decent person proving to be more decent than most people yet, in his own mind is convinced of his own self-worthlessness by his nagging conscience. This conviction lies in the teachings and beliefs of his society at St. Petersburg, which Huck feels he must flee from. However, in nature, Huck's decency shines through and takes over as he becomes a hero defending what he believes and feels is good, even if he is abandoned by society. In this story Twain is able to use his remarkable style of narration to create and develop Huck Finn, a boy who allows the world to judge itself and possesses an innate human decency that makes him both an outcast to society and a traditional hero of the age.

Huck's first display of this innate decency is shown when he plays a trick on Jim making him believe that he had dreamt they were separated in the fog. When Huck tells Jim the truth and makes a fool out of Jim, his conscience begins to gnaw at him as he feels cruel and ashamed for what he has done. This begins Huck's growth in moral insight as he begins to look at Jim like something other than a slave, or a white man's possession. When Jim tells Huck "Dat truck dah is trash; en trash is what people dat puts dirt on de head er dey fren's en makes 'em ashamed" (1222) he is quickly reminded that he is still a boy on the same level as himself. "Huck being the passive observer of men and events" learns by Jim being the "submissive sufferer from them," (Kesterson 65) that they are both EQUAL IN DIGNITY. Humbly Huck is shown his "position in the world, which is not of other boys . . . that he alone must bare the responsibility of a man" (Kesterson 66). In realizing this and taking responsibility for himself, he finally, after fifteen minutes, "worked (himself) up to go and humble (himself) to a nigger . . . and (he) warn't ever sorry for it afterwards, neither" (1223). Finally able to look at Jim and see an equal Huck vows to never play a trick on Jim again, especially knowing how bad it would hurt Jim's feeling. Through this experience Huck and Jim's relationship is allowed to grow and develop into a better and more valued friendship.

THE NEXT BATTLE Huck faces with his conscience is when his ever nagging conscience makes him decide to turn Jim in. He knows, as a decent person, that it is wrong to treat Jim that way because he now sees Jim as an actual person, instead of property or a possession. This "dramatizes Huck's benevolence and his break with a corrupt adult society" (Johnson 96). Here, one is able to see that Huck is capable of rising above this moral corruption through deeds of compassion and sympathy by denying his own needs to help Jim. However, he feels that, by helping Jim, or not turning him in, that he would be betraying Miss Watson someone who, "tried to learn him his books, learn him his manners, and be good to him every way she knowed how" (1232). Every time he tried to justify himself that he was not doing anything wrong, his conscience would start nagging him and say, "But you knowed he was running for his freedom, and you could a paddled ashore and told somebody. That was so- I couldn't get around that, noway" (1232). So now Huck is faced with the dilemma of turning Jim in and being good, thus going to Heaven, or saving Jim from slavery, by helping him get away, thus going to Hell. As he thinks over his decision Huck realizes, making a significant development in the understanding of his moral dilemma, that he would not feel any better if he did turn Jim in especially, "when there wasn't no use in learning to do right, when it's troublesome to do right and ain't no trouble to do wrong, and the wages is just the same" (1234). ultimately his innate decency wins out over societal pressure as he keeps his promise and friendship to Jim and by him not denying his true self.

One of the last significant developments in Huck's story comes when he decides to try and pray to see if he could stop being, in his eyes, a bad boy. Here he realizes that you cannot lie when you are praying because God will always know the truth.

> I was trying to make my mouth say I would do the right thing and the clean thing, and go and write to that nigger's owner and tell where he was; but deep down in me I knowed it was a lie- and He knowed it. You can't pray a lie- I found out (1309).

So to absolve himself he decides to write a letter to Miss Watson telling her where Jim is, but as Huck recalls his past relationship with Jim, he struggles with his conscience, finally making the choice to do what he feels is right. Ripping up the letter, he decides to go t Hell for Jim, abandoning all hope of reform, a high point in the novel, as Huck deepens his commitment to self and to Jim. In doing this Huck "has won his moral struggle; innate goodness has triumphed over the internalized mores of Huck's civilization; through losing his soul, Huck has saved it" (Kesterson 79). By refusing to join the civilization of adulthood, Huck finds a new identity which finally allows him to free himself from his conscience and seek out the freedom he lost; by being entrapped in society.

Huck "transcends ignorance, step by slow step, as any man must, by taking upon his shoulders the knowledge of good and evil" (Hoffman 11). By analyzing these three points of Twain's novel, *The Adventures of Huckleberry Finn* one is able to see, by Huck telling the story and being in constant contact with his thoughts and feelings, how his innate human decency makes him a social outcast and a traditional hero. Huck is a "sign of moral integrity . . . who has ultimately rejected society . . . losing everything except his integrity" (Regan 129–130). Through his courageous struggles with his conscience and the values of St. Petersburg Huck ultimately wins out as he remains true to his inner self, he never gives up his search for freedom, realizing he wants to be free and needs to be free to survive with his innate decency and not be destroyed by society and their beliefs; as he runs off saying, "But I reckon I got to light out for the Territory ahead of the rest, because Aunt Sally she's going to adopt me and civilize me and I can't stand it. I been there before" (1358).

WORKS CITED

Gottesman. *The Norton Anthology of American Literature: American Literature 1865–1914.* New York: W. W. Norton and Company, 1989. pp. 1151–1162

Hoffman, Andrew Jay. *Twain's Heroes, Twain's Worlds.* Philadelphia: University of Pennsylvania Press, 1988.

Johnson, James L. *Mark Twain and the Limits of Power.* Knoxville: The University of Tennessee Press, 1982.

Kesterson, David B. *Critics on Mark Twain and His Characters.* Coral Gables, Florida: University of Miami Press, 1973.

Regan, Robert. *Unpromising Heroes: Mark Twain and his Characters.* University of California Press, Berkly, and Los Angeles, 1966.

Twain, Mark. *The Adventures of Huckleberry Finn.* New York: W. W. Norton and Company, 1989.

WRIGHT'S "THE ETHICS OF LIVING JIM CROW": AN OLD SONG AND DANCE AND A NEW WAY OF LIVING—KAREN KENNEDY

(Karen Kennedy majored in education and minored in English. She is now working on her Master's in Education. After working several years teaching in Beaumont schools, she is hoping to move into administration. At this writing, she also reports that she is engaged.)

"Learning" is a process which involves the mastery of a particular skill and or the acquisition of some sort of mental cultivation in order to feel and be successful. Just as one can master the art of dancing, singing, or writing, he can also learn to be submissive, accept oppression, and thus remain ignorant to the world around him. Unfortunately, the latter part of the previous statement becomes a way of life for so many. Nevertheless, mastering the art of submissiveness is indeed taught, but in no way is such a talent uplifting; instead, it is degrading and laborious.

To insure that Negros were obedient and understood their place in society, they were given a specific duty. They were to learn how to live "Jim Crow." "Jim Crow" was simply a group of laws designed to promote white superiority and black inferiority through the use of racism, segregation and discrimination (Litwack 414). Under no circumstances was a Negro to step out of the boundaries established by these laws; however, should one attempt to do so, he could surely expect to pay the price!

One brave individual who actually mastered the art of writing in spite of "Old Jim Crow" was Richard Wright. While supposedly learning to live "Jim Crow," Wright manages to break every rule of society. Not only does this Negro become a successful writer, he also gains the identity of a unique individual, he is not just a member of that somber Negro race. Nonetheless, to show how he emerges form a life filled with poverty, fear and bigotry, Wright constructs an autobiographical sketch. In the essay "The Ethics of Living Jim Crow," Wright uses symbolism, addresses the subtlety of racism in both the South and North, and demonstrates the dehumanizing effects that "learning to live Jim Crow" has on him personally as well as on others around him.

Wright uses symbolism to compare and contrast the environments of whites and blacks at this time in history. For example, in the beginning of the essay, Wright discusses the black cinders found in the black communities. Naturally, the black cinders are not anything to really boast about or be proud of. The cinders simply represent "fine weapons and can be used nicely in a hot war" (Barksdale 542). Virtually all they really do is enhance the violence that is so prevalent in Wright's community.

In addition, the railroad tracks are symbolic of the separation of whites and blacks in terms of environment and race. Indeed, one side with lovely, clear scenery is dominated by white people; therefore, the area represents "the right side of the tracks." On the other hand, the dark, gloomy area cleverly labeled "the wrong side of the tracks" is predominately occupied by Negros. Evidently because Wright is an impoverished Negro child, he resides in the Negro section of the South. Thus, the railroad tracks do successfully create a white world and a black one. Consequently, the negro is supposed to assume that crossing over to "the right side" is the wrong thing to do because not only is he stepping out of his boundaries, he is infringing on the privacy of white people. Nevertheless, such actions could indeed prove to be deadly.

Moreover, Wright refers to "greenness" several times and links it very closely to aesthetics. Essentially, "greenness" represents beauty, prosperity and success. These are all things that White people are expected to have, but they are things that a Negro can only dream of having. "Greenness" is virtually unseen in the black world. However, one can catch a glimpse of this "greenness" if he crosses over to "the right side." Nonetheless, once the Negro reaches his destination ("the greenness"), he is in for a rude awakening because he does not belong there.

Closely linked to the "greenness" and prosperity that Wright so desires is the white race. White people are symbols just like the railroad tracks and the black cinders. According to Wright, "white people represent fear" (Barksdale 543). To Wright and so many Negros like him, white people are the controllers and oppressors of their race. They (the whites) are really not be toyed with for they hold the destinies of all the Negros in their hands.

Moreover, because his destiny lies in the hands of a white man, Wright knows that one day he will be thrust into the world of "greenness". He is also fully aware that once he is part of their world, he will have no choice but to work with the enemy. As a result of his apprehension, Wright cannot seem to thoroughly prepare himself for things to come and thus remains overwhelmingly anxious. Needless to say, the apprehension he possesses and the fear he tries to avoid foreshadows events to come. Thus "fear" and his warped environment cause Wright to have to deal with problems in the work place, at home, and in public.

Finally, the visions he has as a negro are simply representative of illusions and falseness which are continuously fed to Negros like Wright during this time in history. Wright even goes on to mention the "Horatio Alger Myth" and manages to connect the myth to these unclear visions. In short, the myth simply says that no matter how hard a Negro works he cannot get exactly what he wants; however, he can have dreams about those things he desires. Obviously, such visions become blurry for Wright because somehow all of his dreams are "deferred" (Barksdale 422).

Wright also discusses the subtlety of racism which he encounters not only at work but throughout the Northern and Southern communities as well. For example, Wright is forced to work at a very young age in order to help ends meet. Working at a young age is difficult because not only is he deprived of a childhood, but he has to grow up pretty quickly. More importantly, being tossed into the "green world" at such a tender age does prove to be disastrous. First of all, at the beginning of his interview for his first job, Wright is all ready exposed to subtle racism as the interviewer examines him in the manner that one would examine a prize poodle" (Barksdale 543). Here he is atomically viewed as something other than human. Oddly enough, the interviewer does not even need use degrading words because his looks are damaging! Naturally, Wright is a bit miffed by the expressions of this white man, but does somehow manage to come to the realization that "white men see the Negro as a filthy, repulsive thing" (Unger 486). Consequently, at this point, there is nothing young Wright can do about the situation because he needs the money.

Overall, subtle racism is just as bad as straightforward, blood shedding racism. As a matter of fact, Wright continues to perform his designated tasks at the optical company, and like any normal individual, he wants to become more enlightened. Wright wholeheartedly believes that, as a Negro, he has the ability and the right to broaden his mental capacity; therefore, "he wants to learn something about the mechanics of grinding lenses" (Barksdale 544). When he has the courage to bring forth such suggestions, he is quickly struck down and essentially told to remain "in the dark American underworld like a 'good' Negro should" (Unger 485). As a source of punishment for trying "to get smart, the white men's attitudes towards him change dramatically" (Barksdale 544). Whenever he makes a mistake now or moves at a slow pace, he is bombarded with degrading words. Before, he is just looked at as some sort of dog, but he has now graduated to a higher level. Presently, because he has attempted to learn something other than "Jim Crow," has earned the title of "lazy, stupid dog." Obviously, the racial slurs and the subtle racist actions of his co-workers do indeed cause Wright a lot of pain, but he does continue to work there.

Finally, the last straw occurs when Wright is put into a no-win situation, Wright is falsely accused by his co-workers of disrespecting the boss, Mr. Pease. By law, "Negros are expected to accommodate their speech habits to the expectations of whites. To be 'sassy' after all is to be outspoken" (Unger 479). Therefore, to be accused of such "heinous crime" is literally a Negro's ticket to a lynching or a severe beating. Though Wright and his fellow co-workers know that Wright is not guilty of calling the boss "Pease" as opposed to "Mr. Pease", none of them will come to his defense. Wright surely cannot come forth and call these white men liars. As a result, without any valid and real explanations, Mr. Pease automatically assumes that the Negro is guilty as sin. Thus, this very sin earns him a slap across the face as well. Nonetheless the incident perhaps is an economical one, but subtle racism plays its role well. True enough the white guys fear losing their job to a Negro like Wright, and to insure that they keep their jobs, they conjure up this scheme. Unfortunately, Wright has no choice but to live the lie, quit his job and seek employment elsewhere.

Moreover, Wright encounters more racial subtlety as he works in a clothing store. While working in the store one day, Wright witnesses a black woman being brutally beaten by the store's white owner and his son. A police officer (one's whose job it is to serve and protect) witnesses the entire episode too, but he does absolutely nothing initially.

After their moment of pleasure ends, they simply wash their hands of the lady's blood and carry on with business as usual. Naturally, Wright is puzzled by the beating and the lack on interest on the police officer's behalf. The worst part of this event is yet to come.

As a gesture of "kindness," the son offers Wright a cigarette. The cigarette is also used to warn Wright to keep his mouth closed if he does not intend to receive a similar thrashing. Both Wright and the white boy know that a beating can indeed be arranged and of course the white boy will be able to get his story accepted by all" (Barksdale 545). Now, not only is the white boy's gesture subtlety racist, he has the audacity to toss Wright into the game against his will. Much to Wright's dismay, he eventually learns that Negros have been playing the game all along. Essentially Negros have been trained not to hear, speak or see any evil. Therefore, no matter how gruesome a scene is, it is up to Wright to toss the skeletons in the closet and forget everything he witnesses. How could he adopt this mentality when he sees that same policeman drag a wounded black lady into his car for being drunk when he knows darn well that she has been violated?

To further cope with this specific incident and the new things he has learned, Wright confides in a fellow co-worker only to be told essentially what he has all ready heard. However, now the plot thickens because those white men could have easily laid her when they got through terrorizing her" (Barksdale 545). In other words she is blessed to have only shed a couple pints of blood, for having to submit to the "enemy" sexually, is far more degrading.

Furthermore, Wright encounters subtle racism as he makes some deliveries. Although he is not doing anything illegal, a group of policemen stop him and taunt him. However, they are "unable to find anything incriminating" (Barksdale 546). Rather than apologize for their mistake, they warn him not to let the darkness catch him in a white neighborhood. Little do they know that whether he delivers in the morning or evening, the "darkness" will always catch him in a white neighborhood. Nevertheless, once again racial subtlety rears it ugly head. It, finally demonstrates the dehumanizing effects that learning to live "Jim Crow" has on him personally and others like him as well. For instance, Wright first encounters "Jim Crow" while growing up in the South. One day, young Wright gets into a little altercation with some white boys and is deeply wounded. Like any normal child, he cannot wait to show his mommy his bruise so that she can kiss it and make it better. Instead of getting comfort and sympathy from his mother, he is rejected, scolded, and beaten. Wright's mom literally tries to "beat the dangerous waywardness out of him" (Unger 474). Not only has he disobeyed her teachings, he has disrespected the white man and for that he must be punished. To further avoid such punishment from his mom and other white people, she virtually tells him to stay away from white people whenever possible and respect them whenever its necessary. Though it is a lot of information for one Negro child to process, young Wright takes his mom's advice into consideration.

Another incident in which Wright shows the devastating effects "Jim Crow laws" have on him personally occur when his bike breaks. As he tries to get home, some drunk white boys in a car approach him and offer him a drink, but he refuses. Forgetting the advice of his mom, Wright outright disrespects these white boys because he somehow neglects to use the word "sir" when he turns down the offer. As a result, he is hit in the face with the bottle and starts to bleed. Apparently, being physically wounded by the guys is not humiliating enough. The men continue to taunt him, kick his bike and warn him about his "wicked tongue." Wright stands there and takes everything they say to heart, but somehow he just cannot bring himself to respect some semi-illiterate, incapacitated drunks!

Furthermore, Wright's "Jim Crow" education continues to deepen and broaden as he works in a hotel. Much like his other previous lessons, he learns to try to control his impulses to be "human." For example, one day while he is working, a naked lady gets up to fix herself a drink. Her partner remains in the bed. Like any man (with a sex drive), Wright sneaks a peek at this lady. When her partner realizes what he is doing, he quickly scolds Wright and warns him to stay in his place. He scolds him in a manner in which a master would say to a begging dog, "Down Boy!" After all, Negros are sub-human and therefore are to be guided by their master. As a result, "at the most elementary levels of human existence he (Wright), is forbidden to touch, speak, read, dream or expand unless told to do so by his 'teacher'" (Unger 479). Here not only is Wright dehumanized in terms of his sexuality, he's degraded in many other ways as well.

Wright evidently is an intelligent young man who longs to read and stimulate himself mentally; therefore, he needs to have access to books. However, the only type of "learning" that is readily available to a Negro involves grasping the teachings of "Jim Crow." Subsequently, by accepting the teachings of "Jim Crow," Wright learns to "lie, cheat and steal and play that dual role that every Negro must play if he wants to eat and live" (Barksdale 547). In short, as a means of teaching Negros to live "Jim Crow" without mentally enriched, white people deny them library cards. They actually believe it is in the Negro's best interest to remain ignorant. Apparently, Wright begs to differ for not only does he have access to the best books, he gets them by violating the "Jim Crow laws." As a matter of fact, Wright convinces a white man to allow him to use his library card. Once he gets the books he desires, he forges the man's signature. Not only is he clever enough to break the rules, but he also has an "enforcer" breaking them too. Nonetheless, Wright is a pretty bright kid to say that he has been in darkness much of his life!

The final episode that shows the effects "Jim Crow" has on Wright personally occurs in an elevator. Because Wright is in the elevator with two white men, he is supposed to (by law) remove his hat. However, he fails to do so. As a result, one of the white men takes it upon himself to remove Wright's hat. "Rather than risk a blow to the mouth by saying thanks or grin like a fool out of the corner of his eye, he chooses to remain extremely subservient" (Barksdale 548). In fact, the brilliant, young Wright takes a more clever route, he acts as if his packages are about to fall after the man places the hat on top of them. He does this to make them think that he is about to lose his balance. In actuality, Wright's little "balancing act" shows that mentally he is balanced and has learned to defeat the "system."

Based on all the trials and tribulations Wright endured as a Negro, he has a right to be in a lot of pain, for "Jim Crow" is responsible for much of his grief. In addition to physical abuse, Wright is mentally abused and subjected to racial subtlety too. As a result, the various types of abuse dramatically affect him and other Negros around him and other Negros around him. After being reduced to a sub-human, Wright tries to bring his problems to light and cope with them through the mastering of an art. The art which he has at his disposal is "writing." Now he is able to produce an autobiographical sketch which allows him to discuss the brutality and cruelty he faced while learning the "system." Fortunately, by being allowed to openly vent his anger towards white people and "lick his flesh and mental wounds," Wright becomes an "individual."

Unfortunately, Wright is not the only Negro who feels the pain of "living Jim Crow." Allicin much like Wright, "has been subjected to mere 'nothingness', manipulated by the system, robbed of his personality and cheated out of a sense of self" (Unger 479). To deal with pains, Allicin too resorts to the art of writing. In his novel, *Invisible Man,* Allicin, much like what Wright does in "Ethics" "blends tragedy and complex symbolism to indeed show how a man can be deemed invisible" (Draper 673).

Though both protagonists in the two works indeed have good minds and great potential, they are Negros, and according to white folks everywhere, they are to be kept in their place at all times. On the contrary, Allicin and Wright decide to step outside of the boundaries, challenge the system and develop a sense of self. No longer will they tolerate that "pre-individualistic categorization" (Barksdale 689).

Nonetheless, the more society "insisted on setting artificial bounds to their experiences, the greater their compulsions to trespass, to taste the forbidden fruit of individual success. In addition, the more society conspired against their human rights and presence, the more determined they became to assert themselves, to compel the recognition of their individuality" (Unger 479). Fortunately, both men were successful in their attempts to come to some sort of self-realization despite of "Jim Crow." As odd as it may be, the plights of both Allicin and Wright actually connect them to each personally and to the entire Negro race.

Thus, Wright in "The Ethics of Living Jim Crow," uses symbolism, discusses racial subtlety and sheds light upon the dehumanizing effects of "living Jim Crow." Because Wright does somehow live vicariously through the "system," he manages to become a strong "individual."

Obviously, racism is a sensitive, complex subject. Apparently, a solution to conquer all forms of it has not yet been found. Much like Wright does when subjected to racism in the North, a Negro just has to "grin and bare it." Wright is truly bothered by the subtle racism in the optical company and is angered that the only topics the white people discuss involve sex or religion. Other subjects such as racial equality, specific amendments and social equality are all deemed unacceptable (Wright 547). Nevertheless, the only reason these subjects are 'taboo' is because they make white people uncomfortable. More importantly, Negros are animalistic and pastoral anyhow, so why would they need to discuss anything other than sex? As silly as that previous statement sounds, it indeed represents the mentality of these Northern white people. Nonetheless, to challenge the authority is unthinkable, so Wright waits to get his revenge on paper!

Prior to becoming an artist, Wright turns to a life of violence and crime to show the "system" exactly what he thought of it. He was later found guilty of lying, stealing, and cheating, punished for his wrongdoings and then released. However, the "ultimate crime for which he cannot bring himself to acknowledge any guilt, but for which he nonetheless knows he will be persecuted is the crime of being black" (Unger 480). Unfortunately, the sentencing for this crime endures for a lifetime and his "penal institution" is the black community. Moreover, the saddest part is that he will never be eligible for parole, nor will he get time off for good behavior!

Works Cited

Barksdale, R. and Kinnamon, K. Hughes, L., eds. "Dream Boogie." *Black Writers of America: A Comprehensive Anthology*. New York: Macmillan, 1972, 522.

Barksdale, R. and Kinnamon, K. Wright, Richard., eds. "The Ethics of Living Jim Crow." *Black Writers of America: A Comprehensive Anthology*. New York: Macmillan, 1972. pp. 542–48.

Barksdale, R. and Kinnamon, K. Ellison, R., eds. "Richard Wright's Blues." *Black Writers of American: A Comprehensive Anthology*. New York: Macmillan, 1972. p. 689.

Draper, J. "Background on Ellison." *Black Literature Criticism*. Detroit; Gales Research Inc., 1992. Vol. 1, 673.

Litwack, L. F. "Article on Jim Crow Laws." *The United States Becoming a World Power*. Ed. Kathleen Shiaparelli. New Jersey: Simon and Shuster, 1991. Vol.2, 414.

AN IDENTITY CRISIS: RYDER'S BLAST FROM HIS PAST IN "THE WIFE OF HIS YOUTH"—KAREN KENNEDY

In W. E. B. Du Bois' "The Souls of Black Folk," Du Bois addresses a specific group of black people and labels them as "the talented tenth" (Barksdale 370). According to Du Bois, this "talented tenth represents that portion of the African American society that is capable by 'character and talent' to be trained as teachers, clergymen, and business professionals and who would, as a result of higher education, become community leaders dedicated to their race" (Baechler 76). However, although these people have been blessed with various talents and have reaped the benefits of success, they have also managed to deny their true heritage (Barksdale 370). As a result, Du Bois accuses them of losing their "blackness" due to their desire to be "white" and eagerness to be rewarded monetarily. To prevent the further spread of such ignorance, Du Bois argues that "the talented tenth must first recognize their African American heritage based on folk spirit deriving from African American heritage based on folk spirit deriving from Africa" (Baechler 76). Next, Du Bois encourages them "to embrace African American ideals and culture instead of Anglo Saxon teachings because this is the only way they can conserve their souls from sordid aims and petty passions" (Barksdale 372). Once again, Du Bois speaks of the preservation of black culture and preaches against the adoption of white culture and ideals.

Chesnutt's "The Wife of His Youth," essentially contains situations and people that are similar to the ones presented in Du Bois' "The Souls of Black Folk." Much like Du Bois, Chesnutt favors the "assimilation of people of color into the socioeconomic mainstream of America; however, at the same time, Chesnutt believes that African Americans must maintain their racial heritage as well (Baechler 76). To further develop his arguments, Chesnutt focuses on the Blue Vein society and one of its prominent leaders, Mr. Ryder. As Chesnutt primarily focuses on Ryder (a man who desperately tries to deny his black heritage) and other blue Veins, he also successfully brings to light the interracial prejudice that is enhanced due to the attitudes of people like Ryder and his peers. They actually attempt to escape their "blackness" by adopting "white tastes and characteristics because they feel this is the only manner in which they can separate themselves from the black culture and at the same time, be incorporated into the white culture" (Barksdale 337). In "The Wife of His Youth," Chesnutt concentrates on the cultured and refined members of the Blue Vein society, introduces Ryder who struggles with his past and present identity, and presents Liza Jane as a symbol and a key to Ryder's past in order to show the consequences one must face if he chooses to conceal or avoid his true heritage.

First of all, the Blue Veins are cultured, refined people who attempt to adopt the white culture. For example, Ryder holds an extravagant ball in honor of a young lady whom he wishes to marry. The individuals who attend the dance are very well-dressed. In fact, the women do not arrive in cheap, casual attire; instead, "they come dressed in evening costume, and dress coats and dancing pumps is the rule among the men" (Barksdale 339). Based on their clothing alone, the Blue Veins who are present at the ball manage to display nothing but shear elegance. In addition, at this same ball, a band is present and plays popular music which is perhaps classical in nature unlike sorrow songs often chanted by typical blacks during this particular time in history (Barksdale 339).

Moreover, most of the Blue Veins are of upper middle class standing and are educated. A great proportion of them are doctors, lawyers and school teachers. Not only are they intelligent people with character and grace, they are fairly wealthy and hold some of the most prestigious occupations. Nonetheless, the guests at the ball enhance the respect and recognition of the Blue Vein society "not only because of dress and display, but for the high level of intelligence that helps these people and the gathering as a whole" (Barksdale 339). As a result of their gracefulness and elegance, the Blue Veins heighten their image and also manage to success fully imitate white people.

Finally, the Blue Veins are light-skinned people. Several of them are indeed light enough to pass as white people. "Though many of them are light enough to pass, the members deny that skin color is a prerequisite for acceptance. They argue that 'culture and character' are the only things considered. Furthermore, if most of their members are light-colored, it is because such persons as a rule, have better opportunities to qualify themselves for membership" (Barksdale 339). By utilizing such an argument, the Blue Veins are essentially upholding the beliefs that the closer one's complexion is to that of a white person's, the better the individual is and the more likely he is to be accepted into the Blue Vein society. Not only are the Blue Veins denying the admittance of decent people (of darker complexions), they are promoting separatism. The type of prejudice these people are guilty of promoting is the worst kind of prejudice.

Ryder, a Blue Vein member, is forced to cope with his present and past identity problems. First and foremost, Ryder manages to blend into the Blue Vein society because of his outer appearance. He is fair-skinned, has fine hair, and dresses well which are characteristics of Blue Veins "who always maintain a refined look" (Barksdale 335). Much like his peers, Ryder is also educated. Though he did not have access to the best schools, he learns to read and is fascinated primarily with English poets instead of African American ones" (Chesnutt 336). Ryder can also articulate as well as any white person when he recites poetry with "a poetic soul" (Chesnutt 336).

In comparison with other Blue Veins, Ryder is wealthy. Apparently, to be part of the Blue Vein society, one must possess both intelligence and money. Luckily, Ryder has both. In fact, Ryder manages to save money, and he also owns a fairly extravagant home that is "handsomely equipped with a piano and library along with other valuable commodities" (Barksdale 336). Ryder actually lives like a typical wealthy white man of this time period.

Just as Ryder is similar to his friends in terms of wealth and education, he also resembles them in a more important way. Ryder attempts to suppress his true identity and "blackness" much like his friends do. First of all, Ryder is the name he adopts in order to separate himself from his past. His given name is actually Sam Taylor. More importantly, the culture he tries to escape is the black culture, the one he intends to embrace is the white culture. For instance, unlike many of his "black brothers," Ryder is wealthy, erudite and an admirer of various English poets. Obviously, Ruder does not reach such status by identifying with black people. Instead, Ryder forgets that just twenty-five years earlier he worked as an apprentice to white people. As a result of his "convenient amnesia," Ryder emulates his white counterparts and achieves many wonderful things.

More importantly, despite the fact that Ryder memorizes English poetry, is a Blue Vein and attempts to adopt "white" tastes, he tries to convince himself and others around him that "he has no prejudice; instead, he is obligated to promote self-preservation through the absorption of the white race. Identification with the black race would merely be a ticket to extinction" (Barksdale 336). Apparently, Ryder and the other Blue Veins are intelligent people who all exhibit the same mentalities. Needless to say, when Ryder uses the above statements as a means to justify his acceptance of the white culture as opposed to the black culture, he (along with his peers) seem prejudiced and are completely out of touch with who they really are. Nonetheless, if Ryder cannot Accept his heritage as well as his past and present way of living then there is no way he can totally conserve himself. There will always be a missing link in his life.

Finally, Chesnutt introduces Liza Jane who symbolizes numerous things and is also the missing link of Ryder's past. First of all, she represents an ex plantation slave. She is not physically attractive with "her black skin and blue toothless gums" (Barksdale 337). She is also poorly dressed, indicating she virtually has little or no money. In addition, she is also uneducated. Her dialect is very nonstandard and incoherent. As a result, it becomes somewhat difficult to interpret everything she says.

Liza Jane is also a symbol of devotion. For example, when she is a younger lady, she works hard to help her husband Sam Taylor. He is a mulatto, and because of his lineage," the tasks he is assigned are not nearly as strenuous as those assigned to Liza. Because of her devotion to Sam, the fact that he does little or no work does not phase Liza Jane at all.

In addition, Ryder seems to be somewhat embarrassed by Liza Jane "because he is light and she is black" (Barksdale 340). Evidently, based on this observation, Ryder thinks highly of himself and views Liza Jane as his inferior because of her complexion. Unfortunately, Liza Jane does not have a clue as to how her husband feels, or perhaps she loves him so much she overlooks his attitude.

Liza Jane's devotion also causes her to represent a "wandering soul." For instance, though her husband has been gone for twenty five years now, Liza Jane never remarries, carries his picture around, and travels several miles in search of her long lost husband. In fact, Liza Jane travels "to New Orleans, Atlanta and several other places" (Barksdale 338). Just like other wandering slaves, Liza Jane travels thousands of miles to find someone she has loved and lost.

Liza Jane represents the key to Ryder's past as well. First, before becoming a Blue Vein member, Ryder marries the dark complexioned Liza Jane and promises to send for her once he acquires his freedom. Rather than keep his promise, Ryder enjoys the benefits of success and seeks to take the light complexioned Mrs. Dixon as his wife. The reason he chooses Mrs. Dixon is "because she is attractive, educated, whiter than he and superior, and will be readily accepted by the other Blue Veins" (Barksdale 336). Nevertheless, there is a huge difference in the Ryder of the past and present, and the type of women he chooses differ as well. When Ryder marries Liza Jane, their marriage is neither praised nor hidden; instead, the marriage is virtually worthless and nonexistent. However, Ryder's future marriage to Liza Jane will be highly valued because it will enhance Ryder's credibility as a Blue Vein and the marriage will better his chance of being accepted into the white culture.

As mentioned previously, Ryder is a lover of English poetry. Ironically, as Ryder rehearses a few lines of poetry to describe the lovely Mrs. Dixon, Liza Jane (Mrs. Dixon's complete opposite) approaches him. At this very moment, Ryder's past and his attempt to avoid his "blackness" finally catch up with him. Though Ryder tries to discourage Liza Jane, his attempt fails because her spirit and faith cannot be destroyed.

After speaking with Ryder for quite some time, Liza Jane shows Ryder a picture of her long lost husband. "It is evident that the picture has faded with time, but the features are still distinct and it is easy to see what manner of man it represents" (Barksdale 340). The picture simply indicates that though he has tried for years to hide from his past, Ryder has been fighting a worthless battle. Nonetheless, the photo reveals the "true" Ryder, and there is no place left to hide.

As a result, Ryder has no choice but to recognize "the wife of his youth" because Liza Jane and the picture she possesses are the keys to Ryder's "true identity." However, before he acknowledges her, Ryder presents his situation to his peers without using his or Liza Jane's names. Once he gets their reactions to the story, he introduces everyone to his wife.

In a sense, Ryder's and the Blue Veins' recognition of Liza Jane is somewhat selfish and lacks sincerity. The only reason Ryder accepts her now is because his friends say they would, and naturally he does not want to jeopardize his relationship with the Blue Vein society. As for the other Blue Veins, they only agree to acknowledge her because they want to be viewed as sympathetic and compassionate. In actuality, these are the very people who attempt to escape their "blackness" and would highly likely shun someone like Liza Jane. Therefore, it is virtually impossible for them to label themselves a s compassionate, sympathetic individuals because Liza Jane represents the class of people the Blue Veins conscientiously avoid at all costs!

Thus, Chesnutt through the presentation of the cultured and refined blue Veins, introduction of Ryder and his struggles with his past and present, and use of Liza Jane as a symbol, ultimately demonstrates the consequences one must endure if he promotes interracial prejudice and attempts to deny his true heritage. Nonetheless, if one rises from the detriments of poverty and becomes successful, one should not feel that he is no longer black, nor should he try to avoid his black culture. However, if one does try to escape and forget about his true heritage, someone or something will force him to recognize his past.

WORKS CITED

Baechler, L. and Waltonliz, A., eds. "Background on C. Chesnutt." *African American Writers*. New York: Macmillan, 1991. 66.

Baechler, L. and Waltonliz, A., eds. "Background on Du Bois." *African American Writers*. New York: Macmillan, 1991. 76.

Barksdale, R. and Kinnamon, K., eds. Du Bois, W. E. B. "The Souls of Black Folk." *Black Writers of America: A Comprehensive Anthology*. New York: Macmillan, 1972. pp. 335–40.

Magill, Frank., ed. "Background on W. E. B. Du Bois." *Masterpieces African American Literature*. New York: HarperCollins, 1992. pp. 521–522.

YHWH OR THE HIGHWAY: *THE ILIAD, THE ODYSSEY,* AND THE *BIBLE'S* INFLUENCE—AMANDA SEAMAN

(Amanda Seaman is a former Longman Award Winner for Composition I.)

As one looks back on the history of the Israeli people and the beginnings of Hebrew literature, one might reflect on the legendary accounts that emerged from that time period. How did these stories originate? Who immortalized these chronicles for future generations? Were they fact or fiction, myth or just a folk tale? Is there any relationship between Greek writings such as *The Iliad* and *The Odyssey* and Hebrew literature such as *The Bible?* Transcending cultures, several universal themes unite the Hebrew text with other Ancient World literature. Furthermore, the Hebrew people held religious beliefs that differed from other cultures of that time. The Hebrew people believed in one and only one God, which made the religious literature innovative at that point in history. Although not fully understood in their own time, annals of the Ancient World such as *The Iliad, The Odyssey,* and *The Bible* influence life, as we know it, in the twenty-first century.

The Hebrew people are members of the Semitic race which descended from Abraham. Hebrew means to cross over. The history of the Hebrew people and their literature dates back centuries. Although *The Bible,* as we know it, did not exist until the fifteenth century A.D., its conception began thousands of years earlier. During the Age of Patriarch (2000 B.C.), the survival of history depended on oral tradition to pass stories on from generation to generation. In 1250 B.C., Moses led the Hebrew people out of slavery in Egypt. Thus, they received the name crossing over, or Hebrew. It is believed that the first written account of *The Bible* began during the forty-year period of Israel's (the Hebrews) wandering in the desert dating around 1200 B.C. During this time, Moses wrote the first five books of *The Bible: Genesis, Exodus, Leviticus, Numbers,* and *Deuteronomy*. These five books comprise the Pentateuch. Due to their exodus from Egypt, the Hebrews had no homeland and were considered a Diaspora (wandering Jew). They were relegated to the deserts as one nation with nothing to call their own. The Israeli nation was like no other nation of their time. The Hebrew peoples faced many challenges from internal and external influences. During these forty years, the Hebrews realized the ethical and moral responsibilities that God required of them. Upholding godly standards during this time was a challenge for them. The Hebrew nation also differed from other nations of that time in that they had no earthly king. Their only king was Yahweh (YHWH), the king of everything. The Hebrews believed that everything was "established by God" (32). While considering challenges faced by the Hebrews, one should contemplate Mosaic authorship of the Pentateuch. It is relatively easy to judge while sitting in the air-conditioned 21st century, but pondering life in 1200 B.C. Mesopotamia opens the door for many interesting observations. Moses wrote a significant literary work while walking in a hot, sandy, wind swept desert after leading a million or more people from their homes into the wilderness. What did he use to write? How did he transport and protect the writings? When did he have time to write a noteworthy work the size of the Pentateuch? If one considers all of the circumstances that affected Moses during the time of his writing, one must see that this text was truly inspired by God. It is amazing that such great literature could come out of a nation at such a turbulent time. The history of Hebrew literature is an important part of Ancient World literature and greatly affects us still today.

Hebrew literature at the time in which it was written could be described as revolutionary due to the ideals that were presented. Monotheism, spiritual aspects, relationships between God and man, and opposing ideals are a few qualities that make this literature revolutionary. Monotheism is the belief in a single, all-powerful God. This is the central element in what makes the Jewish faith and the Hebrew text original. The Hebrews also opposed the ideas of many gods, no gods, and the fact that everything is god. To the Hebrews, God (YHWH) was the only divine Godhead. Before Hebrew literature was accepted, polytheism (the belief in many gods) was one of the main beliefs of the time period. There were sun gods, rain gods, gods of love, and many other gods to worship. Many natural events such as earthquakes, volcanoes, and tsunamis were attributed to these gods. In addition to monotheism, spiritual aspects were a new idea for people in the Ancient World. The Hebrew people believed in a sovereign God. They prayed to a personal God who answered prayers. There was a love relationship between the Lord (YHWH) and His people and between the people and their Lord. The Greeks, on the other hand, believed in tangible gods (statues) that they could see and touch. Another quality that makes the Hebrew religious literature revolutionary for its time is the relationship between God and creation which is shown in the first chapter of *Genesis:* "In the beginning God created the heaven and the earth" (17). One can get two principles from this scripture. First, the world has a beginning. God is everlasting, but the world is not. Hence, creation cannot be God, because God is eternal. Also, God created the Earth. Thus, the world is dependant on God for continuation. Therefore, the Hebrew literature clearly defines the relationship between God and creation. These were revolutionary ideals expressed by Hebrew literature, unknown and misunderstood for the time in which it was written. Hebrew literature is factual, a history book through the ages. Other Ancient World literature of the time, *The Iliad* and *The Odyssey,* are mythology. Hebrew literature was revolutionary for the time in which it was written, and inspires many even today.

Universal themes throughout Hebrew literature that connect with other Ancient World literature are also numerous. Although Hebrew text is very different from other texts of the Ancient World, there are still themes that connect the literature. First, a very common theme throughout Greek literature and Hebrew literature is the fact that God or the gods are in control. Also, the fact that all things are subject to fate is addressed in both Greek and Hebrew literature. Other very important themes are good versus evil, the treatment of women, the status of first-born sons, idols, sacrifice, tragedy, and rebellion. In *Genesis* and *Job,* there are many instances of good versus evil. For example, in the book of *Job,* angels "came to present themselves before the Lord" and Satan "present[s] himself before the Lord"(41) which clearly represents the saga of good versus evil in the Hebrew literature. Also, women in Hebrew and Greek literature were not treated with respect. The woman's place in the home was to cook and to present a son to the leader of the house. On that same note, the treatment of the first-born son was with respect second only to his father. The first-born was given all the inheritance and was considered a leader of the home. The son was normally either a farmer or warrior and was very gifted. In so many cultures, the first-born son is held high. Most authors of Ancient literature use this as a detail to help mold the story. These universal themes of Ancient World literature are very important to help connect cultures of different regions. As a result, the universal themes of Hebrew text that connect other literature with the Ancient World are what make the writings so profound today.

History, universal themes, and revolutionary ideals are what make Ancient World literature a work of art. Whether one reads Greek mythology or Hebrew literature such as *The Bible,* one can learn about the ancient world and the cultures that surround the text. Life as we know it now would not be the same without the great writings penned before Christ (B.C.). The Hebrew nation, though not politically, artistically, or militarily powerful in their day has influenced billions through their masterpieces. *The Bible* is a prime example of a misunderstood text, full of cutting edge ideology, that two thousand years later, is the best-selling book of all time.

EDGAR RICE BURROUGHS' TARZAN AND THE ARCHETYPE—BILL SIZEMORE

For virtually all people in America, and many around the world, the character Tarzan is a cultural staple. He is present in all forms of media including representation in film, on television, the radio and comic books. One could stand in practically any shopping center in America and voice the cry of the bull ape made popular by the various movie Tarzans and it would be recognized as just that; the victory cry of Tarzan. Most Americans however, are not aware that Tarzan began as serialized fictional literature.

The Tarzan character would become one of the most successful and well know literary characters of all time, transcending the print medium and subsequently including the aforementioned film, television, radio and other media. While Tarzan, and several other franchises created by Burroughs, was a huge financial success, Burroughs was not particularly well regarded critically. His stories were thought to be formulaic and they relied too much on coincidence. Why is it, then, that Burroughs has been remembered long after many other more popular and critically successful authors of his time? How has it come about that such an enduring character as Tarzan has lost his literary roots while growing in popularity? What is it about Tarzan that appeals to so many people across so many social, cultural and temporal boundaries?

The answer lies in Burroughs's ability to fashion characters that transcend these differences. This is possible because, at our core, we are all attracted to the same types of beings. In Tarzan, Burroughs created a character that is representative of a type of character we can all readily identify within our conscious, as well as our unconscious mind. The psychologist Carl Jung identified several of these character types, naming them "archetypes."

In his analysis of Jung's work, A Primer of Jungian Psychology (1973), Dr. Calvin S. Hall states that Jung believed an archetype to be "the contents of the collective unconscious" (40), or, more specifically, an inherited pattern of thought or symbolic imagery derived from the past collective experience and present in the individual unconscious. In simple terms, an archetype is an idealized model of an aspect of a person. According to psychologist Dr. Cate Carabelle, adjunct professor at Lamar University, Beaumont, Texas, Jung believed that archetypes were innate prototypes for these ideals, and could be used to interpret observations of a subject. There are many archetypes including the Hero, Trickster, Savior, Lover and the Wild man. Burroughs was able to combine several of these archetypes into one package; Tarzan. In essence, Tarzan is an easily accessible collection of archetypes that we are so ready to accept because they exist in all of us.

Edgar Rice Burroughs began his writing career only after working in a variety of other trades. During his stint as a pencil sharpener salesman he was checking an ad he had run in a pulp magazine and he decided to try his hand at writing. "If people are paid for writing such rot," he said of the writing he found in the pulp mag, "then I can write something just as rotten!"

His first story, written in 1911, a sci-fi thriller called *Under the Moon of Mars,* was published in installments in early 1912, and netted him $400.00, which was a staggering sum for the time. Thomas Metcalf, the editor of All-Story Magazine, who accepted Burroughs' story, suggested he write something along the lines of an Arthurian legend. Burroughs responded in May of 1912 with a story called Tarzan of the Apes. Metcalf published the story in its entirety as a monthly serial and Burroughs earned a resounding $700.00. It was this that convinced him to take up writing full time.

Burroughs received many rejection slips, but eventually got an offer from a major publishing house in Chicago, A. C. McClurg & Co., who published the earlier serialized Tarzan of the Apes in book form in 1914. It immediately became a best seller. Burroughs would go on to publish 29 more books for this publisher between 1914 and 1929 but decided in 1931 to incorporate himself and publish his own books. This successful ploy resulted in 24 first edition books and made him vast amounts of money. What kept consumers coming back to his various works was his ability to craft the Jungian archetypal characters that connected with our psyche time and again.

"Jung describes the Hero as an "archetype of transformation and redemption," (Guerin 163). Tarzan is the ultimate Hero, facing situations that would certainly defeat any normal mortal. In the first book, Tarzan of the Apes (1914), Tarzan fights Kerchak, the leader of the ape troupe to whom Tarzan belongs. Jealous Kerchak picks a fight with Tarzan, whom he sees as an inferior creature. Tarzan, armed with the intelligence of man and a sharp hunting knife left behind by his biological father, steps up to Kerchak's challenge. The author writes, "Awaiting him stood Tarzan, himself a mighty muscled animal, but his six feet of height and his great rolling sinews seemed pitifully inadequate to the ordeal which awaited them" (84).

Even so, faced with such odds that he must surely fail, Tarzan uses these tools, as well as those learned through his ape upbringing, and courageously faces the ferocious ape. Burroughs continues, "As his antagonist came roaring toward him, Lord Greystoke tore his long knife from its sheath, and with an answering challenge as horrid and bloodcurdling as that of the beast he faced, rushed swiftly to meet the attack" (86). Burroughs goes on to describe a vicious fight between Tarzan (Lord Greystoke) and Kerchak. The fight ends thus; "The greater strength of the ape was slowly prevailing, and the teeth of the straining beast were scarce an inch Tarzan's throat when, with a shuddering tremor, the great body stiffened for an instant and then sank limply to the ground.

Kerchak was dead" (94).

Against all odds Tarzan has defeated Kerchak and becomes the king of the apes himself This is only one example of the countless similar moments Tarzan is forced to face as he battles incredible foes against insurmountable odds. Yet time and again he is victorious.

Other archetypes are just as evident in Tarzan. The Wild Man archetype clearly shows in Tarzan's upbringing in the jungle, raised by apes. How much more wild can one get? He is distanced from civilization and technology and relies solely on his own strength and intelligence to ensure his survival.

As the Savior, Tarzan ensure the safety and well being of others. His sense of morality, fair play and the "law of the jungle" often force him to confront issues that are faced by his family and close friends, as well as those who are not closely connected to him, yet are in need of help. In chapter 21 of Tarzan of the Apes (1914) Tarzan responds to the sounds of fighting near a native village that he knows to contain cannibals. He also knows, due to the sounds of gunfire, that the fighting was between the cannibals and a group of white men whom Tarzan has just discovered are in the jungle. The sounds soon change from that of fighting to the sounds of celebration by the cannibals, who are preparing to torture, kill and feast on a captive, whom Tarzan correctly assumes is one of the white men. Though the man means nothing to him, the flesh eating practices of the cannibals bother him greatly and so he goes swiftly to end the suffering of the prisoner. Upon arriving at the village, Tarzan decides that rather than just kill the captive to frustrate the cannibals, he can save him, and does so not only because he believes the villages are wrong, but he knows that it will demoralize them as well, which is the only way he can effectively fight the cannibals without killing them outright. He does save the man, a French army officer named Lt. D'Amot, and they begin a lifelong friendship. So not only does Tarzan act the part of Savior, he also accepts ongoing responsibility for those he helps.

Much of the research centering on Jung and archetypes indicates that Jung connected the archetypal image with that of what he called "complexes." Writing for the publication Creative Loafing (1998), author Cliff Rostock says that these complexes are not like those of Freud, and do not imply a pathology, but rather they are the aggregate of thoughts and feelings that center around a particular archetype. The tone of each complex an individual may experience has much to do with the experience one has with one's primary archetypal example figure. It is this ongoing positive message of the archetypal image given to us through Tarzan by Burroughs, that attracts us to the character and endears him in our hearts.

Not only has Burroughs created these powerful archetypal characters, Tarzan being foremost amongst them, he has taken the time to include the flaws necessary to make them more believable. It is hard to care about a perfect character; they're boring! Flaws add flavor. Tarzan enjoys alcohol and smokes cigarettes. He also has a penchant for jungle princesses even though he is a married man. Burroughs plots his stories so that these traits often lead to moral decisions that force the character to choose between right and wrong. In Burroughs stories the characters always choose right, or if they do choose wrong there is a reason for it, such as a lack of a bit of crucial information or some similar device. Even so, the good guys are always good and the bad guys are always bad. There is little or no middle ground. Often times the bad guys are ambiguous to the good guys in the stories, but Burroughs always makes it clear for the reader. Eventually the "bad" comes out and the antagonist takes on the traits of the archetypal figure of the Shadow. Hall states that "the Shadow is probably the most powerful, and potentially the most dangerous of all the archetypes. It is the source of all that is best and worst in man, especially in his relations with others of the same sex" (48). So it is even more important that Tarzan vanquish the Shadow aspect of the villains in the stories. It is the inevitable defeat of the Shadow, and the creation of a positive relationship of archetypal images in Burroughs characters, especially Tarzan, and the complexes that dwell around them, that keep the reader coming back for more.

Along with the successful creation of the archetypal character, Burroughs does have other literary devices which help to attract and keep the reader. While Burroughs was criticized for his formulaic writing, he was lauded, then and now, for his sense of pacing and exciting cliffhanger chapter endings. It was his style to open the story with an exciting event and grow upon it from there. As the characters developed through the plot, they inevitably became separated and went through their own harrowing sequence of events, culminating in an eventual rejoining of the storyline with other main characters for a dramatic climax and satisfying resolution. This scheme of constantly changing point of view helped to maintain interest in the plot by leaving the character during a point of distress and going back to a previous character who had been left in a similar position the last time. This writing style increases the tension by ebbing and flowing the various dramatic plot points around different character, giving us time to assimilate what has happened to one, while we move on with another plot line.

Burroughs has given us many iconic characters from which to choose, Tarzan being among the most favorite and enduring of them. It is unfortunate that more of the young readers today are not familiar with his writing as it still has a lot to offer. He has a simple, easy to read style that grabs hold and is relentless in providing conflict to move the story forward at a blinding pace. While Burroughs is admittedly not a literary giant, his stories hold up even today as entertaining and exciting. They do not come across as too dated as they are told simply and straightforward in a literary landscape that is easily detached from the now. He was considered a true pioneer of the fantasy/science fiction genre due to these elements and his use of the archetypal character, and he has left us with a worldwide cultural icon in Tarzan of the Apes.

Works Cited

Burroughs, Edgar Rice. *Tarzan of the Apes.* Chicago: A. C. McClurg & Co., 1914 Bostock, Cliff.

"Archetypes:A short course in their (misunderstood) meaning." (Originally published in the "Paradigms" column of Creative Loafing, Atlanta, Jan. 31, 1998)

Carabelle, Cate. Personal Interview. 15 March 2006.

Cowart, David. "The Tarzan Myth and Jung's Genesis of the Self." *Journal of Popular Culture* 2.2 (Sumr 1979): 220–30.

Guerin, Wilfred L., Earle G. Labor, Lee Morgan. *A Handbook of Critical Approaches to Literature.* 2nd Edition. Oxford, 1979. 162–165.

Hall, Calvin S. *A Primer in Jungian Psychology.* New York: Mentor, 1973

Section

5

Advanced English Essays

The Lamar University English Department sponsors the Rowe Award, which is given to the best critical essay written in a 3000 or 4000 level English course for a particular year. In the following are a couple winners.

While students may not want to major in English, they can see these essays as examples of what English teachers ultimately expect. They will also reveal the kind of critical thinking that goes not just into a literary analysis but any kind of critical analysis.

THE HOLLOW MAN REVISITED: NARRATOR JIM BURDEN IN *MY ÁNTONIA*—ELISE DAVENPORT

(2005 Rowe Critical Essay Award Winner, Lamar University)

Willa Cather's Jim Burden is intrinsically complicated simply because not much is ever revealed about him. Cather gives scant information to fill in the blanks as to Jim's background, beliefs, and even his life after Ántonia. Jim Burden is as much an "outcast" as anyone in the story—he begins as an uprooted orphan, and ends as an uprooted lawyer. The adult Jim also seems disconnected from his childhood: he has no longing to return to life on the farm or to Ántonia until the close of the book, when he is trapped in a very probable loveless and sexless marriage and in a job that keeps him constantly uprooted. Burden continually detaches himself from his surroundings and his peers for the sake of propriety. This voluntary disconnection and general lack of development of the narrative character may be explained by one of several factors. The fact Cather, a lesbian, chose to write from a man's perspective presents immediate problems. Cather wrote *My Ántonia* at a time in her life when women had disappointed her and thus, Jim keeps his distance from the opposite sex, and perhaps, Cather intended Jim's life to seem hollow to offset the fullness of Ántonia's.

Jim may lack background and depth simply because Willa Cather's experience with men was limited. She had two brothers, and had a good relationship with her father, Charles Cather. Woodress states that "Charles and Willa had always been very close" (24). However, it seems she never formed a romantic attachment to a man. Writing from the perspective of the opposite sex is difficult enough, but Cather was a lesbian, a lifestyle that can severely limit insight onto the opposite sex and sex itself. Cather did not participate in heterosexual sex, and it seems neither does Jim. Burden's sexless and loveless marriage adds to the feeling that he is essentially a flat character. Even in his younger years, before his marriage, Jim is unable or unwilling to form any sort of romantic relationship with Lena, even though he states that he was "in love with Lena" (Cather 227). Instead of deepening the relationship with a woman he is supposedly in love with, he chooses to leave, saying "I'll never settle down and grind if I stay here. You know that" (Cather 230). So, ultimately, love and sex seem to be distractions throughout Jim's life. He suppresses love and desire and reverts to his bland world of propriety and work.

147

Cather's men in general seem to be all work and no play. Jim's grandfather only reserves time for prayer and Bible readings. There is no show of affection between Jim's grandfather and grandmother at all. This temperament may be a reflection of her grandfather's disposition: an "inflexible will and evangelical zeal" (Woodress 22). Perhaps it is also a reflection of how marriages were formed at the time—usually more of a business merger than a matter of love or affection. Otto and Jake seem to be a sort of male couple who have no interest in anything but work and, after the family moves to town, adventure on the western frontier. Anything more between them is as forbidden in the contemporary social world as is Cather's own sexuality. Mr. Shimerda obviously finds little joy in his daughters or his wife since he commits suicide and leaves them to the care of Ambrosch.

Perhaps Cather simply did not have enough observation and certainly little experience with heterosexual relationships to create a male character that interacts normally with women. One of the only male characters to have "relationships" with women, Wick Cutter, is a despicable character. The adulterous relationships Cutter has with women always end in shame and ruin for the female characters. Women are tainted by mere association with him, like Ántonia. The general opinion in Black Hawk is "if you go to work for the Cutters, you're likely to have a fling that you won't get up from in a hurry" (Cather 166). Even the more respectable characters have dysfunctional relationships with women. Mr. Harling seems oppressive. When he is home, he keeps his wife locked up with him, and his children are expected to be silent and unseen. These strained relationships seem to be a theme throughout Cather's fiction. This could be a failed attempt to "[transform] her emotional life and experiences into acceptable, heterosexual forms and guises" (Lambert 120). Gelfant agrees: "Though the tenor of her writing is normality, normal sex stands barred from her fictional world" (80).

Jim also seems to act artificially in some situations. He doesn't seem to act like a young man might in the company of girls like Lena and Ántonia. He does, briefly, succumb to enjoying the presence of the opposite sex when he attends the firemen's hall dances. However, the loss of his grandmother's high opinion is all it takes for Jim to withdraw from the girls again and throw himself into his studies. Jim seems easily deterred from girls, and likewise, easily engaged in studying, two things which are not typical behavior for a young man. Jim's marriage is never mentioned in the book proper, but the introduction mentions that "his career was suddenly advanced by a brilliant marriage" (Cather 2). Cather seems to suggest that this marriage came about only because the woman had been slighted by a better suitor, and felt like doing something spiteful (2). His marriage is not a relationship of love, but a vehicle to advance his career. Yet, the speaker in the introduction says Jim has a "naturally romantic and ardent disposition" (Cather 2–3). This seems contradictory. A "romantic" and "ardent" man would presumably have married for love, not to climb another rung on the career ladder. These vague and contradictory behaviors from Jim are quite possibly a result of Cather's small range of experience with the opposite sex.

Also, Cather's experience with women at the time she wrote *My Ántonia* had disappointed her. Stephanie Vaughn states in her introduction that the woman that Cather had probably been much in love with, and spent a great deal of time with, Isabelle McClung, married a man (xxi). Cather had obviously expected more of Isabelle than Isabelle herself intended to give. This very great disappointment coupled with the illness of her mother came just before Cather began *My Ántonia*. In a letter to Dorothy Canfield Fisher, Cather writes, "Loss of Isabelle is a severe one" (56). Later on in the year, Cather wrote Elizabeth Sergeant, "Isabelle's marriage still hard to accept" (58). Clearly, Cather was deeply affected by the event. "By the time she went back to New York in the autumn, [1916] she had written several chapters of *My Ántonia*. So, though it draws deeply on the material of her childhood, it was strongly coloured too by these recent feelings: her desolation at Isabelle's betrayal" (Lee 136). This may have given Jim his lackluster stance on love and women. Jim never mentions his marriage, we only learn that he is really married from the introduction, so he does not seem to be "happily" married. Lee sums it up, calling his marriage "an offstage failure" (154). The evidence in Cather's introduction suggests that Jim and his wife rarely see each other, and she is an unpleasant woman with a disposition very different from his own (2). Jim's "quiet tastes irritate" his wife, and her flagrant behavior must irritate him. Cather's speaker in the introduction even goes so far as to suggest Jim's marriage is a "disappointment," though not severe enough to "chill his naturally romantic . . . disposition" (2). Perhaps Cather was writing a warning on what was to come for Isabelle, or perhaps she was bitter and broken up over Isabelle's marriage, and so her narrator, Burden, rejects marriage and women thus.

Jim is likewise disappointed in Ántonia in several instances in the novel, and withdraws from her. After her father's suicide, and Ántonia works in the fields like a man, Jim is disappointed not to see her but also that she will stoop to such work voluntarily. Ántonia seems to prefer this sort of work to learning and housework, saying "I can work like mans now. . . . School is all right for little boys" (Cather 100). Later she says "Oh, better I like to work out-of-doors than in a house! . . . I not care that your grandmother say it makes me like a man. I like to be like a man" (Cather 111). Chapter 18 contains the episode with Ambrosch and Jake over the horse collar, in which Jim withdraws even further from Ántonia due to her spiteful jeers and taunts. Now Jim is distanced from Ántonia not because he has no chance to see her but because he has no *wish* to see her. Jim is offended by Ántonia's taunts, and she instantly is no longer a friend, but an ungrateful Czech. Jim feels that her behavior is as bad as Ambrosch's. It is Jim's grandfather who ends the frigid spell between them by riding over to invite Ántonia to come and work in the Burden house helping in the kitchen.

Jim's biggest disappointment in Ántonia is later, after the Burdens move to Black Hawk, and Ántonia is working next door at the Harlings'. Ántonia's refusal to stop going to the dances and decision instead to go work for Wick Cutter shames her in Jim's eyes. Her defiance is as shameful to Jim as the Cutters' reputation. Perhaps Cather is using Jim to represent the present society and its ideals, and using Ántonia to express a progressive idea of women. Ántonia is not bothered by propriety, as perhaps Cather wishes she were free to express herself. Jim clings to the established social mode because Cather herself does.

Still, Jim agrees to tend Cutter's house. It is after Cutter has beaten him on Ántonia's account that Jim withdraws completely to the university and his studies. At this point, Ántonia seems to disappear from the novel. Jim is let down even by Lena's mentions of Ántonia. Lena tells him that Ántonia is engaged to Larry Donovan, and Jim responds "I think I'd better go home and look after Ántonia," but he never does (Cather 211). Jim does not seem as concerned for Ántonia's well-being as he might've before the Cutter episode. The incident at Wick Cutter's house that night seems to have been the breaking point in their "relationship," as Isabelle's marriage was in Cather's life. Though Cather continued to visit Isabelle until she died, things would never be the same between them.

Jim withdraws from not only Ántonia, but all the "hired girls" for the sake of propriety. Though he "hoped that Sylvester would marry Lena, and thus give all the country girls a better position in town," Jim himself would never think of marrying one of the hired girls, no matter how attached he might become to Ántonia or later, Lena (Cather 163). This may be a reflection of Cather's own withdrawal from women at the time. In her youth, Cather kept her hair short, dressed unconventionally, and sometimes signed her name as "William" rather than "Willa." Vaughn suggests in her introduction that once Cather realized she was to have a career as a writer, she began wearing silk dresses, let her hair grow out, and changed her name back to "Willa" (ix-x). Jim undergoes a similar almost slavish return to propriety when he stops attending the Firemen's Hall dances. In doing so, he cuts off his closest contact with women since he played with Ántonia on the farm. He has one more brush with Lena before he plunges into studies, profession, and a loveless marriage. Though Cather put up her façade of propriety, she used Jim as a tool to express her feelings as she felt unable to do in reality.

Cather was unwilling or unable to express her homosexuality freely. "In her society it was difficult to be a woman and achieve professionally, and she certainly could not be a woman who loved women," and as a result of this, Lambert says, "she began to deny or distort the sexuality of her principal characters" (120). Jim is not alone in this, indeed he "belongs to a remarkable gallery of characters for whom Cather constantly invalidates sex" (Gelfant 80). She "denies Jim's erotic impulses and Ántonia's sexuality as well; and she retreats into the safety of convention by ensconcing Ántonia in marriage and rendering her apotheosis as earth mother" (Lambert 126). Cather's inability or unwillingness to express her own sexuality colors all her characters with a similar lack of contact with the sexual world. Cather's characters may marry and bear children, but sex and love are rarely present on any other terms, and thus the marriages do not seem fulfilling or healthy. This seems to be one of Cather's greatest failings: because she was unable to freely love in her society, her characters constantly find themselves in the same situation. Cather seems unable to write about love or sex, and so her characters suffer a lack of development and depth without it.

Jim also could be little more than a literary foil to Ántonia. Where Jim's life is hollow, Ántonia's seems that much fuller. Jim is childless, lives without a meaningful relationship, and is often away from home, uprooted. Ántonia, in the final chapters, has a loving husband, sons, daughters, and a prosperous farm which has become her real home. Of course, neither Jim nor Ántonia seems to have a real sex life, but when compared to Jim, Ántonia certainly seems to have lived a fuller life. In the end, Ántonia has become a flat-chested, toothless, rough and brown-skinned woman, which seems a terrible change from her beautiful youth. However, when we compare her to Jim, who in the introduction is said to still appear young, her condition seems trivial in light of the fact that her life is full and happy (Cather 3). Jim is such a near perfect foil to Ántonia in the end that it is hard to imagine that it was not at least partially intentional. Thus, perhaps, Cather considered it necessary for Jim Burden to be a flat character to give Ántonia the roundness she needed. Without the example of Jim's sexless marriage and rootless existence, Ántonia's cozy farm life might not seem as inviting. Though the farm is prosperous, the Cuzak family is still at poverty level because of the sheer number of children they have. Jim obviously enjoys a comfortable lifestyle and makes enough to not feel the pangs of poverty, but this does not give him half the enjoyment in life that Ántonia has from her home and family. Indeed, in the end, after meeting Ántonia's boys, Jim vows to make time to go hunting with them soon. Jim makes time not for his wife, or to be home, but to cling to the feeling of Ántonia's happiness. Jim's lack thereof brings out just how much family and home mean in the novel. "Whatever Ántonia may have lost, it does not define the person she has become. Jim, however, is defined, sadly, by unfulfillment, a longing to belong" (Kvasnicka 106). This absence of home and family in Cather's fiction results often in "alienation, loss of identity, or spiritual paralysis" (Kvasnicka 103). Ántonia, although she has constantly rejected social rules and mores, leads a full and happy life (except for the absence of sex that affects all of Cather's characters). Thus, perhaps it is Cather's understated point that in rejecting society's strict confines, Ántonia has enabled herself to enjoy life in a way that Jim simply cannot.

However, placing Jim as Ántonia's foil does not make all the pieces fall into place. If Jim is simply a literary device, then why does Cather choose to use him rather than focusing on Ántonia? "It is . . . difficult to determine who is the novel's central character. If it is Ántonia . . . why does she entirely disappear from two of the novel's five books? If . . . we decide that Jim Burden, the narrator, is the central figure, we find that the novel explores neither his consciousness or his development" (Lambert 119). Hermione Lee suggests that Jim allows Cather "to speak from her own sexual identity and express her own emotions for women" (153). Obviously, Cather felt unable to love women openly, so she may not have been comfortable attempting to express herself through a female character. Jim allows her a mask of normalcy with which she is more free to express appreciation and admiration of women, though she is still unable to express any sexual or romantic feelings.

Thus, though there is little background on Jim, he is still a complex character. To understand why he behaves as he does, it is imperative to look at Cather herself. Cather's limited experience with men and her devastating break with Isabelle McClung certainly could account for Jim's seeming lack of complexity, inability to deal with women, and disappointment and withdrawal from the opposite sex. Or perhaps Jim is simply intended to foil Ántonia in order to make her life seem fuller. Whatever the case, to gain an understanding of Jim Burden, it is important to first look at Cather's treatment of him. When we look at Cather's life at the time *My Ántonia* was written, some of Jim's inexplicable behaviors begin to possibly make sense, and from this knowledge, we can begin to fuller understand the "hollow man" that Jim Burden seems.

Works Cited

Cather, Willa. *My Ántonia.* New York: Bantam, 1994.

Cather, Willa. "Letter to Dorothy Canfield Fisher, Mar. 15, 1916." *A Calendar of the Letters of Willa Cather.* Ed. Janis Stuart. Lincoln, London: U of Nebraska Press, 2002.

Cather, Willa. "Letter to Elizabeth Sergeant, Aug. 3, 1916." *A Calendar of the Letters of Willa Cather.* Ed. Janis Stuart. Lincoln, London: U of Nebraska Press, 2002.

Gelfant, Blanche. "The Forgotten Reaping-Hook: Sex in *My Ántonia.*" *Modern Critical Interpretations: Willa Cather's My Ántonia.* Ed. Harold Bloom. New York, Philadelphia: Chelsea House, 1987. 79–97.

Kvasnicka, Mellanee. "Fragmented Families, Fragmented Lives in 'Paul's Case,' *My Ántonia,* and *A Lost Lady.*" *Willa Cather: Family, Community, and History.* Ed. John J. Murphy. Provo: BYU Humanities Publications Center, 1990. 103–108.

Lambert, Deborah. "The Defeat of a Hero: Autonomy and Sexuality in *My Ántonia.*" *Modern Critical Interpretations: Willa Catehr's My Ántonia.* Ed. Harold Bloom. New York, Philadelphia: Chelsea House, 1987. 119–131.

Lee, Hermione. *Willa Cather: Double Lives.* New York: Pantheon, 1989.

Vaughn, Stephanie. "Bringing the Muse Into the Country." Introduction. *My Ántonia.* New York: Bantam, 1994. vii-xxv.

Woodress, James. "A Dutiful Daughter." *Willa Cather: Family, Community, and History.* Ed. John J. Murphy. Provo: BYU Humanities Publications Center, 1990. 19–31.

EDWIN ARLINGTON ROBINSON: A KIND OF SPIRITUAL KINDERGARTEN—AMBER PLACETTE

(2006 Rowe Critical Essay Award, Lamar University)

"Suffering is but another name for the teaching of experience, which is the parent of instruction and the schoolmaster of life," once wrote the Greek poet Horace. Horace's theory denotes a particular subject in modern American literature: the poetry of Edwin Arlington Robinson. Robinson's life and literary works are both examples of perpetual conflict. His life was in constant turmoil from the moment of his birth to the last minutes of his death. His poetry and other forms of writing were also drenched in conflict, causing critics to debate and "call Robinson an idealist, Platonist, a transcendentalist, a pantheist, and many combinations thereof" (Cary ix). If Horace is correct in his evaluation, Robinson's poetry should be ingenious as he had one of the harshest schoolmasters of life and learned the lesson of suffering well. Perhaps the question is not of Robinson's genius, but rather where to place that genius in accordance with other types of literature. Some critics maintain that Robinson was a traditionalist, a cousin to poet Robert Frost in his imagery and his attention to tradition. Others would argue that Robinson is simply a mediocre writer of verses, a type of poetic coming attractions for the poets of the modern movement. However, Robinson does not conform to either of these assumptions, but rather defies any type of categorization or labeling. To truly understand the poetry of Robinson, one must not only examine his own biographical information but also the impact of traumatic events that would later influence his choices involving characterization, diction, and themes in his writings. Robinson was obsessed with the ideas of isolation and failure within his own life as well as the lives of his subjects. He focused on individuals and individual relationships in society and how ultimately, ever single individual feels a sense of isolation, desperation, and failure. In actuality, Robinson was ahead of his time; he was preoccupied with the failure of his subjects and yet creates a sense of irony and compassion for them, making him a true pioneer of the modernist movement.

Edwin Arlington Robinson was born in Hide Tide, Maine, on December 22, 1869 (Coffin 17). From the moment he uttered his first cry, Robinson was predestined to become a man who understood the complexity of failure as well as individual isolation from a surrounding environment and other human beings. Throughout his childhood in Maine, Robinson was constantly reminded of the success of his two adult brothers by his parents (Barnard 12). His mother, often cited as "New England's first colonial poet" (Coffin 19), and his father, who had reached the age of retirement at the time of Robinson's birth, recognized the boy's exceptional intelligence and yet tended to ignore their youngest child (Barnard 14). His family often viewed him as a disappointment, and his parents' preoccupation with material achievements handicapped him, forcing him to face the world with a jaded and disillusioned outlook. Following his graduation from secondary school, Robinson spent four years in a state of apparent inactivity, endlessly studying literature and struggling to write his own lines of poetry. The fledging poet then studies philosophy, literature, and languages at Harvard University for two years but had to withdraw from the institution due to the death of his father in 1893 (Barnard 20–23). The years that followed marked a time of great depression and mental anxiety for the young man as he suffered with a chronic ear infection, the depletion of his family's wealth, the death of his mother, and the end of an important love affair (Anderson 44).

Robinson moved to New York in 1895 after his mother's death relieved him of his obligations to his family and continued to pursue his literary career. Despite the fact that he had already managed to publish two volumes of poetry, Robinson struggled financially, relying heavily on the aid of friends and infrequent, temporary jobs (Coffin 24). In 1905, President Theodore Roosevelt's son Kermit read Robinson's collection of poems, *The Children of the Night,* in school and urged his father to take an interest in the poet. At his son's insistence, Roosevelt presented Robinson with a job at a customs house which was deliberately structured to enable him to work as little as possible in order to devout the majority of his time to poetry. However, Robinson did not find the situation ideal and decided to recommit himself to revising his old poems as well as writing new ones (Anderson 42). Suddenly, with the poetic revival that preceded the First World War, Robinson found an audience for his poetry. He was awarded the Pulitzer Prize three times during the 1920s for his works, *Collected Poems, Tristram,* and *The Man Who Died Twice* (Franchere 34). Robinson continued to write poetry for the remainder of his life, working himself into a state of exhaustion. As Hoyt C. Franchere notes, "He lost the power of compression and precision; he lost much of the control of structure (45). Robinson died in a hospital in New York City while revising his final work *King Jasper* in 1935.

In the time following Robinson's death, the volumes of critical interpretation are both immense and conflicting. Although the critics are generally in agreement about the basic aspects of his works, differing opinions about the interpretation of Robinson's verse are as numerous as the critics who strive to understand this deceased visionary. The consensus remains that Robinson was an original individual, obsessed with the themes of human isolation, the tormented introversions of the human conditions, and the frustrations and pain of humanity as it struggles to inhabit a world in which God has apparently shunned (Cary 112). James Dickey concludes, "No poet ever understood loneliness or separateness better than Robinson or knew the self-consuming furnace that the brain can become in isolation" (qut. In Lowell 99). Therefore, his poetry's subject matter often deals with individuals who are perplexed, unfulfilled, and unsuccessful to various degrees. The characters in his verse tend to be victims of modern conceptions of success (Cary 155). The question as to why Robinson devoted the majority of his writings to characterizations of failure is often debated. Possibly he was motivated by his own sense of failure from both his family's perspective and his own as an unappreciated writer (Lowell 165). Also, the plight of his morphine-addicted brother, the bankruptcy of his father, his own alcoholism, and his financial struggles possibly contributed to Robinson's obsession with characters who had failed either spiritually or who appeared to be failures to society, but in actuality had succeeded in wisdom (Cary 45).

Despite Robinson's pessimistic attitude, he refused to adopt a naturalistic point of view in which human beings must struggle relentlessly against the uncontrollable elements of the physical world (Anderson 37). Robinson was naturally introspective and conscious of the psychological depths of the human mind as well as intensely aware that man was a spiritual being and interested in man as a social creature only as is related to his internal composition (Lowell 87). Therefore, Robinson is indeed modern and writes in an existentialism manner, concerning himself with humanity's very being, with its perpetual, anguished struggle to exist. He is a modern writer who deals with the idea of outcasts, individuals on the outskirts of society and how society views those it rejects. In this way, Robinson is revolutionary, analyzing the isolated individual far earlier than other modernists such as Truman Capote, Saul Bellow, and Flannery O'Conner.

Robinson's most infamous poetic work is "Richard Cory," a shining example of modernism centered on a man who is the typical flawed failure that dominates much of Robinson's works. This poem is a thriving example of Robinson's observation regarding conventional success: that outwardly a man may maintain the appearance of accomplishment while internally he succumbs to an internal sense of disappointment (Cary 64). In this poem, a man's life is condensed into sixteen lines as seen through the eyes of the "people on the pavement" who believe that the title character seemingly has everything. The poem is a powerful statement of the inner turmoil of a man who fails to connect with the world around him and therefore becomes the fatal character of his own tragedy. Robinson does not explain why Cory feels the desperation and the isolation, which ultimately leads to his suicide, creating an even more shocking sensation for the reader upon the discovery of the final line of the poem. As previously stated, the theme of many of Robinson's character sketches is one of seclusion from the surrounding society, and it is within this framework that Robinson weaves an intricate yet simplistic web of words. Robinson approaches this particular poem as well as the entirety of his work with a philosophical point of view, perfecting each choice of words and agonizing on the desired message he was striving to reverberate (Cary 55). The end result of such attention to detail is a piece like "Richard Cory" which is an enduring and severe work that transcends generations. The crashing climatic moment when the man outwardly has achieved much commits the ultimate act of desperation generates a sharp sense of emptiness, of a life wasted, and of failure—all themes that characterize the modern movement.

"Mr. Flood's Party" is another of Robinson's poems which emphasizes his adherence to modern themes with its solitary figure saturated in isolation and failure. The poem centers on a man, Eben Flood, who has positioned himself atop a hill overlooking his town and his life. Flood is older, an alcoholic, and contemplating his life and failures by talking to his alter ego. He is "climbing alone" to his "forsaken upland hermitage," which holds "as much as he should ever know/On earth again of home" (Robinson 34). Therefore, Flood has no wife, no family, no true companions, and very few possessions. He is the true isolated figure, talking in fragments only to himself in a manner which constitutes as a soliloquy (Franchere 45). However, Flood was not always been alone.

Robinson explains that in his town "friends of other days had honored him." He has simply out-lived his friends and must cope with the deadening solitude. Mirroring the poet's own life, Flood uses alcohol to combat his loneliness and poverty, ultimately creating a sense of complete desolation and sadness.

As in most of Robinson's work, "Mr. Flood's Party" is about a man challenged by hardships, loss or personal failure, consequent defeat, and isolation. In this way, Flood is an example of an existential character. Robinson is struggling to understand the "I" within the man. Robinson envisions that a man's inner being was a force within him that is isolated from the outside world. As critic W. R. Robinson notes, "The self, Robinson therefore came to understand, is not identified with character or personality, with, that is, the conscious social aspects of a man's being, but is an activity, a truth-determining, moral creative force not identifiable with or derivable from a role, idea, institution, community, state, or culture (114). In other words, a person is truly isolated, like Flood, and can ultimately look inward to determine the true nature of their being. In terms of modernism, Flood is somewhat of an archetype. He is a man on the outer edges of society who appears to be insane according to social standards. He is standing on a hilltop in the middle of the night speaking to an alternate personality he has created while drinking alcohol. Also, there is no true resolution at the end of the "party;" Flood is "alone again" after his final drink and travels back toward Tilbury Town and faces the truth about his life: "There was not much that was ahead of him/And there was nothing in the town below—/Where strangers would have shut the many doors/That many friends had opened long ago" (Robinson 34). Flood will obviously die alone and lonely, completely rejected from the social world. Using traditional language, Robinson is commenting on the modern ideas of isolation and disillusionment with the world. Robinson's picture is not a sugar-coated, pastoral view of New England's countryside; his portrait is a bleak, desolate landscape of abandonment of the individual by all others and the segregation of the self.

In the greatest example of poetic irony, a man whose name would continue to be studied by students of American poetry did not receive it until some months after his birth (Barnard 12). It is therefore not unfounded to say that Edwin Arlington Robinson was destined to become a man whose life was a reflection of irony and a sense of isolation, the boy who lacked even the most basic of human recognition was born to voice to the pain and desperateness of separation. But perhaps the greatest ironies of Robinson's life and works continue to be that the man who felt like his existence was riddled with failure is often viewed as one of the greatest poets of the twentieth century and that his ability to express his own sense of loneliness unites him with humanity on innumerable levels. "The world is not a 'prison house,'" Robinson stated, "but kind of a spiritual kindergarten, where millions of infants are trying to spell "God" with the wrong blocks" (qt. In Lowell 78). Robinson saw himself and his poetic characters as member of such a group of infants: individuals whose minds could never encompass the truth about the world in which they inhabit but who nevertheless keep on trying to do so. His own life is a testimony to his destiny to become one of the first writers of the modern movement. One critic notes, "If Robinson's life sometimes seems a reflection of his poetry, there is no doubt that his finest poems are in part a reflection of his life (Cary 66). In this way, Robinson is more modern that most critics will ever allow. Despite his obvious adherence to traditional form and devices, Robinson is a lone figure; he is a poet who defines categorizations or labels and emerges as a modern writer, isolated by greatness and genius.

Works Cited

Anderson, Wallace Ludwig. Edwin *Arlington Robinson: A Critical Introduction.* Cambridge: Harvard U. P., 1968.

Barnard, Ellsworth. *Edwin Arlington Robinson: A Critical Study.* New York: Octagon, 1977.

Cary, Richard. *Appreciation of Edwin Arlington Robinson: 28 Interpretive Essays.* Waterville: Colby C. P., 1969.

Coffin, Robert Peter Tristram. *New Poetry of New England: Frost and Robinson.* New York: Russell & Russell, 1964.

Franchere, Hoyt C. *Edwin Arlington Robinson.* New York: Twayne, 1968.

Lowell, Amy. "Edwin Arlington Robinson." *Tendencies in Modern American Poetry.* New York: Houghton, 1921.

Robinson, Edwin Arlington. "Mr. Flood's Party." *Selected Poems.* New York: Macmillan, 1965.

———. "Richard Cory." *Selected Poems.* New York: Macmillan, 1965.

Robinson, W. R. *Edwin Arlington Robinson: A Poetry of the Act.* Cleveland: The Press of Western Reserve University, 1967.

Printed in the USA
CPSIA information can be obtained
at www.ICGtesting.com
JSHW060855020923
47697JS00003B/23